THE
KOREAN CONFLICT

Other Titles in the
Greenwood Press Guides to Historic Events of the Twentieth Century
Randall M. Miller, Series Editor

The Persian Gulf Crisis
Steve A. Yetiv

World War I
Neil M. Heyman

The Civil Rights Movement
Peter B. Levy

The Breakup of Yugoslavia and the War in Bosnia
Carole Rogel

Islamic Fundamentalism
Lawrence Davidson

Frontiers of Space Exploration
Roger D. Launius

The Collapse of Communism in the Soviet Union
William E. Watson

Origins and Development of the Arab-Israeli Conflict
Ann M. Lesch and Dan Tschirgi

The Rise of Fascism in Europe
George P. Blum

The Cold War
Katherine A.S. Sibley

The War in Vietnam
Anthony O. Edmonds

World War II
Loyd E. Lee

The Unification of Germany, 1989–1990
Richard A. Leiby

The Environmental Crisis
Miguel A. Santos

Castro and the Cuban Revolution
Thomas M. Leonard

The End of Apartheid in South Africa
Lindsay Michie Eades

THE
KOREAN CONFLICT

Burton I. Kaufman

Greenwood Press Guides to
Historic Events of the Twentieth Century
Randall M. Miller, Series Editor

Greenwood Press
Westport, Connecticut • London

Library of Congress Cataloging-in-Publication Data

Kaufman, Burton Ira.
    The Korean conflict / Burton I. Kaufman.
    p.   cm.—(Greenwood Press guides to historic events of the
twentieth century, ISSN 1092–177X)
  Includes bibliographical references and index.
  ISBN 0–313–29909–9 (alk. paper)
  1. Korean War, 1950–1953. I. Title. II. Series.
  DS918.K39   1999
  951.904′2—dc21   98–48905

British Library Cataloguing in Publication Data is available.

Library of Congress Catalog Card Number: 98–48905
ISBN: 0–313–29909–9
ISSN: 1092–177X

First published in 1999

Greenwood Press, 88 Post Road West, Westport, CT 06881
An imprint of Greenwood Publishing Group, Inc.
www.greenwood.com

Printed in the United States of America

The paper used in this book complies with the
Permanent Paper Standard issued by the National
Information Standards Organization (Z39.48–1984).

10 9 8 7 6 5 4 3 2 1

Front cover photo: Truman presents MacArthur with medal. Library of Congress.

Back cover photo: Two army privates operating a bazooka. Library of Congress.

For Heather and Daniel

Contents

A photo essay follows p. 78

Series Foreword

As the twenty-first century approaches, it is time to take stock of the political, social, economic, intellectual, and cultural forces and factors that have made the twentieth century the most dramatic period of change in history. To that end, the Greenwood Press Guides to Historic Events of the Twentieth Century presents interpretive histories of the most significant events of the century. Each book in the series combines narrative history and analysis with primary documents and biographical sketches, with an eye to providing both a reference guide to the principal persons, ideas, and experiences defining each historic event, and a reliable, readable overview of that event. Each book further provides analyses and discussions, grounded in both primary and secondary sources, of the causes and consequences, in thought and action, that give meaning to the historic event under review. By assuming a historical perspective, drawing on the latest and best writing on each subject, and offering fresh insights, each book promises to explain how and why a particular event defined the twentieth century. No consensus about the meaning of the twentieth century emerges from the series, but, collectively, the books identify the most salient concerns of the century. In so doing, the series reminds us of the many ways those historic events continue to affect our lives.

Each book follows a similar format designed to encourage readers to consult it both as a reference and a history in its own right. Each volume opens with a chronology of the historic event, followed by a narrative overview, which also serves to introduce and examine briefly the main themes and issues related to that event. The next set of chapters is composed of topical es-

says, each analyzing closely an issue or problem of interpretation introduced
in the opening chapter. A concluding chapter suggesting the long-term implications and meanings of the historic event brings the strands of the pre-
ceding chapters together while placing the event in the larger historical
context. Each book also includes a section of short biographies of the principal persons related to the event, followed by a section introducing and re-
printing key historical documents illustrative of and pertinent to the event. A
glossary of selected terms adds to the utility of each book. An annotated bibliography—of significant books, films, and CD-ROMs—and an index conclude each volume.

The editors made no attempt to impose any theoretical model or historical
perspective on the individual authors. Rather, in developing the series, an ad-
visory board of noted historians and informed high school history teachers
and public and school librarians identified the topics needful of exploration
and the scholars eminently qualified to examine those events with intelligence and sensitivity. The common commitment throughout the series is to
provide accurate, informative, and readable books, free of jargon and up to
date in evidence and analysis.

Each book stands as a complete historical analysis and reference guide to
a particular historic event. Each book also has many uses, from understanding contemporary perspectives on critical historical issues, to providing biographical treatments of key figures related to each event, to offering excerpts
and complete texts of essential documents about the event, to suggesting and
describing books and media materials for further study and presentation of
the event, and more. The combination of historical narrative and individual
topical chapters addressing significant issues and problems encourages students and teachers to approach each historic event from multiple perspectives and with a critical eye. The arrangement and content of each book thus
invite students and teachers, through classroom discussions and position papers, to debate the character and significance of great historic events and to
discover for themselves how and why history matters.

The series emphasizes the main currents that have shaped the modern
world. Much of that focus necessarily looks at the West, especially Europe and
the United States. The political, commercial, and cultural expansion of the
West wrought largely, though not wholly, the most fundamental changes of
the century. Taken together, however, books in the series reveal the interac-
tions between Western and non-Western peoples and society, and also the tensions between modern and traditional cultures. They also point to the ways in
which non-Western peoples have adapted Western ideas and technology and,
in turn, influenced Western life and thought. Several books examine such in-

creasingly powerful global forces as the rise of Islamic fundamentalism, the emergence of modern Japan, the Communist revolution in China, and the collapse of communism in eastern Europe and the former Soviet Union. American interests and experiences receive special attention in the series, not only in deference to the primary readership of the books but also in recognition that the United States emerged as the dominant political, economic, social, and cultural force during the twentieth century. By looking at the century through the lens of American events and experiences, it is possible to see why the age has come to be known as "The American Century."

Assessing the history of the twentieth century is a formidable prospect. It has been a period of remarkable transformation. The world broadened and narrowed at the same time. Frontiers shifted from the interiors of Africa and Latin America to the moon and beyond; communication spread from mass circulation newspapers and magazines to radio, television, and now the Internet; skyscrapers reached upward and suburbs stretched outward; energy switched from steam, to electric, to atomic power. Many changes did not lead to a complete abandonment of established patterns and practices so much as a synthesis of old and new, as, for example, the increased use of (even reliance on) the telephone in the age of the computer. The automobile and the truck, the airplane, and telecommunications closed distances, and people in unprecedented numbers migrated from rural to urban, industrial, and ever more ethnically diverse areas. Tractors and chemical fertilizers made it possible for fewer people to grow more, but the environmental and demographic costs of an exploding global population threatened to outstrip natural resources and human innovation. Disparities in wealth increased, with developed nations prospering and underdeveloped nations starving. Amid the crumbling of former European colonial empires, Western technology, goods, and culture increasingly enveloped the globe, seeping into, and undermining, non-Western cultures—a process that contributed to a surge of religious fundamentalism and ethno-nationalism in the Middle East, Asia, and Africa. As people became more alike, they also became more aware of their differences. Ethnic and religious rivalries grew in intensity everywhere as the century closed.

The political changes during the twentieth century have been no less profound than the social, economic, and cultural ones. Many of the books in the series focus on political events, broadly defined, but no books are confined to politics alone. Political ideas and events have social effects, just as they spring from a complex interplay of non-political forces in culture, society, and economy. Thus, for example, the modern civil rights and woman's rights movements were at once social and political events in cause and consequence. Likewise, the Cold War created the geopolitical framework for deal-ing with competing ideologies and nations abroad and served as the touchstone for political and cultural identities at home. The books treating political events do so within their social, cultural, and economic contexts.

Several books in the series examine particular wars in depth. Wars are de-fining moments for people and eras. During the twentieth century war be-came more widespread and terrible than ever before, encouraging new efforts to end war through strategies and organizations of international coop-eration and disarmament while also fueling new ideologies and instruments of mass persuasion that fostered distrust and festered old national rivalries. Two world wars during the century redrew the political map, slaughtered or uprooted two generations of people, and introduced and hastened the devel-opment of new technologies and weapons of mass destruction. The First World War spelled the end of the old European order and spurred communist revolution in Russia and fascism in Italy, Germany, and elsewhere. The Sec-ond World War killed fascism and inspired the final push for freedom from European colonial rule in Asia and Africa. It also led to the Cold War that suffocated much of the world for almost half a century. Large wars begat small ones, and brutal totalitarian regimes cropped up across the globe. Af-ter (and in some ways because of) the fall of communism in eastern Europe and the former Soviet Union, wars of competing cultures, national interests, and political systems persisted in the struggle to make a new world order. Continuing, too, has been the belief that military technology can achieve po-litical ends, whether in the superior American firepower that failed to "win" in Vietnam or in the American "smart bombs" and other military wizardry that "won" in the Persian Gulf.

Another theme evident in the series is that throughout the century nation-alism has continued to drive events. Whether in the Balkans in 1914 trigger-ing World War I or in the Balkans in the 1990s threatening the post–Cold War peace—or in many other places—nationalist ambitions and forces would not die. The persistence of nationalism is yet another reminder of the many ways that the past becomes prologue.

We thus offer the series as a modern guide to and interpretation of the historic events of the twentieth century and as an invitation to consider how and why those events have defined not only the past and present but also charted the po-litical, social, intellectual, cultural, and economic routes into the next century.

Randall M. Miller
Saint Joseph's University, Philadelphia

Preface

If there remains a neglected war in the history of the United States, it is the Korean War (1950–1953). Indeed, the lack of interest in the Korean War among high school and college students as compared with the Vietnam War is striking. Since the formal end in 1973 of U.S.'s participation in what has often been referred to as the nation's most unpopular war (Vietnam), courses on that war have been among the most popular on college campuses throughout the country. Even today they continue to draw large enrollments despite the fact that most students in these courses were not even born when the war in Vietnam ended. The Vietnam War Memorial in Washington, D.C., continues to be among the most popular tourist attractions in the nation's capital.

Interest in the Korean War also seems to be growing. Over the last ten or fifteen years, scores of new books have been published, many of them drawing on newly available materials not only from the United States and its allies in the conflict, especially Great Britain, but also from its former adversaries, the former Soviet Union and the People's Republic of China (Communist China). As a result, we now have a more complete and comprehensive account of the conflict than we do for the Vietnam War. The magnificent new memorial in Washington, D.C., to veterans of the Korean War, which flanks the side of the Lincoln Memorial opposite the Vietnam War Memorial, stands as a belated recognition of the nation's gratitude to the thousands of Americans who fought, suffered, and died in the forbidding hills and mountains of Korea.

Still there has never been an outpouring of national interest in the Korean Conflict even remotely resembling that which has characterized the Vietnam War. The fact that the Korean Memorial was constructed more than a decade after the Vietnam Memorial even though U.S. military involvement in Korea preceded its similar involvement in Vietnam by more than a decade is a testimony to the nation's relative interest (or lack thereof) in the two wars. In contrast to the Vietnam War, there have also been very few, if any, undergraduate courses dealing exclusively with the Korean conflict. Personally, I have been struck in my more than thirty years of teaching by how few students, especially my more recent students, know, or have heard, about the Korean War.

Yet in historical terms the Korean War was just as, or even more, important than the Vietnam War. Indeed, it is not too much to argue that, without the Korean War, there may not have been direct American military involvement in Vietnam. As most historians now recognize, the war in Korea greatly expanded America's military commitments worldwide and shifted the focus of the nations policymakers from an almost exclusive interest in developments in Europe and the Middle East to one that embraced Asia as well. It also had a profound impact on Washington's allies and enemies, making America's European friends reluctant to follow the United States's military lead in places like Vietnam, gaining new respect for Communist China, especially among Third World nations, and contributing to the growing division between China and the Soviet Union. Regionally, it left Korea permanently divided, began Japan's economic "miracle," and made possible South Korea's own economic growth. Occurring at the middle of the twentieth century, it helped shape the course of international affairs for the rest of the century. All this I hope the following pages make clear.

In preparing this book, I wish to acknowledge the support, the patience, and the assistance of Randall M. Miller of St. Joseph's University, the editor of the series to which this volume is a contribution. Not only did Randall do an extremely careful job of editing the manuscript, he made numerous helpful comments and suggestions for changes, all with the gentle prodding of a fine editor who must deal with a sometimes prickly author. I appreciate very much the help he gave me throughout the preparation of this book. I also want to thank Randall and the Greenwood Press for granting me the extension of time needed to complete the book. Once more, I am grateful to my son, Scott, who made available to me documents he found while conducting his own research at the British Public Records Office in London and for repeatedly making me aware of new titles having to do with the Korean War that I might otherwise have overlooked. I also thank my wife,

Diane, for her love and support over more than thirty-three years of marriage (and for help with the bibliography). But I dedicate this book to my daughter and my new son-in-law, Heather Bank and Daniel Bank.

Chronology of Events

1904–1905	Russo-Japanese War; Korea annexed by Japan
March 1, 1919	Beginning of Korean demonstrations against Japanese rule
December 1, 1943	Cairo Conference; Roosevelt, Churchill and Chiang Kai-shek state that "in due course Korea shall become free and independent"
August 15, 1945	Japan agrees to surrender, thereby ending World War II
September 2, 1945	Instrument of Japanese surrender signed in Tokyo Bay
September 8, 1945	American occupation forces land in Korea
October 1945	Syngman Rhee returns to Korea
December 1945	Moscow foreign ministers' conference agrees to joint Soviet-American commission to prepare Korea for election of a provisional government and trusteeship lasting as long as five years; demonstrations follow
May 1946	Joint Commission disbanded
September 17, 1947	The United States refers issue of Korean reunion and independence to United Nations
September 29, 1947	U.S. Joint Chiefs of Staff declare South Korea of little strategic value
October 1947	The United States presents a resolution at United Nations calling for separate elections in U.S. and Soviet zones. A United Nations Temporary Commission (UNTCOK) would be established to supervise elections for a Korean government

January 1948	Soviet Union refuses to allow UNTCOK to enter its zone in Korea
February 1948	UN approves U.S. resolution giving UNTCOK authority to supervise elections "in such parts of Korea as might be accessible to the Commission."
May 10, 1948	National Assembly elected in South Korea; names Syngman Rhee as the first president of the Republic of Korea (ROK)
August 15, 1948	Republic of Korea formally established
September 9, 1948	In North Korea, Democratic People's Republic of Korea formally established
October 1948	Mutiny of South Korean constabulary about to embark for island of Cheju to put down rebellion there; lasts until January 1949
November 1948	Rhee imposes martial law over most of South Korea
December 10, 1948	The United States agrees to $300 million in military aid to South Korea
January 1, 1949	The United States formally recognizes Seoul government
March 1949	National Security Council recommends withdrawal of all American forces by June 30, 1949
April 8, 1949	Soviet Union vetoes South Korean membership in UN
January 12, 1950	Secretary of State Acheson delivers speech placing Korea outside the U.S. defense perimeter
April 1950	National Security Council sends to President Truman NSC-68, which becomes the blueprint of the Cold War
May 5, 1950	Rhee's party loses elections
June 19, 1950	CIA determines that North Korea could capture much of South Korea, including Seoul, without help from Communist China or the Soviet Union
June 25, 1950	North Korea invades South Korea; UN seeks cease-fire
June 27, 1950	UN calls for military sanctions against North Korea
June 30, 1950	Seoul falls to North Korean forces
June 30, 1950	Truman authorizes the use of American ground forces in Korea under UN command
July 1, 1950	American task force arrives in Korea from Japan
July 3, 1950	U.S. troops engage North Koreans for first time
July 3, 1950	General Douglas MacArthur begins plans for amphibious operation against North Korean forces
July 8, 1950	MacArthur appointed Supreme Commander of UN forces in Korea

July 19, 1950	Truman asks Congress for $10 billion for military weapons
July 13–20, 1950	U.S. ground troops at Taejon suffer casualties of almost 30 percent
July 19, 1950	Truman asks Congress for substantial increase in military and defense spending
July 21, 1950	National Guard and reserves called up
July 26, 1950	Great Britain, Australia, and New Zealand commit troops to Korea under UN command
August 1, 1950	Soviet Union returns to UN Security Council
August 4, 1950	Soviet Union calls for cease-fire in Korea
August 14, 1950	MacArthur ordered not to authorize any attack from Formosa against the Chinese mainland
August 26, 1950	Release of MacArthur's statement to Veterans of Foreign War urging defense of Formosa
September 4, 1950	The United States announces Soviet flier found in plane shot down in Korea
September 7, 1950	UN forces successfully defend Pusan perimeter
September 8, 1950	Defense Production Act passed giving Truman broad discretionary power over the economy
September 12, 1950	George C. Marshall appointed Secretary of Defense
September 15, 1950	Amphibious landing at Inchon
September 16, 1950	UN forces begin breakout from Pusan Perimeter
September 27, 1950	Seoul recaptured
September 27, 1950	Truman approves directive for UN forces to cross 38th parallel
September 28, 1950	Communist China threatens intervention if North Korea is invaded
October 7, 1950	UN adopts resolution authorizing UN forces to cross into North Korea
October 15, 1950	Truman meets MacArthur on Wake Island
October 19, 1950	North Korean capital of Pyongyang falls to UN forces
October 24, 1950	MacArthur orders U.S. forces to march to Yalu River
October 26, 1950	First Chinese troops taken prisoners by UN forces
October 27, 1950	South Korean forces reach Yalu River
November 6, 1950	MacArthur announces that Chinese forces have entered Korea
November 9, 1950	UN Security Council fails to take action on British proposal to establish a buffer zone around Yalu River
November 20, 1950	U.S. forces reach Manchurian border

November 24, 1950	UN forces begin "home by Christmas" offensive
November 25–28, 1950	200,000 Chinese troops invade North Korea
November 30, 1950	Truman refuses at press conference to reject possible use of atomic weapons against Chinese
December 3, 1950	UN forces withdraw south of Pyongyang
December 5, 1950	British Prime Minister Clement Attlee begins two weeks of talks in Washington with Truman
December 15, 1950	Truman declares state of emergency in the United States
December 22, 1950	Joint Chiefs of Staff inform MacArthur that no additional troops will be sent to the Far East until Truman administration decides future courses of action
December 26, 1950	General Matthew Ridgway assumes command of Eighth Army
January 1, 1951	Communist forces advance below 38th parallel
January 4, 1951	UN forces abandon Seoul to communists
January 5, 1951	Senator Robert Taft of Ohio accuses Truman of usurping authority by sending troops to Korea to fight in an undeclared war without congressional approval
January 24, 1951	Communist offensive halted along line approximating 37th parallel
January 25, 1951	UN forces begin new offensive known as Operation Thunderbolt
February 1, 1951	UN approves American resolution branding China an aggressor nation
February 11, 1951	UN forces again cross 38th parallel
February 18, 1951	Chinese counterattack halted
March 14, 1951	Seoul reclaimed by UN forces for second time
March 24, 1951	MacArthur threatens Chinese with extension of Korean War unless they agree to a truce
April 5, 1951	In letter released by House Minority Leader Joseph W. Martin, General MacArthur questions the administration's foreign policy
April 11, 1951	MacArthur relieved of commands by Truman; Ridgway named to succeed him as Supreme Commander of UN forces in Korea
April 14, 1951	Lieutenant General James A. Van Fleet assumes command of Eighth Army
April 17, 1951	MacArthur returns to United States; receives hero's welcome in San Francisco
April 19, 1951	MacArthur addresses joint session of Congress

April 22, 1951	Chinese launch first phase of a major spring offensive
May 3, 1951	U.S. Senate opens hearings on MacArthur's recall
May 16, 1951	Chinese launch second phase of spring offensive; suffer heavy casualties
May 23, 1951	UN forces begin counteroffensive
June 10, 1951	UN forces break into communist "iron triangle"
June 23, 1951	Soviet Union calls for Korean cease-fire
July 2, 1951	Communists agree to begin armistice negotiations
July 10, 1951	UN and Communist negotiators begin truce talks at Kaesong
July 25, 1951	Agreement reached at Kaesong on agenda for negotiations
August 5, 1951	Truce talks suspended after Ridgway charges communist violations of neutral zone
August 10, 1951	Talks resume after North Koreans promise to respect neutral zone
August 24, 1951	Communists suspend negotiations again, claiming UN violations of neutral zone
September 8, 1951	Signing of Japanese Peace Treaty in San Francisco
September 13, 1951	Battle for "Heartbreak Ridge" begins
September 24, 1951	Communist negotiators at Kaesong leave meeting after rejecting plan to reopen peace talks
October 6, 1951	UN troops retake "Heartbreak Ridge"
October 25, 1951	Truce talks transferred to Panmunjom
November 12, 1951	General Ridgway adopts military policy of "active defense"
November 25, 1951	Negotiators at Panmunjom reach tentative agreement on truce line
January 2, 1952	UNC proposes voluntary repatriation of POWs
January 5, 1952	British Prime Minister Winston Churchill arrives in Washington, D.C., to confer with President Truman
January 10, 1952	UN delegation at Panmunjom rejects armistice when North Koreans refuse to ban building of new air bases
February 18, 1952	Major clash between UN guards and POWs at Koje-do POW camp
March 4, 1952	Communists accuse UN forces of using germ warfare
April 11, 1952	Dwight Eisenhower leaves NATO, presumably to run for president
April 15, 1952	President Truman signs Japanese peace treaty
May 7, 1952	Commander of Koje-do POW camp, General Francis T. Dodd, taken prisoner

May 7, 1952	Armistice negotiations stall over repatriation of POWs
May 7, 1952	General Mark Clark succeeds Ridgway as UN Commander
June 3, 1952	U.S. forces, supported by tanks, retake Koje-do POW camp
June 4, 1952	The United States and Britain protest President Syngman Rhee's purge of South Korean Assembly
June 23, 1952	Over 500 UN planes attack Suiho, heavily damaging five of North Korea's largest hydroelectric plants
August 29, 1952	UN planes bomb and destroy much of Pyongyang in heaviest attack of war
October 23, 1952	Republican presidential candidate Dwight Eisenhower promises in Detroit to "go to Korea" if elected
November 4, 1952	Eisenhower elected president in landslide victory
December 2, 1952	Eisenhower begins three-day visit to Korea
January 30, 1953	Eisenhower announces that he will pull Seventh Fleet out of Formosa Straits
February 27, 1953	F-84 Thunderbirds raid North Korean base on Yalu River
March 5, 1953	Soviet Premier Joseph Stalin dies of stroke
March 23, 1953	Battle of Pork Chop Hill begins
March 28, 1953	Communists accept UN plan for exchange of sick and injured POWs
April 20, 1953	Operation Little Switch (exchange of sick and injured POWs)
May 23, 1953	South Korea's President Syngman Rhee threatens to remove ROK army with UNC in protest over armistice terms
June 14, 1953	Chinese begin series of major attacks against ROK forces in the biggest battle since 1951
June 18, 1953	Eisenhower rebukes Rhee for releasing North Korean POWs without UN authority
July 27, 1953	Armistice ending Korean War signed at Panmunjom
August 23, 1953	Operation Big Switch (exchange of POWs) begins
April 26, 1954	Opening of Geneva Conference on the reunification of Korea and other Asian matters
April 27, 1960	President Syngman Rhee forced to resign after nationwide demonstrations against his regime; instability and martial law follow
July 19, 1965	Syngman Rhee dies
January 30, 1968	North Korea captures U.S. intelligence ship *Pueblo*; ship later released after its commander, Lloyd Bucher, signs confession (later renounced by him) that ship was engaged in espionage

August 18, 1976	North Koreans kill two Americans in demilitarized zone
October 27, 1979	South Korean President Park Chung Hee assassinated
September 16, 1980	North Korea names Kim Jong Il to succeed his father, Kim Il Sung
September 1, 1983	Korean Airlines Flight 269 downed by Soviet jet killing 269 passengers after straying over Soviet airspace
July 8, 1985	President Ronald Reagan condemns North Korea as one of five "terrorist states"
July 8, 1994	Kim Il Sung dies

THE KOREAN CONFLICT
EXPLAINED

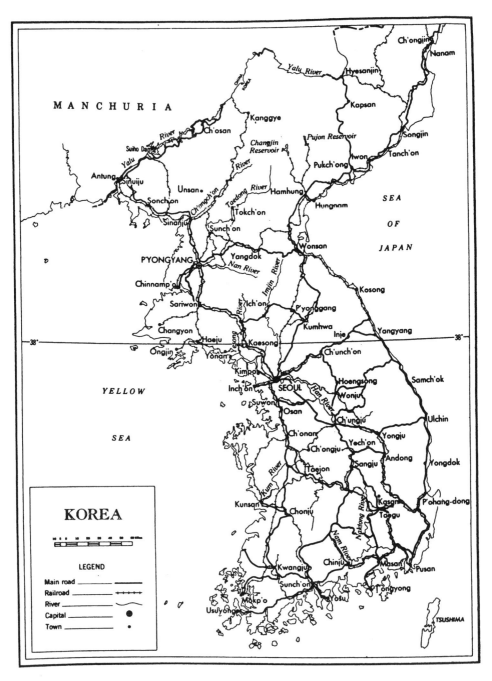

Map 1. From United States Army, Center of Military History, *Korea: 1950* (Washington, DC: Government Printing Office, 1997).

1

Historical Overview

On Sunday, June 25 (Korean time), 1950, the armed forces of North Korea am Independence, approved orders to General Douglas MacArthur in Tokyo to sttacked South Korea below the 38th parallel, which had divided the Korean peninsula since the end of World War II. Informed of the attack while he was at home in Independence, Missouri, President Harry S Truman responded by approving a proposal for an emergency meeting of the United Nations Security Council. The Security Council met the next day (June 25, New York time) and approved a U.S. resolution calling for the end of hostilities and the withdrawal of North Korean forces above the 38th parallel. Later that day, Truman, who had flown back to Washington, D.C., froend supplies and a survey team to Korea. Over the next four days, as the North Koreans continued to advance further south, Truman escalated America's military commitment in Korea. On June 29, he authorized the sending of a regimental combat team to Korea. Over the next three years, approximately 1.4 million American soldiers, serving as part of a United Nations Command (UNC), fought North Korean and Chinese communist forces in a conflict that dramatically changed the complexion of the Cold War and served as a precedent for U.S. involvement in Vietnam a decade later.

The great irony of the Korean Conflict was that at the time the North Koreans invaded South Korea, most Americans had never heard of Korea. The Korean peninsula, moreover, was not part of an American defense perimeter in East Asia that Secretary of State Dean Acheson had described in a speech to the National Press Association just six months earlier. Furthermore, even though the Korean Conflict drastically upped the ante of the Cold War and led to twenty years of especially bitter relations between the United States and Communist China (People's Republic of China or the PRC), neither the Soviet Union nor the PRC had been particularly anxious to have North Korea invade South Korea.

The reasons for the outbreak of hostilities on June 25 and the response it engendered are far more explicable today than they were nearly fifty or even fifteen years ago. For one thing, it is now clear that the Korean War was part of a continuing civil conflict in Korea since the end of World War II. During most of the twentieth century, Korea had been ruled by Japan as a rice-producing colony. Although Korea had a long and proud history going back nearly 2,000 years, the Japanese had tried to extinguish all vestiges of Korean national identity. But they had failed. After the war, a number of groups sought to assume the mantle of leadership. All groups believed that Korea, which, according to an agreement reached immediately following the end of the war in August, was to be occupied above the 38th parallel by the Soviet Union and below that line by the United States, should be reunited and given its independence. Otherwise, they were divided ideologically and politically. On the one hand was a conservative elite of landowners, businessmen, and manufacturers who had enjoyed a privileged status under Japanese rule that they sought to retain. On the other were political leftists, including large numbers of peasants and workers, who sought a fundamental change in the social and political structure of Korea. Even before World War II officially ended in August 1945, clashes had taken place between the opposing groups as workers and peasant unions flourished and communist strength grew.

This was the situation that faced the American occupation force under the command of Lieutenant General John Hodge when it landed in September 1945. Hodge's instructions were to not recognize any political group as the legitimate government of Korea but instead to proceed with the establishment of an American military government (AMG). Disturbed by the political and social chaos he found in Korea, however, Hodge was soon working closely with rightist elements, particularly with Syngman Rhee, a tenacious Korean nationalist who had spent most of his adult life in the United States working for Korean independence. Hodge believed that Rhee represented the best chance to restore order and stability in Korea.

Yet Rhee's goal of immediate Korean independence conflicted with American policy. At the Cairo Conference of 1943, President Franklin Roosevelt, Prime Minister Winston Churchill of Great Britain, and Generalissimo Chiang Kai-shek of China declared that "in due course Korea shall become free and independent." The Potsdam Conference of July 1945 reaffirmed the Cairo statement. But what Roosevelt had in mind at Cairo was a multipower trusteeship, which would include the United States, the Soviet Union, Great Britain, and China and which could last up to forty years. He did not think that Korea was ready for immediate independence after the war. He also opposed having Korea occupied by a single power because he thought that could lead to a great power struggle over Korea similar to the conflict between Russia and Japan that resulted in the Russo-Japanese War of 1904.

After Truman took office in 1945, he adopted the basic outlines of Roosevelt's policy for Korea. At a Moscow meeting of foreign ministers in December, both the United States and the Soviet Union agreed to an American proposal providing for the election of a provisional government and the establishment of a trusteeship lasting for as long as five years. A joint Soviet-American commission was established to prepare Korea for the election of the provisional government. But although the commission met several times, all-Korean elections for the establishment of a provisional government were never held. Because the Moscow agreement delayed Korean independence for as much as five years, it was greeted with demonstrations and work stoppages by Koreans of all political persuasions.

Even more important in preventing elections was the hardening of relations between Washington and Moscow. The United States and the Soviet Union had been at odds with each other politically and ideologically since the Bolshevik Revolution of 1917. The United States had intervened in the Russian Civil War of 1918 and had not even recognized Moscow until 1933. For its part, the Soviet Union had called for world revolution and the end of capitalism. The exigencies of fighting a common enemy had brought the two powers together during World War II. For a short time after the war, President Truman had sought to maintain the grand coalition that had won the war. But traditional distrusts and misperceptions surfaced once more. The Soviet Union maintained tight control over eastern Europe and posed a threat to Greece, Turkey, and Iran. The United States refused to supply Moscow with badly needed economic assistance and subtly reminded the Soviets of its nuclear monopoly.

In a long telegram from Moscow in February 1946, George Kennan, a State Department expert on the Soviet Union, warned that the United States was faced with an implacable foe and wrote about the need to contain further Soviet expansionism. This doctrine of containment became the basis of the "get tough" policy that President Truman adopted toward the Soviet Union by the spring of 1946; it was also the foundation of American foreign policy throughout most of the Cold War. Kennan intended to "contain" the Soviets through economic means, such as the Marshall Plan of 1948. That he meant to rely on such a strategy is hardly surprising. Until the Korean War, most American leaders thought the greatest danger from the Soviet Union would come from a communist takeover of the economically devastated nations of western Europe. They never really feared overt Soviet aggression across Europe. The purpose of the Marshall Plan was, therefore, to bring about European economic recovery in order to prevent communist parties in countries like France and Italy from seizing political power. Not until the formation of the North Atlantic Treaty Organization (NATO) in 1949 and the war in Korea a year later did the doctrine of containment assume a more military orientation.

The onset of the Cold War directly affected developments in Korea. Increasingly, American policy within its occupation zone became one of supporting rightist elements and limiting leftist political activity. An effort to establish a moderate centrist coalition of Korean leaders failed when one of its most prominent members was killed by an unknown assassin. In their zone, the Soviets established a Communist Provisional People's Committee led by Kim Il Sung, a thirty-five-year-old former resistance fighter against the Japanese who had received military training from the Soviets during the war.

In May 1948, elections were held in South Korea under the auspices of the United Nations, and two months later the newly established legislative assembly elected Rhee as the first president of the Republic of South Korea (ROK). A separate regime, the Democratic People's Republic of Korea (DPR), led by Kim Il Sung, was established in the north, in December, but the United Nations (UN) declared the South Korean government as the lawful government in Korea.

During the two years that followed, political conditions in Korea remained very unstable. Civil war raged in South Korea as political leftists engaged in various guerrilla activities that included attacks on towns, burning of villages, and the kidnaping and murder of rightist leaders and the police. The violence that continued to spread throughout South Korea undermined political confidence in the security forces and exposed the weakness of the Rhee government, which became increasingly oppressive and imposed martial law on the country.

Despite the instability of the Rhee regime and considerable opposition from the State Department in Washington, which was concerned about the military threat to South Korea from North Korea, American policy was to withdraw from Korea as soon as possible. Military leaders believed that Korea lacked military and strategic value in case of a war in Asia. In the wake of the communist victory in China, they were also reluctant to make military commitments on the Asian mainland, and they shared the administration's view that Europe and not Asia would be the main area of confrontation with the Soviet Union. Secretary of State Acheson's speech before the National Press Association in January 1950, in which he placed Korea outside of the American defense perimeter in Asia, was merely public confirmation of what was already existing policy.

Meanwhile, Kim Il Sung, who had built an impressive military force outfitted by the Soviet Union, made plans for an invasion of South Korea. He had been allowed to build such a force because Moscow viewed North Korea as part of a security blanket around its borders. Ironically, the United States refused to equip South Korea in a similar way because it feared that South Korea might use its military strength to invade North Korea, thereby precipitating a major conflict between the United States and the Soviet Union.

In the spring of 1950, Kim visited Moscow and Peking (Beijing) where he tried to persuade Soviet leader Joseph Stalin and Chinese leader Mao Zedong (Mao Tse-tung) to approve his plans for an invasion. Neither leader was particularly anxious to give him the green light. Both Stalin and Mao were concerned that an attack on South Korea might lead to an American response. The Soviet leader, moreover, was preoccupied with the West, whereas the Chinese leader was fearful of any action that might divert his attention away from his own plans to attack Formosa (Taiwan). However, Stalin agreed to the invasion after being reassured that South Korea could be defeated within three days, and Mao had little choice except to go along with him.[1]

The North Korean attack on June 25 was a smashing success. Equipped by the Soviets with more than 1,400 artillery pieces and 126 modern tanks, the North Korean force of 110,000 soldiers quickly drove the ill-equipped and badly outnumbered South Korean (ROK) forces into hasty retreat. By the third day of the invasion, the North Korean forces had captured the South Korean capital of Seoul. By the fifth day, they had driven another twenty-five miles south of Seoul. Despite Truman's decision to commit U.S. forces to the defense of South Korea, there was really little that he could do immediately to halt the North Korean advance. In order to prevent the Korean War form serving as a diversion for an attack on or from Formosa, Truman ordered the Seventh Fleet into the Formosa Straight. On June 27, he also won approval from the United Nations, which the United States still dominated, of a resolution calling for military sanctions against North Korea, thereby securing the imprimatur of the UN on U.S. actions. But neither of these developments had much immediate bearing on the fighting in Korea.

Even though the Pentagon had expressed major reservations about the military and strategic value of Korea, once North Korea attacked South Korea, the president felt that he had little choice other than a military response. In the first place, Truman and most foreign policy officials believed that North Korea was merely serving as a proxy for the Soviet Union, who, they were convinced, had ordered the invasion. Geopolitical concerns also weighed heavily on their minds. By 1950 the United States was committed to resurrecting Japan as a major power in East Asia. Korea was regarded as important both as a future market for Japanese goods and as a source of rice for Japan, just as it had been during the Japanese occupation. Conversely, the loss of Korea to the communists would pose a real danger to Japan separated as it was by only 100 miles from the Korean port of Pusan.

The administration also believed that its credibility both at home and abroad, both among U.S. allies and its enemies, was at stake in Korea. By 1950, a "red scare" had spread throughout the United States. For many Americans, the United States was imperiled by the threat of communism both at home and abroad. Events of the previous year augured ill for the future: the Soviet Union's successful testing of an atomic bomb in September; the fall of China to the communists a month later; the conviction of Alger Hiss, a former high State Department official of perjury for denying under oath that he had been a communist in the 1930s; and the admission by Karl Fuchs, a high-level atomic scientist, that he had given atomic secrets to the communists. The red-baiting junior senator for Wisconsin, Joseph McCarthy, made the State Department one of his prime targets, accusing it of harboring known or former communist agents. Secretary of State Dean Acheson was pillored by McCarthy and his followers, who held Acheson and other high-ranking State Department officials largely responsible for the loss of China.

To allow Korea to fall to the communists so soon after China had fallen, therefore, would turn the American people even more against an already unpopular president and administration, especially if it were revealed how sadly unprepared the United States was for war. It also would damage American prestige in Europe and the Middle East, and smack of appeasement, which could lead to further aggression, just as the Munich Agreement of 1938 had nurtured Adolf Hitler's expansionist ambitions. At the same time, bringing the invasion to the UN made sense to the administration. The United States had earlier acted within the framework of the UN, and taking the matter to the Security Council let the world know just how seriously it regarded the fighting in Korea. It was also a way to achieve a collective response to the invasion rather than a unilateral action by Washington.

But the employment of American and other UN forces under the aegis of the United Nations Command (UNC) led by General Douglas MacArthur took time. In the interim, the North Koreans were able to continue their advance against the ROK army and the small American contingent that Truman had ordered to Korea immediately after the North Korean invasion. By August 1950, the only part of Korea not captured by the North Koreans was an eighty-mile defense perimeter around the Korean port of Pusan. But in the two months since the invasion, a steady stream of American personnel and equipment had been sent to Korea. On September 15, the conflict changed dramatically when UN forces successfully conducted an amphibious flanking operation at Inchon, twenty-five miles west of Seoul. About the same time other UN forces broke out of the defense perimeter around Pusan. The Joint Chiefs of Staff (JCS) had been opposed to the amphibious operation, warning MacArthur that Inchon had some of the highest tides in the world and that the city itself was protected by a seawall, both of which would make an amphibious operation extremely hazardous. But MacArthur, a brilliant but vainglorious commander with a towering ego and supreme sense of self-confidence, countered that it was precisely these conditions that would assure the element of surprise essential to the success of his amphibious operation. Because MacArthur was such a commanding and persuasive figure, who, in the view of many Americans, was one of the great military commanders in history, the JCS was reluctant to challenge him. Instead, they deferred to his judgment, and the Inchon operation proved every bit as successful as MacArthur said it would be. Most of the North Korean forces were able to escape form the trap of the two pronged pincer operation against them. But by the end of September, Seoul had been retaken, and the North Korean armies had retreated north of the 38th parallel. Had the UN command been ordered to stop at the 38th parallel, the United States might have been able to declare victory in Korea.

Even before the landing at Inchon, however, the White House had begun to consider the possibility of not stopping at the 38th parallel but, instead, of "rolling back" communism by crossing this artificially set line and advancing all the way to the Yalu River separating Korea from China. Most of the American public favored expanding the war into North Korea. Even the conservative *Life* magazine and the liberal magazine *The New Republic*, polar opposites politically, agreed that UN forces should cross the 38th parallel. "The restoration of the status quo ante [in Korea was] no longer a matter of negotiation with the USSR," *The New Republic* concluded.[2] According to *Life*, the authority of UN forces to march above the 38th parallel was implicit in the 1943 agreement in Cairo that "in due course" Korea was to become free and independent.

The White House's major concern was how the Soviet Union and China would respond to such an advance northward. Although there were some skeptics, the general feeling within the White House and at the State Department and Pentagon was that the time for Moscow's involvement in the conflict had passed and that the Chinese would stay out of the war if they were given adequate assurances that UN forces would stop at the Yalu river and not attack China. Republican and Democratic leaders in Congress said much the same thing.

If there still remained any doubts about the possibility of intervention into Korea by Beijing and Moscow, the Wake Island conference of October 15 between President Truman and General MacArthur served to dispel them. Truman later said that he made the 18,000 mile trip from Washington to Wake Island because he had never met his Far East commander and thought that it was time to do so. In truth, the president wanted to be in the same public spotlight that shined on MacArthur because of his success at Inchon, while also getting the measure of the man by personal interviews. Truman distrusted the arrogant, even insubordinate, general, whom he referred to in his diary as "Mr. Prima Donna." He was infuriated especially by a message MacArthur had delivered in August to the Veterans of Foreign Wars (VFW) in which the general stressed the need to defend Formosa against invasion from the mainland. Truman wanted to make clear to him that the Far East was only part of America's larger global responsibilities and that messages such as the one he had sent to the VFW were inappropriate.

At the Wake Island meeting, MacArthur apologized for his earlier remarks to the VFW and stated that the war in Korea would be over by November. He dismissed out-of-hand a warning China made through diplomatic channels that it would enter the conflict if UN forces crossed the 38th parallel. In MacArthur's view, China made the threat only because it was greatly embarrassed by the turn of events in Korea. Encouraged by MacArthur's comments, Truman left the Wake Island meeting saying that he had "never had a more satisfactory conference" since becoming president.

Influenced by these winds of war and displaying considerable hubris, therefore, the administration gave UN forces in Korea orders to continue their advance northward. On the western side of the Korean peninsula, which was divided in the center by a spine of mountains, the Eighth Army moved northward under the command of General Walton Walker. In the east, the X Corps, consisting of the First Marine Division and the Army's Seventh Infantry Division, advanced under the command of General Edward M. Almond.

Although Beijing had agreed only reluctantly to North Korea's invasion of South Korea, it had begun to prepare for entry into the war as early as August. There is considerable controversy about what motivated the PRC to intervene in Korea in November. Recent scholarship suggests that even had the UN decided not to march to the Yalu, China's leader Mao Zedong would have intervened, believing that American imperialism had to be contained, that China's intervention in the war afforded him an opportunity to eliminate counterrevolutionary opponents in China and to expand China's influence in East Asia, and that he had a responsibility to support revolutionary wars such as the one being fought in Korea.[3]

These considerations aside, there can be little doubt that the UN's almost unimpeded march toward the Yalu assured China's entry into the war. At the end of October, intelligence confirmed that Chinese forces had entered North Korea, and in early November, UN forces encountered Chinese troops for the first time. But almost as soon as the Chinese engaged in battle, they broke off the fighting. Whether this maneuver was intended as a warning to the UNC not to advance any further or was part of a trap to lure UN forces further north before attacking in full force is unclear. What is clear is that General MacArthur dismissed the Chinese action and continued the UN march northward, even promising on November 24 to have American troops home for Christmas.

Two days later, the Chinese struck in massive numbers against the overextended, ill-equipped, and outnumbered UN troops, inflicting what military historian Roy Appleman has called "one of the worst defeats an American army has ever suffered."[4] Although there were moments of great heroism, such as the breakout of the 1st Marine Division from its trap at the Chosin Reservoir in the brutally cold wastelands of northeast Korea, by the time Chinese forces were stopped, at the end of January, the Eighth Army had withdrawn more than 300 miles, the longest retreat in American military history. Once more the South Korean capital of Seoul was in enemy hands. Instead of having as its objective the liberation of North Korea from communist control, the purpose of the war returned to the original one of keeping South Korea from falling to the communists.

The Chinese intervention had an immediate and shocking impact on the American public. Americans were now faced with the possibility of a humiliating defeat in a country that, until six months earlier, few had ever heard of, in a war they had come to embrace only as overwhelming victory seemed imminent, and at the hands of a people whom, historically, the United States had treated with a curious mixture of paternalism and disdain, much of which had been racially motivated. For those who believed that President Truman had courted disaster in Asia by misdirected attention to Europe, their worst fears seemed realized. Indeed, the Chinese intervention touched off a great debate in the United States over its proper role in the world that lasted well until 1951. In December 1950, former President Herbert Hoover outlined in a speech his "Gibraltar" concept of American defense, which, he said, should be based on air power and economic self-sufficiency in the Western Hemisphere. Although his remarks were dismissed by some critics as nothing more than the isolationist mutterings of a failed president grown senile, his speech received enormous press coverage and filled the airwaves and media with charges and countercharges of isolationism and misguided internationalism.

The Chinese offensive, however, had not been an unqualified success for the Chinese or an unmitigated disaster for UN forces. As the Chinese advanced below Seoul, they faced an increasing barrage of artillery fire, which took a heavy toll on them. Their supply lines also grew thin, and they began to run out of supplics. Following the accidental death of General Walker in December, moreover, the Eighth Army was placed under the command of General Matthew B. Ridgway, a tough and demanding field commander who had led the 82nd Airborne Division during World War II and had jumped with the division at Normandy. The X Corps was also merged into his command.

On February 21, Ridgway launched "Operation Killer," which resulted in the recapture of Seoul and forced the communists to withdraw their troops from most of South Korea. By the end of April, UN forces had established a new defensive line, "Line Wyoming," which again took them above the 38th parallel and which, in the center, reached almost to a heavily defended area known as the "iron triangle" (Pyonggang-Chorwon-Kumhwa). But this time, the decision to cross the 38th parallel was based purely on the need to interrupt enemy offensive operation; no longer was serious consideration given in Washington to marching north to Yalu River.

Despite the Chinese intervention into the war, General Douglas MacArthur had continued to oppose strongly anything short of total victory. On April 11, President Truman relieved MacArthur of all his commands after House Minority Leader Joseph W. Martin made public a message in which the general publicly challenged the president's foreign policy.[5] To replace MacArthur, Truman named Ridgway. To replace Ridgway as commander of the Eighth Army, the president appointed Lieutenant General James A. Van Fleet, commander of the 2nd Army at Fort Meade, Maryland.

Truman's firing of MacArthur touched off one of the most bitter political backlashes in the nation's history. Arriving in San Francisco and then flying to Washington, D.C., to deliver a speech to a hastily called joint session of Congress, MacArthur was greeted by an outpouring of emotion rarely extended to any individual. His own eloquent address to Congress in which he stated that there was "no substitute for victory" and ended by referring to himself as just an "old soldier" trying to do his duty as he viewed it, added to the public outrage against the White House. In some places, effigies of Truman were even hung or burned at the stake. On Capitol Hill, there were calls for the president's impeachment.

Very quickly, however, the public tumult began to subside. Although Truman remained a very unpopular president, as much for his domestic politics as for his conduct of the Cold War, cooler heads began to prevail. MacArthur's own proposals for expanding the Korean War to include targets inside China also came to be viewed as dangerous. At Senate hearings convened by the Senate Foreign Relations and Armed Services Committees to examine the administration's Far East policy, General Omar Bradley of the Joint Chiefs of Staff effectively put to rest the arguments for an expanded conflict when he remarked that MacArthur's plans would put the United States "in the wrong war, at the wrong place, at the wrong time, and with the wrong enemy." Although the hearings dragged on for seven weeks, by the time they concluded, even Republican members of the two committees holding the hearings conceded that MacArthur had exceeded his authority by directly challenging the president's foreign policy and that "the removal of Gen. MacArthur was within the constitutional power of the President."

At the end of April, even as the hearings were continuing in Washington, the Chinese again went on the attack, launching their greatest military effort of the war and recapturing Seoul for the third time. But in contrast to the UN withdrawal of December and January, this retreat was orderly and extremely costly to the communists. By May, the Chinese offensive, which had been carried out in two phases, had been stopped, and once more UN forces were able to drive the Chinese and North Koreans back roughly to where they had started their offensive. Indeed, the communist forces had become so disorganized and demoralized that some field commanders, including Van Fleet, wanted to move farther north. But the Truman administration decided to halt the advance in order to test the chances for peace. Although tough fighting and some major battles lay ahead over the next two years on hills known as Old Baldy, Capital, Pork Chop, and Heartbreak Ridge, the positions occupied by the two opposing military forces at the end of May were roughly the same ones as the ones they would hold when the armistice ending the war was signed in July 1953.

By the middle of 1951, the helicopter had begun to play a major role in the war. Referred to during the war as "whirlybirds," helicopters also started replacing jeeps for reconnaissance purposes; in one battle, Lieutenant General Edward M. Almond actually commanded the Tenth Army from a helicopter flying over the battlefield. Helicopters were also used to carry equipment and infantrymen to forward areas and to search for enemy mines in the waters of both coasts of Korea. It was the helicopter's ability to land beside a wounded soldier and then carry him quickly to a mobile Army surgical hospital near the battlefront (the so-called M.A.S.H. units, later made famous in one of the nation's most popular television shows of the same name) or hospital ship off-shore that made it such an indispensable tool of the war. Nurses, who worked alongside doctors in the M.A.S.H. units and in flights carrying the wounded from Korea, began to receive some of the recognition that had been denied them in earlier wars. *Reader's Digest*, the country's most widely read magazine, even featured a story from *Everywomen's Magazine*, in a series it ran on heroes of the conflict, of one nurse who nearly lost her life rescuing evacuees after an accident.

During the early months of the war, however, there were only a few helicopters in Korea, and they had been designed for peacetime purposes. Lacking guns and armor and being small, they were easy prey for enemy sharpshooters, and wounded men had to be placed in them crosswise on stretchers. Later "pods" were attached to the outside of the helicopters to carry the wounded. But by the end of the war, a Piasecki helicopter plant in Pennsylvania was manufacturing a helicopter outfitted for war that could carry as many as twelve patients and two medical officers; together with the M.A.S.H. units, they saved countless soldiers who might otherwise have died.

During the war, a real effort was made to make the lives of the frontline soldiers as comfortable as possible. Whenever possible, they were supplied with at least one hot meal a day. By the end of the conflict, new footwear, consisting of two thin rubber boots separated by a vacuum, had replaced the old combat boot, which, despite layers of woolen socks, could not prevent wet feet and frostbite. The new boots kept feet warmer, drier, and freer of frostbite. Soldiers on the front also received new lightweight fragmentation-proof vests, which were discarded by the thousands because they were still uncomfortable to wear, but which undoubtedly prevented even more fragmentation casualties. Much of the back-breaking work along the front, such as carrying rations, chopping down trees, and digging trenches was done by South Korean laborers known as "cargadores" rather than by the troops themselves. And if they were not killed or wounded, soldiers could look forward to five-day rest and recuperation visits to Japan and rotation home after about thirteen months.

Yet the old adage that "war is hell" certainly applied to the Korean War. Almost every American in Korea hated being there, exposed as they were to bitter cold in winter and roasting heat during the summer. Many of those doing the fighting, especially in the early months of the war, were inactive reservists who had fought during World War II and resented the fact that they had been called up before active reservists and National Guard units and that able-bodied college students could easily get draft deferments. The complex of trenches that ran across much of the battlefield were often no more than 400 yards from enemy lines and were only shoulder-deep, so that soldiers walking the trenches had their necks and heads exposed to enemy bullets. Bunkers, which were shored up by logs and roofed with other logs and sandbags, generally provided a safe haven for those inside them, but they were crowded, muddy, and lice-ridden. In the rainy season, they sometimes collapsed, suffocating the inhabitants in the muddy sand. Despite President Truman's 1948 call for desegregating the armed forces, black soldiers continued to fight in segregated units and were often maligned as being incompetent and even cowardly in combat. Desegregation of the armed forces was simply not pursued with much vigor.

By 1952 the Chinese had developed into a major air power with more than 1,400 aircraft, about half of which were estimated to be modern Mig-15s able to outclimb and outrun the F-86, America's best jet fighter. Indeed, after World War II, the U.S. Air Force had concentrated its efforts on building bombers rather than fighters, believing the speed of its first jet bomber, the B-45, would make it invulnerable to fighters. But it was no match for the Mig-15, and not until the B-47 became operational in 1951 did the United States have a bomber whose speed presented a problem to the Mig-15. What superiority the United States enjoyed in the skies was due more to the skill of its pilots and the willingness of the Chinese to risk its aircraft by straying deep into Korean air space than to the superiority of American technology. At the same time, American jets provided indispensable ground support for troops fighting along the front (See Map 2).

Although not nearly as costly for the United States in terms of casualties as World Wars I and II and the American Civil War, the Korean War nevertheless took its toll of dead, wounded, and missing in action. By the time the war ended in 1953, U.S. casualties numbered over 157,000; Korea suffered more than 1.3 million casualties, including 415,000 deaths. Other UN casualties amounted to more than 16,000, including 3,100 dead. Communist casualties were estimated at more than 2 million.

The cost in casualties for the United States, however, was only part of the picture. The draft had interfered with the careers of more than 1.4 million American youth who had fought in Korea. In tangible goods, the war consumed about 12 percent of gross domestic production, including 11 percent of all steel produced, 17 percent of all copper, and 24 percent of total aluminum production. The shortage of goods as a result of the war also led to an in-

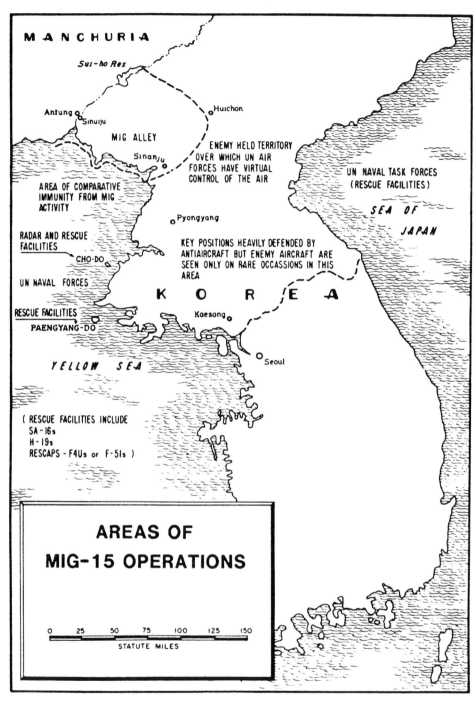

MANCHURIA

Sui-ho Res

Antung   Huichon
Sinuiju

MIG ALLEY

Sinanju

ENEMY HELD TERRITORY
OVER WHICH UN AIR
FORCES HAVE VIRTUAL
CONTROL OF THE AIR

AREA OF COMPARATIVE
IMMUNITY FROM MIG
ACTIVITY

UN NAVAL TASK FORCES
(RESCUE FACILITIES)

SEA OF
JAPAN

Pyongyang

RADAR AND RESCUE
FACILITIES

CHO-DO

KEY POSITIONS HEAVILY DEFENDED BY
ANTIAIRCRAFT BUT ENEMY AIRCRAFT ARE
SEEN ONLY ON RARE OCCASSIONS IN THIS
AREA

UN NAVAL FORCES

KOREA

RESCUE FACILITIES

PAENGYANG-DO

Kaesong

Seoul

YELLOW SEA

(RESCUE FACILITIES INCLUDE
SA-16s
H-19s
RESCAPS - F4Us or F-51s)

AREAS OF
MIG-15 OPERATIONS

0   25   50   75   100   125   150

STATUTE MILES

Map 2. From Office of Air Force History, United States *Air Force, Air Superiority in World War II and Korea* (Washington, DC: Government Printing Office, 1983).

crease in the cost of living for an American family of 12 percent between 1950 and 1953, an inflation rate that might seem modest by modern standards but was widely regarded as highly inflationary in the early 1950s. Tax payments jumped from $35 billion to $65 billion a year. By the end of the conflict, few Americans thought the war had been worth the human and material toll it took.

As early as March 1951, when UN forces were driving the communists once more out of most of South Korea, President Truman had planned to announce that the UNC was ready to enter into armistice talks. The president was under great pressure from America's European allies to launch a peace initiative. But MacArthur had purposefully undermined the peace initiative by issuing a statement effectively portraying the enemy as being militarily defeated and offering them a chance to sue for peace before being totally annihilated. As the general well knew, the Chinese would never agree to what amounted to an ultimatum from the UNC to surrender. As he anticipated, they remained silent.

With the war having reached a military stalemate by June, however, and still under great pressure both at home and abroad to end the conflict, the White House decided to try again to get armistice talks started. Using quiet diplomacy, the State Department let the Soviet Union know that it desired to arrange an armistice or cease-fire. After some delay, during which the United States hinted that it might accept the 38th parallel as the armistice line, Moscow responded in somewhat ambiguous language that negotiations might be possible. China also indicated that it was ready to start the peace process. In response, the administration ordered Ridgway to announce that he was prepared to appoint a representative to meet with the communists to begin armistice negotiations. After a short delay over where the talks should begin, both sides agreed to start negotiations at the Korean village of Kaesong, near the demarcation line between UN and communist forces (See Map 3).

The talks, which began on July 10, stretched over two years. During this time, the negotiations were moved to Panmunjom, a small village about five miles east of Kaesong. On a number of occasions, the negotiations were broken off by the UN and/or Chinese negotiators because of lack of progress or over alleged violations of the neutral zone where the negotiations were taking place. Yet although the bargaining was hard, most of the issues that separated the two sides were settled expeditiously. These included such questions as the demarcation of the armistice line, the renovation or rehabilitation of airfields destroyed as a result of the war, the regular rotation of forces on both sides, and the number of ports of entry for bringing in replace-

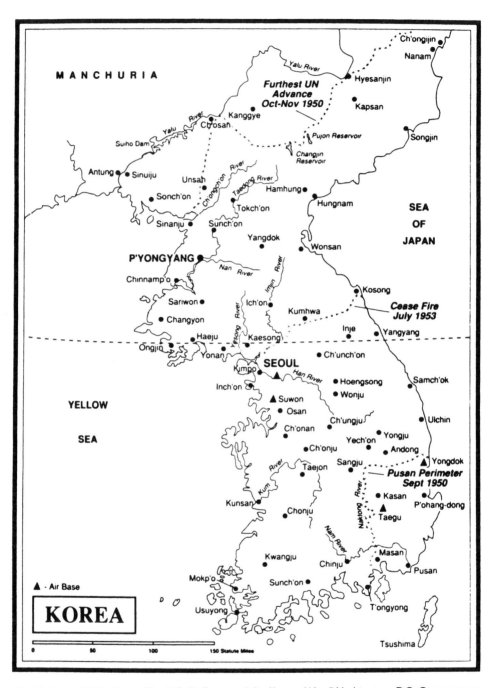

Map 3. From *Within Limits: The U.S. Air Force and the Korean War* (Washington, DC: Government Printing Office, 1996), p. 3.

ment of supplies and personnel. At the same time, the administration resisted most, but not all, appeals from Ridgway, Van Fleet, and, later General Mark Clark, who replaced Van Fleet in May 1952, to apply greater military pressure on the Chinese, including bombing bridges and hydroelectric plants along the Yalu River and bombing Chinese air bases in Manchuria.

Indeed, the only issue that held up a peace agreement was the issue of the voluntary repatriation of captured prisoners-of-war (POWs). The Chinese negotiators insisted that all POWs should be repatriated as provided by the Geneva Convention of 1949; the Truman administration was just as determined that no prisoner should be forced to return against his will. For Truman, the issue of returning POWs was a moral issue; for the Chinese, it was also one of pride. Not until 1953, following a breakdown of negotiations that lasted from October 1952 to April 1953, was the issue resolved. A complex formula was agreed upon by both sides according to which POWs not wanting to be repatriated would be given a period of time to change their minds and then their cases would be turned over to a Neutral Nations Repatriation Commission, which would help relocate them. In the end, only 137 of the communist nonrepatriates elected to go home and only 10 of the UNC nonrepatriates chose to return home. The rest were eventually released the following January.[6]

At Panmunjom, the negotiators had agreed to hold within thirty days of the armistice a political conference to discuss Korean unification and other related matters. But the meeting, which was held in Geneva, did not begin until April 1954 and then became quickly deadlocked over the supervision and conduct of elections that were supposed to result in unification. No agreement was ever reached, and Korea remains a divided nation with North Korea and South Korea still technically at war.

NOTES

1. For a more extended analysis of Soviet and Chinese reasons for agreeing to North Korea's attack of South Korea, see Chapter 3 in this volume.

2. *New Republic* 123 (October 16, 1950): 3.

3. On this point see Chapter 3.

4. Roy E. Appleman, *Disaster in Korea: The Chinese Confront MacArthur* (College Station, TX: Texas A&M University Press, 1989), 305–18, 332–53.

5. For the events surrounding MacArthur's firing and the repercussions that followed, see the biographical entry in this volume on MacArthur.

6. For a more extended discussion of the POW issue, see Chapter 5 in this volume.

2

The Western Alliance, Great Britain, and the Korean Conflict

The Korean Conflict, though generally supported by the United States's major allies, placed great stress on the Western alliance that had developed after World War II. European leaders were worried that the conflict might place undue pressure on them from Washington to rearm at a cost they could not afford and at a price—German rearmament—they did not want to pay. They also feared that Europe could become the battleground of an expanded war between the United States and the Soviet Union. Finally, many of them came to resent the unilateral manner in which the United States conducted the war and, until April 1951, they were disturbed by the power that General Douglas MacArthur appeared to assert over the Pentagon and, indeed, the White House itself. Even after MacArthur was fired by President Truman in 1951, Europeans worried about the influence of right-wing elements in the United States.

In no nation were these concerns more evident than in Great Britain. Much has been written about the "special relationship" that has existed between the United States and Britain, especially since World War II, and there can be no doubt that, over the last fifty years, London has been the United States's closest ally. But during the Korean War, London and Washington differed over a number of issues, especially with regard to the Chinese after they entered the war in November 1950. Even though London always supported Washington publicly, privately Britain sought, with some success, to get the United States to moderate some of its more militarily dangerous inclinations. It also may have helped speed up the peace process. Yet the result of the war was to tarnish Anglo-American relations. Much the same also can be said of U.S. relations with its other Western European allies.

Once North Korea invaded South Korea on June 25, 1950, and the United States made clear its intention not to let the invasion go unchallenged, there was never any doubt that Western Europe would support Washington's position at the United Nations (UN). In the months prior to, and just following, the outbreak of the Korean War, the fabric of European unity and Atlantic community had grown tighter. Major steps in this direction included the formation of the North Atlantic Treaty Organization (NATO) in 1949 and the establishment in 1950 of the European Payments Union. European leaders also believed that the North Koreans should be punished for committing aggression. Recalling the Munich Conference of 1938, during which British Prime Minister Neville Chamberlain tried to appease Germany's Adolph Hitler by effectively allowing him to move into Czechoslovakia, they concluded that appeasement would only lead to further aggression. Indeed, there was considerable concern about a possible Soviet invasion of Western Europe. The British had additional reason to support the United States. Not only was London anxious to cement its "special relationship" with Washington, it was concerned that if the attack in Korea went unanswered, the Soviet Union might feel free to move into Iran, where vital British oil interests would be threatened.

At the UN, therefore, Britain voted on June 27 in support of a Security Council Resolution sponsored by the United States calling for an international military action in support of South Korea. The next day, Britain placed its air and naval units stationed in Japan under the command of General Douglas MacArthur, commander in chief of U.S. forces in the Far East, who was named a week later as Supreme Commander of UN forces in Korea. France undertook to raise fifteen divisions with American aid. By June 30, the Netherlands also had committed forces to Korea. Over the rest of the summer and fall, Europe continued to support the war effort. In August, the British sent two infantry battalions from Hong Kong to help defend the Pusan perimeter and even began a partial mobilization of its reserves. It also extended the period of national service from eighteen months to two years. Other British dominions, including Australia, New Zealand, and Canada, committed their own forces to the UN command.

By August, however, important differences had begun to surface between the United States and its European allies over the issue of European rearmament and the conflict in Korea. Although North Korea's invasion of South Korea had raised fears about a Soviet invasion of Europe and seemed to underscore the need for European rearmament, by August fear of an invasion had diminished considerably. At the same time, the terrific costs of rearmament dulled the enthusiasm for a rapid military buildup, and in France, Belgium, and the Netherlands, there remained strong opposition to German rearmament.

Britain also disagreed with Washington's decision to send the Seventh Fleet into the straits separating mainland China from Formosa (Taiwan), believing that the United States exaggerated the PRC's threat to Formosa and that the action would drive Beijing closer to Moscow. Similarly, London was greatly concerned that the Chinese communists might enter the war, which could imperil its colony of Hong Kong and other interests in East Asia. Indeed, because of Britain's commitments in Hong Kong and Malaysia (as well as in Europe), the British Chiefs of Staff had been reluctant to send military forces into Korea. Most important, Britain wanted to avoid escalating the fighting in Korea into a major war involving both the United States and the Soviet Union.

Although the United States's European allies continued to follow its lead on most issues involving the war in Korea, including supporting its decision in September to cross the 38th parallel, the issues of German rearmament and the conduct of the war in Korea remained bones of contention within the Western alliance. British Prime Minister Clement Attlee found himself increasingly between a rock and a hard place, especially within his own Labour Party. Left-wing Labourites strongly opposed Washington's efforts to strengthen Europe's defenses by establishing a unified command for NATO and by creating a ten-division German army as part of a European defense system. Although Attlee went along with the United States, his government's support for German rearmament was only lukewarm, and the French remained adamantly opposed to the idea. As a result, in December, NATO approved the concept of a unified command but agreed only in principle to German participation as part of an integrated force. In Korea, the British became increasingly frustrated over their lack of input into military decision-making and increasingly fearful that General MacArthur might send troops into China after reaching the Yalu River.

Once it was confirmed in early November that the Chinese had sent forces into Korea, alarm bells went off throughout Europe. More than ever, the British were determined that the United States must avoid war with China. At the UN, Britain urged the establishment of a buffer zone between China and Korea, but Secretary of State Acheson, who earlier had entertained the possibility of such a zone, spoke out against the plan, maintaining that the zone could be used by the Chinese as a staging area for the further buildup of their forces. He even raised the possibility that the United States might have to send aircraft across the border in order to defend the airspace over the Yalu River. The British warned that they would withdraw their forces from the United Nations Command (UNC) if Washington forced Beijing into an all-out war. American newsman Howard K. Smith reported from London that British attitudes toward the United States had not been so turbulent and testy for several years. Similar reports of discontent were filed in other European capitals.

The massive Chinese offensive launched at the end of November and the retreat of the Eighth Army from the Yalu River had a profound impact on Europeans. "There is no doubt that confidence in General MacArthur . . . has been shaken badly as a result of the events of the last few days," wrote James Reston of the *New York Times*. "Similarly, there is no doubt that the United States leadership in the Western world has been damaged by President Truman's acceptance of the bold MacArthur's offensive."[1] After inspecting the battlefields, British General Leslie Mansergh delivered a secret report to the British Chiefs of Staff in which he criticized American forces for their "lack of determination and their inability . . . to stand and fight" and warned that "British troops, although sympathetic to the South Koreans in their adversity, despise them and are not interested in this civil war."[2] Indeed, British troops in the field and the British public at home were appalled by incidents reported in the press of women and children being massacred by retreating South Korean forces.

MacArthur became a symbol for most European leaders about what was wrong in U.S. foreign policy. The UN commander was thus bitterly attacked for wanting to escalate the fighting in Asia while leaving Europe virtually defenseless. Europeans remained terribly afraid that the Korean Conflict might escalate into a global war between East and West, most of which would be fought on their continent. They also nursed other grievances, mainly having to do with Washington's failure to consult them often enough.

Differences between Europe and the United States came to a head after President Truman announced at a press conference on November 30 that the United States would use whatever military means were necessary to bring an end to the war in Korea and then refused to exclude atomic weapons when pressed by reporters. Western Europe was shocked and outraged by Truman's statement. In Vienna, the story was the lead in all the morning newspapers, while in Rome one paper even reported that the Tokyo bomber command was prepared to take off with an atomic bomb one hour after it was ordered to do so by Washington. News commentator Howard K. Smith referred to the European reaction as "one of the most amazing political upheavals in Europe since the war."[3]

Responding to the clamor in London and throughout the capitals of western Europe, British Prime Minister Attlee flew to Washington seeking reassurances that the United States would not use atomic weapons or expand the war against China. His decision to go to Washington was widely hailed throughout Europe. The visit to London of French Prime Minister Rene Pleven, who had just received an overwhelming vote of confidence for his foreign policy of "preventing the [Korean] conflict from spreading," was taken by some observers to mean that Attlee would represent all of Western Europe.[4]

Although Truman, clearly influenced by Allied opinion, told the British leader that he did not anticipate using nuclear weapons in Korea and would inform him of any change in policy, Attlee failed to gain the reassurances that he wanted. In fact, although the talks resolved some of the differences that had developed in Anglo-American relations, they were more significant for underscoring the disagreements that still existed, especially with respect to China. While Attlee continued to press the Americans on the question of Chinese membership in the United Nations, Truman and Secretary of State Acheson stuck firmly to their position that that was not a negotiable item so long as China continued its aggression in Korea.

In the months that followed, Britain, the United States, and most of Western Europe continued to disagree over China policy. At the UN, the United States resisted efforts, supported by London, to call a conference on Far Eastern affairs to deal with such matters as the China question, stating that such a meeting would smack of appeasement. Indeed, with considerable diplomatic and political finesse, it was able to get through the United Nations a resolution condemning China as an "aggressor nation." Even so, it did not have its way at the UN without causing a deep rift within the Western coalition. All of America's Western allies objected to the American proposal, maintaining that it would make it all the more difficult to negotiate with the Chinese and might even lead to Soviet involvement in the Korean Conflict. Within Britain's Labour Party, a split developed between moderate and more radical Labourites who believed that London was following too closely the dictates of its erstwhile ally.

During the winter of 1950–1951, a great debate took place in the United States over whether the United States should make Europe or Asia its first line of defense. Senator Robert Taft of Ohio, the likely Republican candidate for president in 1952, and other Republican leaders spoke out against any large contingent of American soldiers going to Europe, much less without the prior approval of Congress. "Is Europe our first line of defense?" Taft asked. "Is it defensible at all?"[5] Europe's widely publicized criticism of

America's foreign policy and conduct of the war in Korea and Europe's own procrastination in rearming caused some in the United States to ask similar questions. Meanwhile, other Americans talked about the likelihood of a nuclear war and made preparations, including building bomb shelters, in case the United States was attacked by the Soviet Union. There was even talk of a "preventive war," and sentiment grew for using nuclear weapons against the communists.

Europeans watched with growing concern the debate taking place in the United States. They were fearful of both the isolationist sentiment and talk about a nuclear war that seemed to coexist in America. Many of them believed that this reflected the whimsical and erratic nature of American foreign policy. Concerned that the United States might abandon Europe in favor of Asia or retreat altogether from its world responsibilities, they remained even more fearful of a nuclear war between the United States and the Soviet Union in which they would be the first casualties. Seeking to resolve differences between East and West, they persisted in their protests against Washington's China policy. Lastly, they criticized American smugness and took issue with the United States's contention that it was carrying most of the responsibilities for containing communist expansion in the Far East. James Reston sensed the attitude—and frustration—of many of America's allies when he remarked in January 1951, that there "was something of a rebellion within the Western coalition against the past United States policy in the Far East."[6] One correspondent for the *New Yorker* wrote from London that "isolationist utterances" had "produced a wave of alarm here and across the channel," a statement validated in the press throughout Europe.[7]

Also muddying relations between Washington and its European allies was the long-standing European conviction that General MacArthur, whom the Europeans assailed for wanting to plunge the United States into a major Asiatic war, had undue influence in Washington. They were especially angered by MacArthur's action in March 1951, in turning what was intended as a peace initiative from Washington into an ultimatum to the Chinese either to surrender or face total destruction. The Norwegian ambassador to the United States referred to the general's statement as a "pronounciomento," and the pro-American London *Economist* called it a piece of unmitigated "mischief." "Our principal difficulty is General MacArthur," Britain's new foreign secretary, Herbert Morrison, even commented in April 1951, to Sir Oliver Franks, Britain's ambassador in Washington. "He seems to want war with China. We do not. It is no exaggeration to say that by his public utterances, he has weakened public confidence in this country and in Western Europe in the quality of American political judgement and leadership."[8]

It was with much relief, therefore, that Europe received the news of MacArthur's firing on April 11 following the release of a telegram he had sent to House Minority Leader Joseph Martin criticizing the administration for fighting a limited war in Korea. In the House of Commons, cheers went up at news that MacArthur had been relieved of his commands. Defending Truman's action, the *Manchester Guardian* predicted that "in every domestic country except his own [the president's] action would be received with almost unmixed approval and relief." From London, Howard K. Smith reported that the British press had reiterated that there was only one question at issue: "whether generals may make foreign policy."[9] Important papers like *Le Monde, L'Observateur*, and *Franc-Tireur* emphasized the great danger MacArthur might have created by bombing Manchuria.

The firing of MacArthur, however, narrowed the differences only marginally between the United States and its Western coalition partners. Washington made clear to its allies that MacArthur's dismissal did not mean any change in U.S. policy in the Far East. It thus refused a request from London that Beijing be allowed to participate in a Japanese peace treaty and remained firmly opposed to giving the PRC a seat at the United Nations. Indeed, it increased pressure at the UN for harsh economic sanctions against China. More important, Truman approved a request from MacArthur's replacement, General Matthew Ridgway, that he be allowed to attack Chinese air bases across the Yalu in the event that they were used for a major air offensive against UN forces in Korea, a request that Ridgway made in response to a buildup of Chinese air power in Manchuria. The Europeans, especially the British, were taken back by the administration's decision both because it did not provide for prior consultation with them before an attack was carried out (although the United States emphasized it would try to consult before approving any actions against Manchurian bases) and because they did not think the Chinese had the capability to launch a major air offensive. Furthermore, the American decision provided a loophole that would allow Ridgway to order an air strike without first consulting Washington, something the British opposed. In response, Foreign Minister Morrison told Secretary of State Acheson that although his government would accept "in principle" retaliatory bombing of Manchurian air bases, it could not "divest" itself of final responsibility for approving such an attack. Despite British objections, the administration refused to modify its position, but as the historian William Stueck has pointed out, "[f]ortunately circumstances never arose in which the consultative process was put to the test."[10]

In July, the Korean War entered a new phase. Following an unsuccessful Chinese offensive in April and May and a UN counteroffensive that once more drove the communists above the 38th parallel along most of the battle-front, the Chinese and North Koreans agreed to commence armistice nego-tiations with the UNC at the ancient Korean capital of Kaesong, located in no-man's land between the two opposing forces. Throughout the two years of negotiations that followed, first at Kaesong and then at Panmunjom, about five miles to the east, American and European leaders, particularly the Brit-ish, continued to be adroitly evasive over matters involving the war and the Far East. Anxious to end a war that had caused considerable strain between Washington and London and that could still escalate into a general war with the PRC, Britain welcomed the opening of cease-fire negotiations on July 10. What the Foreign Office wanted was a speedy armistice agreement to be followed by a political conference on the unification of Korea and an even-tual settlement of all Far Eastern questions. Such a settlement would allow Britain to devote its attention to its more strategic interests in Europe and the Middle East.

It soon became clear, however, that an armistice agreement would not come speedily or lead to an agreement on Korean unification. Very quickly, the negotiations became bogged down over whether the cease-fire line should be the 38th parallel (as the communists wanted) or the military line dividing the two sides at the time of a cease-fire (the UN's position). The British tended to blame American recalcitrance for the slow progress on this and other issues. Dismayed by the lack of headway at Kaesong and then Pan-munjom, they increasingly expressed their frustration at not having their own representative on the negotiating team. The Foreign Office also contin-ued to insist that if the West showed a more conciliatory policy toward the PRC, China would quickly agree to a cease-fire. Even the new Conservative government of Prime Minister Winston Churchill, which took office follow-ing the defeat of the Labour Party in elections in October and was highly supportive of U.S. policy, felt that its voice was not always heard or heeded in Washington. "We do not always get a chance to influence American pol-icy in the formative stages, and are apt to be confronted with a firm decision and a request for an immediate answer," the diplomat in charge of the For-eign Office's department on China and Korea, R. H. Scott, told Foreign Sec-retary Anthony Eden in a lengthy memorandum with which Eden fully agreed.[11]

In November, the United States announced that the negotiators at Pan-munjom had finally agreed on a military demarcation line. In a concession to the Chinese (and the British), Acheson also told Eden that the United States would not insist on a strict policing of an armistice agreement when it was concluded. In return, however, Washington pressured the British and its other allies in Korea into agreeing to the "greater sanctions" policy, a public warning to China, to be signed and issued by all sixteen nations under the UNC command after an armistice had been signed, that if the PRC broke the armistice, it would be subject to retaliation by the United States and its principal allies.

Revelations about the "greater sanctions" policy created political havoc on Britain and led to a major attack on the government by Labourites and even some Conservatives. Churchill was able to beat back this challenge to his government, but not before stating that he would never agree to an expansion of the war, thereby virtually nullifying the "greater sanctions" policy. The Korean War also weighed heavily on the internal politics of America's other coalition partners. Ever since the United States had decided to support the rearming of Germany following the outbreak of the Korean War in 1950, the issue had been raised time and time again. In France, Belgium, and the Netherlands, opposition to the establishment of a German army remained strong. Instead of a separate German force, the French had proposed the creation of a European Defense Community (EDC) that would include Germany but would not give Germany control over their own forces or membership in NATO.

Even then, strong opposition remained in France and elsewhere against rearmament of any kind, much less German rearmament. Neutralism in the confrontation between Washington and Moscow became a broad-based movement throughout the continent. Great emphasis was placed on substituting disarmament for rearmament through negotiations with the Soviet Union. Complicating matters even more for many Europeans, the Soviet Union offered the West a new proposal for a neutralized and unified Germany with its own army. Obviously meant to prevent Germany from aligning militarily with the West, the Soviet proposal nevertheless enjoyed considerable support among advocates of neutralism throughout Europe. Continuation of the Korean War, much less its expansion, was viewed by many of these Europeans as a significant obstacle, indeed a major threat, to the type of negotiated end of the Cold War envisioned by them.

Communist charges that the United States had engaged in bacteriological warfare, albeit unsubstantiated, also were quite effective in weakening America's moral weight in Europe, particularly among neutralists, and in stirring worldwide reaction against the United States. Communist newspapers in France denounced the new NATO commander, Matthew Ridgway, as a "microbe killer." Large demonstrations against the United States were held in the spring of 1952 in France, Belgium, Italy, Holland, and Germany.

All the more reason, therefore, that Europeans responded angrily in June, when more than 250 planes under UN command bombed five power stations along the North Korean side of the Yalu River. For millions of Europeans, anxious for a four-power conference with the Soviet Union to resolve the German question and to settle other world problems, including ending the Korean War, the raids along the Yalu River represented a dangerous escalation of the war that imperiled the already slim chances for world peace. In Britain, a radical group of Labourites, headed by their fiery leader, Aneurin Bevan, charged that the United States posed as great a threat to world peace as the Soviet Union. The bombing also deeply upset Churchill both because it was taken without his consent and because he feared that it could result in a wider war.

Worse, the attack on the power stations also threatened to undermine the negotiations underway to resolve the question of repatriation of prisoners of war (POWs), the one matter preventing an armistice agreement. At issue was whether all POWs should be returned home or only those who wanted to be repatriated. The communist negotiators held that all POWs should be repatriated, which was in accordance with the Geneva Convention of 1949 on the treatment of POWs. However, President Truman refused to force captured Chinese and North Koreans to return home against their will. For months, neither side in the negotiations at Panmunjom had been willing to give ground on the matter.

Publicly, London gave its strong public backing to the American position. In May 1952, Foreign Secretary Eden told the House of Commons that "it would clearly be repugnant to the sense of values of the free world to send [POWs] home by force."[12] Nevertheless, the British had been dismayed by the seizure in February of a prisoner-of-war camp on Koje-do Island, off the coast of Korea, by the imprisoned Chinese. After gaining control of the camp, the Chinese were able to take its commander hostage, and then force him to "confess" to mistreatment of POWs. Hitherto London had dismissed charges that thousands of POWs had been intimidated by their brutal South Korean guards to claim falsely that they did not want to be repatriated. But these accusations took on more substance as a result of the camp seizure. Furthermore, the British were embarrassed by the use of British and Canadian troops in restoring order to the island after bitter fighting in which a number of POWs were killed. Former Prime Minister Attlee stated that the fighting would never have happened had the prison compounds been under British control.

The Foreign Office had serious misgivings, moreover, about the UN's negotiating posture at Panmunjom, blaming American intransigence for the deadlock on the POWs. The head of its Korean desk, J. M. Addis, observed that the "manner in which the United Nations Command have conducted the negotiations—rapid and unexplained changes of front on the main question and a policy of sometimes stepping up demands after concessions have been made—has not contributed to removing the suspicion that undoubtedly exists on the Communist side that the Americans do not sincerely want an armistice."[13]

Behind the scenes, therefore, Britain worked hard to resolve the POW question. At the United Nations, it supported an Indian peace initiative, providing for the formation of a neutral nations repatriation commission to handle the repatriation problem until an armistice was concluded. It would then be left to a postwar conference to decide the fate of POWs who, after ninety days, still did not want to be repatriated. At first, the outgoing Truman administration opposed the resolution because it left the repatriation issue unresolved at the end of the war. Furthermore, the United States had introduced its own resolution calling upon the Chinese to agree to an armistice based on voluntary repatriation and raising the possibility of new sanctions against China if it refused to do so. But under heavy pressure from its own allies, including the British and a bloc of Arab-Asian nonaligned nations, Secretary of State Acheson agreed to support the resolution after it was amended to assure that within three months after an armistice the repatriation process would end and the United Nations would determine the disposition of the remaining nonrepatriates. On December 3, the resolution was approved by the UN General Assembly.

In the interim between Washington's rejection of the Indian resolution and its acceptance of an amended version of the proposal, however, U.S. relations with its European allies reached a low point. The secretary of state was furious at its allies for supporting the Indian resolution, warning them that their failure to support the American position at the UN would jeopardize American support for NATO "and other arrangements of the same sort." For their part, Europeans had grown increasingly agitated at what they regarded as the uncompromising position of the United States on the repatriation issue and at the stepped-up bombing raids the Pentagon had ordered against North Korea, including an attack on an oil refinery close to the Soviet border. In France, a form of anti-Americanism had developed that ran the gamut from opposition to American high tariffs to American high ideals. In 1952 the French were particularly indignant at America's rigid anticolonialism, especially on North Africa, and bitterly resented America's recent decision to side with the Asian-Arab bloc in putting the question of French colonialism on the agenda of the UN General Assembly. The highly influential newspaper *Le Monde* accused Americans of meddling in French affairs and forecasted increased tension between the two countries unless the United States changed its policies.

This was the situation facing President-elect Dwight D. Eisenhower as he prepared to assume office in January 1953. Regarding him as both a moderate and internationalist, Europeans had generally welcomed Eisenhower's victory for the Republican presidential nomination over Senator Robert Taft of Ohio, whom they regarded as a right-wing isolationist. But because of Eisenhower's own appeals to Republican right-wingers during the campaign and the more moderate and urbane tones of his Democratic opponent, Adlai Stevenson, a shift had taken place in European sentiment away from Eisenhower and toward Stevenson. Following the Republican candidate's victory in November, Prime Minister Churchill even commented that his election had made an expanded war much more likely.

The new president did little to assuage European concerns. Not ruling out the possible use of tactical nuclear weapons, Eisenhower made it clear that he was prepared to use whatever means were necessary to end the stalemate in Korea. Furthermore, he announced that the "Seventh Fleet [would] no longer be employed to shield Communist China."[14] In ordering an end to the fleet's patrolling of the Formosa Strait, Eisenhower was effectively warning Beijing that if a truce was not forthcoming, Chiang Kai-shek's forces might be used against mainland China. This and hints from Secretary of State John Foster Dulles that the United States was prepared to increase the military pressure on the Chinese to bring an end to the war alarmed Europeans, many of whom regarded Dulles as reckless and irresponsible. What worried them as much as the harshness of the secretary's statements was their conviction that the administration was being taken over by the Republican right wing and that the red-baiting junior senator from Wisconsin, Joseph McCarthy, whose appeal in the United States perplexed Europeans, was dictating foreign policy.

During a meeting with the secretary of state in March, British Foreign Minister Eden urged that the United States launch no major new offensive in Korea without consulting with the British. He also expressed his opposition to a naval blockade of China, which, he said, could lead to a clash with Moscow. An end to the Korean War, however, was soon in sight. In March, Soviet leader Joseph Stalin died. Shortly thereafter, the Chinese agreed to a proposal, first suggested by the International Red Cross in December, to exchange sick and wounded POWs. They also offered to turn over to a neutral state all nonrepatriated POWs and to resume the negotiations at Panmunjom, which had been recessed since October. Although Eisenhower was reluctant to restart the talks until the prisoner exchange had taken place, London urged him not to be overly rigid. "I do not . . . think we should at this stage insist rigidly on conclusion of exchange [of sick and wounded POWs] before resumption of main negotiations," Eden wrote Dulles at the beginning of April. "We should retain flexibility so as to exploit developments to our best advantage."[15] Eden's letter was unnecessary, for a few days later the Chinese concluded arrangements for the swapping of 5,800 POWs held by the UNC for 600 POWs held by the Communists and on April 16, armistice talks were resumed at Panmunjom. All this created tremendous excitement and optimism at the United Nations and throughout Europe that peace was finally at hand.

The negotiations that followed were difficult because the United States still held out for an earlier release of POWs refusing repatriation than was acceptable to the communists. Washington also did not want India as part of a neutral nations commission that would make the final determination on nonrepatriates. However, on June 8, agreement was reached on an armistice that provided for the release of nonrepatriated POWs after 120 days if a political conference that was to be held after the war did not resolve the issue of their final disposition. The agreement was almost sabotaged when, a week later, South Korea's president, Syngman Rhee, unilaterally freed Korean nonrepatriates in camps operated by his guards. Though Rhee's action gave the communist negotiators cause to recess the talks indefinitely, they were clearly anxious to end a war that had become extremely costly for both sides. Instead of breaking off negotiations, therefore, they remained at the negotiating table. On July 2, a final agreement was reached. Having in the interim won major concessions from the United States, including a promise from the White House to sign a mutual security pact with South Korea, Rhee reluctantly acquiesced in the agreement.

Europe, particularly Britain, had played a significant role in pressuring the United States to resolve the POW question and to end the war. In fact, the pressure on the United States from its allies had been unrelenting after the United States balked at a Chinese proposal in May to turn nonrepatriates over to a neutral nations repatriation commission in the camps where they were being held. When the administration responded cooly to the proposal because it did not provide for their final disposition within a specified period, Churchill accused the United States of dillydallying.

The effort by Rhee to sabotage an armistice by freeing the POWs under his control absolutely infuriated Europeans, some of whom were even convinced that Rhee had acted with the knowledge and tacit approval of Washington. Indeed, Europe had become haunted by this time by the specter of the

United States in the grip of a hysterical witch-hunt and of a president cowering before the power of Senator McCarthy and his followers. As the *Atlantic Monthly* commented, "It is progressively more difficult to persuade Europeans that McCarthy does not speak for the United States."[16] British Prime Minister Churchill even threatened not to sign the "greater sanctions" statement. Even though the United States considered the warning essential to any peace agreement, Churchill made it clear that Britain had no intention of being drawn into a war with China because of Rhee. Once an armistice was reached, Britain and the other fifteen nations with armed forces in Korea signed the "greater sanctions" statement. But even then the pact was not made public until August 7 because Britain and the other signatories thought that the language was too warlike, would be too unpopular at home, and would tie them too closely to the Rhee government. Even when it was made public, Churchill left no doubt that he viewed the document in a limited way, that it was not meant to concede to the United States a free hand in responding to renewed trouble with China over Korea.

U.S. relations with its European allies, then, had survived the Korean War intact. And at key moments, such as in the final months of negotiations, the British in particular had been able to act as a restraining force on the United States. Yet on almost every occasion where there had been differences between Washington and its coalition partners, the latter had yielded to the former. The fact was that the partnership was not one of equals. Europe was far more dependent on the United States militarily, economically, and politically than Washington was beholden to Europe. In particular, the United States was needed to contain the Soviet threat in Europe.

Yet Europeans clearly resented the subordinate role they had been forced to play in Korea. The British were especially annoyed by what they regarded as their lack of input in military decision-making and the uncompromising position of the United States in negotiations with the Chinese and North Koreans. After the Chinese entered the war in November 1950, the British feared that the conflict in Korea could expand into a world war involving nuclear weapons. And they had a hard time understanding why Washington refused to recognize Beijing or allow it a seat at the United Nations. A *quid pro quo* involving these concessions by the United States in return for peace in Korea, they believed, might have ended the conflict long before the summer of 1953. If there was one lesson they drew from the Korean War, therefore, it was not to allow the United States to drag them into another conflict in East Asia, such as the one still taking place in Indochina between the Viet-minh and the French.

NOTES

1. *New York Times*, November 30, 1950, p. 17.

2. Max Hastings, *The Korean War* (New York: Simon and Schuster, 1987), 173.

3. *New Yorker* 26 (December 16, 1950): 78–90.

4. *Nation* 171 (December 9, 1950): 521–22.

5. *Life* 30 (January 18, 1951): 10–13.

6. *New Republic* 124 (January 8, 1951): 9.

7. *New Yorker* 26 (January 13, 1951): 46.

8. Trumbull Higgins, *Korea and the Fall of MacArthur: A Precis in Limited War* (New York: Oxford University Press, 1960):110.

9. *New Yorker* 27 (April 21, 1951): 66.

10. William Stueck, Jr., *The Korean War: An International History* (Princeton, NJ: Princeton University Press), 187–89.

11. M. L. Dockrill, "The Foreign Office, Anglo-American Relations and the Korean Truce Negotiations July 1951–July 1953," in James Cotton and Ian Neary, eds., *The Korean War in History* (Atlantic Highlands, NJ: Humanities Press, 1989), 100–3.

12. Quoted in Richard Whelan, *Drawing the Line: The Korean War, 1950–1953* (Boston: Little, Brown and Co., 1990), 101.

13. Quoted in Dockrill, "The Foreign Office, Anglo-American Relations and the Korean Truce Negotiations July 1951–July 1953," 105.

14. Stephen E. Ambrose, *Eisenhower: The President* (New York: Simon and Schuster, 1984), 47.

15. Memorandum for the President, April 1, 1953, Box 9, Subject Series, John Foster Dulles Papers, Dwight D. Eisenhower Library, Abilene, KS.

16. *Atlantic Monthly* 192 (July 1953): 9–10.

3

The Soviet Union, China, and the Korean Conflict: New Sources, New Insights

Until recently, Western scholars writing on the Korean Conflict did not have access to the archives and other records of the People's Republic of China (PRC) and the Soviet Union. Thanks, however, to the end of the Cold War and a growing exchange of historical information between Beijing, Moscow, and Washington, these records have become increasingly available to historians. Although the materials from Russia and China still have to be studied with considerable caution because they remain incomplete, they do provide essential information on three important questions upon which historians could only previously speculate:

1. What role, if any, did Moscow and Beijing play in encouraging the leader of North Korea, Kim Il Sung, to invade South Korea on June 25, 1950?
2. Why did the PRC enter the war in October and November 1950?
3. Why did the PRC agree to an armistice in July 1953? The answer to this question raises yet another one: Was President Dwight D. Eisenhower's threat to use nuclear weapons against China a factor in bringing an end to the fighting?

With respect to the first of these questions, it now seems clear that the Soviet Union and the PRC played a reluctant but, nevertheless, significant role in Kim Il Sung's decision to invade South Korea in the early summer of 1950. Simply put, without their acquiescence, North Korea would almost certainly not have attacked. At the same time, it is also apparent that Kim was more than a lackey of Moscow and Beijing as he had been commonly portrayed by historians for much of the period after the war.[1] A nationalist committed to the reunification of Korea as well as a communist, Kim had planned, and sought Soviet support for, the invasion since at least 1949. Following Secretary of State Dean Acheson's well-known failure, during a speech to the National Press Club in January 1950, to include Korea within the U.S. defense perimeter, Kim renewed his overtures to Moscow and Beijing. In the spring, he traveled to the two cities where he visited Soviet leader Joseph Stalin and Chinese leader Mao Zedong and discussed his plans for attacking South Korea with both of them. Although Stalin approved the plan to reunite Korea and even promised to supply North Korea with arms and other military equipment, he did so reluctantly and only after Kim Il Sung promised that he could defeat South Korea within three days. Stalin was genuinely concerned that the war in Korea could lead to a world war involving the United States and the Soviet Union. But he did not want to put himself in the same embarrassing position that he had found himself a year earlier by not giving the Chinese communists nearly the support they expected in their successful civil war against the Nationalists. Indeed, according to several authors, Stalin waited until the Chinese agreed to support the invasion before he gave it his unequivocal backing. Should the United States intervene in the war, he anticipated that the Chinese would enter the conflict, thereby diminishing the need for Soviet intervention while forcing Beijing to be more dependent on Moscow, something he preferred. At the same time, he hoped that a war in Korea might force the United States to redefine its interests and redeploy its resources away from Europe and offset America's efforts to reestablish Germany and Japan as major economic and political powers.

As for the Chinese, they had cooperated with Kim Il Sung for more than a year in repatriating North Korean soldiers who had fought with them against the Nationalists. Mao Zedong also deeply resented Washington's support of Nationalist leader Chiang Kai-shek, and like Stalin, he was angered and worried by U.S. efforts to turn Japan into a major regional power that could once more pose a threat to China, just as it had before World War II. But he was concerned also that the North Korean invasion might become entangled with his own plans to attack Formosa.

As for the reasons why the PRC decided to send its troops into Korea in October and November 1950, clearly concern for its own national security was a major consideration. Even after the United States entered the war in July, Chinese leaders proceeded cautiously. Although they transferred 90,000 of their best troops close to the border between China and North Korea, they believed that the United States lacked the military strength to counter the Soviet Union's military power in Europe and fight a war against China in East Asia. The visit to Formosa in July by the commander of UN forces in Korea, General Douglas MacArthur, the continued buildup of American forces in Korea, and growing concern that the United States would seek to reunify Korea led the Chinese in August to prepare for military intervention. The Inchon invasion of September and the American decision to roll back communism by marching to the Yalu River almost certainly weighed heavily in Beijing's decision to enter the war.

Yet there is now reason to believe that Chinese leader Mao Zedong may not have been as reluctant a participant in the Korean Conflict as had once been thought and that he had decided to send troops into Korea as early as August, a month before the Inchon invasion and before UN troops were sent across the 38th parallel. A revolutionary nationalist throughout his life, Mao despised the United States, which, even before the Korean Conflict, he regarded as the greatest threat to revolutionary nationalism throughout East Asia. Accordingly, he was convinced that a war with the United States was inevitable, and he was certain that he could defeat the United States in Korea. Furthermore, he viewed China's participation in the war as a way of expanding Chinese influence in East Asia, and eliminating counterrevolutionary elements in China.

A number of political and military leaders, including the commander of forces in northeast China, Gao Gang, remained leery about engaging the United States in combat. They pointed to the country's need to continue with its economic reforms and to wipe out the last vistiges of Nationalist guerrillas still on the mainland. But Mao, who remained in complete control in China, maintained that the United States was overextended and that Korea's geography placed limits on the capability of UN forces to launch offensive operations on the peninsula. His views, which also had support within the military, ultimately prevailed.

The limited Chinese military engagement in Korea in October, therefore, may not have been, as previously believed, a warning to Washington to stop its advance northward before the Chinese intervened in massive numbers but a strategy intended to encourage UN forces to advance further north, stretching their supply lines before the Chinese intervened in massive numbers. As the historian Chen Jian has argued, "Three fundamental and interrelated rationales had dominated Beijing's formulation of foreign policy and security strategy: the party's revolutionary nationalism, its sense of responsibility toward an Asian-wide or worldwide revolution, and its determination to maintain the inner dynamics of the Chinese revolution. Beijing's management of the Korean crisis cannot be properly comprehended without an understanding of these rationales and the mentality related to them."[2]

If Chen is correct, then, it was not traditional national security concerns that dictated China's behavior toward the United States both before and during the Korean War. Furthermore, there was very little that the United States could have done, such as stopping its advance at the 38th parallel, to prevent China from entering the war in November. But a word of caution is in order, for as most historians acknowledge, the documentation is not so patently clear one way or the other as to allow for a definitive answer as to why Mao decided to enter the war. The best guess is that there were competing, albeit related, concerns and interests that dictated China's policy, although ultimately it was Mao's revolutionary fervor and his conviction that the PRC could win in Korea that carried the day.

The PRC's decision to send its troops into Korea caused the Soviet Union considerable concern and led to new tensions between Moscow and Beijing that were never resolved. Initially, Stalin supported China's plan to intervene—indeed, he desired Chinese intervention—as a way of making Beijing more dependent on Moscow without involving the Soviet Union in a war with the United States. But in reaction to the speed with which Washington responded to the North Korean invasion and its heavy military commitment to the war, the Soviet leader began to have second thoughts. He became increasingly worried that the Soviet Union might find itself in a nuclear war with the United States. In fact, the Sino-Soviet alliance, which had been signed only a few months earlier, obligated Moscow to intervene militarily if the United States attacked China. As a result, he reneged on an earlier promise he had made to provide China with military assistance should it enter the war. Mao felt betrayed. According to the Chinese leader, he spent sixty sleepless hours before deciding on October 13 to send his forces into Korea. Although the Soviet Union later sent two air force divisions to defend northeast China, Mao never forgave Stalin for what he regarded as his treachery.

China's intervention changed both the complexion and the outcome of the war. On one hand, it became virtually a conflict between China and the United States. Although the tattered remnants of North Korea's army fought on and forces from South Korea and America's UN allies also contributed significantly to the war effort, most strategic decisions were made in Beijing and Washington. On the other hand, the Chinese intervention led to a military stalemate lasting more than two years before an armistice agreement was completed in July 1953. The question then becomes: Why did Beijing finally agree to an armistice? Related to that question is another—the role of nuclear diplomacy in ending the conflict. Here again historians have greatly benefited from the increasing availability of Chinese sources. It had been widely assumed that the Chinese agreed to an armistice only after President

Dwight D. Eisenhower made known to the Beijing government in 1953 that he was prepared to use nuclear weapons to end the war. According to this interpretation, first stated by Secretary of State John Foster Dulles in a 1956 *Life* magazine article, the secretary had given the Chinese, through the government of India, "an unmistakable warning" that the new administration was prepared to use nuclear weapons and that it was "a pretty fair inference" to conclude that it was this threat that finally persuaded the Chinese negotiators to end the war.[3] This view was very much in keeping with another common assumption—that the lack of progress on ending the war was due to the recalcitrance of the communist negotiators at Panmunjom.

There can be no question that Eisenhower, like President Harry Truman before him, considered the nuclear option in Korea. Indeed, the possibility of using tactical nuclear weapons had been discussed at the first wartime meeting following North Korea's invasion of South Korea on June 25, 1950. It was discussed again in July, once more following the Chinese invasion in November 1950, and then again in April 1951, just before and after the massive military offensive of that month. Bombers outfitted to carry atomic bombs were even deployed to Guam for possible use in Korea, and the Strategic Air Command (SAC) sent a command and control team to Tokyo to coordinate an atomic strike if the order were given. Without ever threatening the Chinese directly, the administration also let Beijing know that the United States had the ability to set back China's development for decades. Even after the armistice talks began in July 1951, the president never entirely discarded the nuclear option.

This suggests, however, that the Chinese could not have been taken by surprise by an explicit, or even implicit, threat from President Eisenhower about the possible use of nuclear weapons against them since there had been discussion in Washington about the same subject since the beginning of the war. Although the Chinese, of course, were not privy to these talks, it is hard to believe that they were unaware of them, especially since President Truman had shocked even U.S. allies by refusing at a press conference on November 30, 1950, to disclaim the nuclear option.

Indeed, it is now known that the Chinese always had considered the possibility of a nuclear strike against them in the event they entered the Korean War. Although they did not totally discount that option, they thought it unlikely because the Americans knew that the Soviet Union could respond with a nuclear strike of its own somewhere in Europe. Beijing also believed that nuclear weapons offered little tactical advantage in Korea. At a meeting in August 1950, Chinese military leaders concluded that human forces, not nuclear weapons, would carry the day in Korea. In fact, Mao expected a short, regional, and conventional war in Korea and refused to be intimidated by American nuclear power. Even if the United States should attack China with atomic bombs, he thought they would be unable to incapacitate the country's war-making power because, unlike the Western industrial powers, China was a vast country without a concentrated industrial center. For the Chinese leader, the atomic bomb was a "paper tiger."

The suggestion that the deadlock at Panmunjom was largely China's doing—and that, therefore, it took the nuclear threat to get the communist negotiators to adopt a more flexible posture—also has been largely discredited. As the historian Rosemary Foot has pointed out, most of the concessions at Panmunjom were, in fact, made by the communist, not the UN, negotiators. The one issue holding up a negotiated settlement was the refusal by the White House to countenance the forced repatriation of North Korean and Chinese prisoners-of-war (POWs) even though that was mandated by the Geneva Convention of 1949, which called for quick and compulsory repatriation.[4] On other issues—such as the agenda for negotiations, the cease-fire line, the withdrawal of foreign troops from Korea after the fighting ended, the rotation of forces and equipment, and the inspection of ports to ensure compliance with an armistice—the communist negotiators had made most of the concessions. Even on the POW issue, Foot concludes, the PRC "might have accepted nonforcible repatriation provided the principle itself was masked and the prisoners were taken out of the hands of those who had allowed them to be influenced or intimidated."[5] Concerns other than a nuclear attack, in other words, influenced Chinese negotiators at Panmunjom.

Not until a crisis in 1954 over the islands of Quemoy and Matsu did Mao begin to take seriously the possibility that the United States might use nuclear weapons against China. The crisis began with the Chinese shelling in September of Quemoy and then Matsu, both only two miles off the Chinese mainland and both garrisoned with Nationalist forces. In response the Eisenhower administration gave serious thought to using nuclear weapons. Only then did the Chinese leader begin to display concern about how willing Moscow would be to retaliate against an American nuclear attack or how the Chinese might react to the danger of such an atomic strike. After the crisis was over, he started, for the first time, to consider the development of China's own nuclear capability.

If it were not fear of a nuclear attack that led China to agree to an armistice in Korea in July 1953, what were the considerations that resulted in its decision to end the war? Here foreign sources have so far not been as helpful as on other questions. Nonetheless, they do offer some insights. In the first place, they confirm what a number of historians have always suspected—that the unanticipated length of the war and the huge losses that both the Chinese and North Koreans sustained during the conflict took their toll on Beijing's leaders. Instead of the short, conventional war with limited Chinese losses anticipated by Chairman Mao, the United States remained determined to carry on the war until a satisfactory armistice could be signed providing for the voluntary repatriation of POWs.

As a result, the conflict dragged on for two more years. Meanwhile, China lost an estimated 900,000 men, and the North Koreans suffered the loss of nearly 520,000 personnel. Similarly, the war showed just how ill-prepared China was to fight an enemy outfitted with the most modern military technology. By the end of the conflict, Chinese military leaders had concluded that their country was especially deficient in its air force, air defenses, and logistics. Anticipating that China would continue to confront American military power, Chairman Mao determined that China would have to correct these deficiencies, in the process building up its military infrastructure and industrial base. Ending the Korean War was crucial to the task at hand. At the same time, China had fought the most advanced military power in the world to a virtual standstill. Beijing could, therefore, claim a great victory in Korea.

In short, there was no compelling reason to continue the conflict while there was a compelling reason to end it. As part of a "peace offensive" following the death of Soviet Premier Joseph Stalin in February 1953, the Soviet Union appears also to have pressured the Chinese and North Koreans to end the conflict. Almost certainly this too influenced China's decision to conclude an armistice.

Foreign sources have thus forced historians to take a second look at various aspects of Korean War. In many cases, they have merely confirmed what historians have long maintained, such as the approval the Soviet Union and the PRC gave for North Korea's invasion of South Korea in 1950. But even in this regard, they have added nuances, such as the reluctance that accompanied the Soviet Union's and the PRC's consent, the tensions between Moscow and Beijing that were exacerbated as a result of the Soviet Union's unwillingness to support China on the eve of its intervention into Korea, and the civil nature of the conflict, which changed with American and, then, Chinese entry into the war. On other matters, such as the rationale behind China's decision to send its troops into Korea, they have provided a dimension that had hitherto been lacking in most histories of the war.

NOTES

1. The standard work on the Korean War remained for many years, David Rees, *Korea: The Limited War* (New York: Hamish Hamilton, 1964). But see also

Allen S. Whiting, *China Crosses the Yalu: The Decision to Enter the Korean War* (Stanford, CA: Stanford University Press, 1968), 45.

2. Chen Jian, *China's Road to the Korean War: The Making of the Sino-American Confrontation* (New York: Columbia University Press, 1994), esp. 211–20.

3. James Shepley, "How Dulles Averted War," *Life* (January 16, 1956).

4. For a more extended discussion of the POW issue, see Chapter 5 in this volume.

5. Rosemary Foot, *A Substitute for Victory: The Politics of Peacemaking at the Korean Armistice Talks* (Ithaca, NY: Cornell University Press, 1990), 218.

4

From Rollback to Rollback: The Chinese Communist Intervention

Had United Nations (UN) forces stopped their military advance at the 38th parallel following the hugely successful invasion at Inchon, the United States might have been able to claim a major victory. North Korea's invasion of South Korea would have ended in humiliating defeat for the communists. Military containment would have been tested successfully. Indeed, had UN forces advanced to the narrow waist of Korea, along a line running roughly from Wonsan on the east to Pyongyang on the west, the United States could have proclaimed an even greater victory, not only stopping communist aggression but liberating land previously held by the communists. Even had Communist China (the People's Republic of China, or PRC) entered the war, UN forces would have been in a much better position militarily to stave off a Chinese offensive.

Despite repeated Chinese warnings not to advance to the Yalu River, however, UN forces, with the approval of President Harry Truman and the Joint Chiefs of Staff (JCS), barely caught their breath once the orders had been given in September 1950 to cross into North Korea. By November, the first elements of the American 7th Division had reached the town of Hyesanjin, in northeast Korea and could look across the Yalu River. By November 24, UN forces held a line that extended from So-dong in the northeast to Hyesanjin on the Yalu and then on a south/southwesterly line to Chongju and the Yellow Sea. General Douglas MacArthur was promising to end the war by Christmas. Instead, the Chinese, who had secretly crossed into Korea in massive numbers, launched an offensive at the end of November that led to one of the most humiliating defeats the United States ever suffered on the battlefield. What had been the "rollback" of communism now became the "rollback" of containment.

As indicated in the previous chapter, historians still debate the question of whether China would have entered the Korean War had UN forces not advanced to the Yalu River. Until recently, most writers believed that this would not have happened. Now, however, some scholars claim that Mao Zedong had decided as early as August, before the Inchon invasion and UN march to the Yalu, to commit his forces to Korea. Regardless of when the Chinese intervention became inevitable, there was considerable warning that China would not countenance the stationing of UN forces on its border with Korea. For example, Hanson Baldwin of the *New York Times* reported in October that there were between 200,000 and 250,000 Chinese soldiers mobilized along the Yalu River. Even the Central Intelligence Agency (CIA), which had concluded in September that an invasion of Korea by either China or the Soviet Union was highly unlikely, determined in October that the Chinese would enter the war, but only for the purpose of defending its power stations along the Yalu. Between November 1 and 3, Chinese troops attacked the ROK (Republic of Korea) II Corps and the U.S. 1st Cavalry Division, inflicting heavy casualties before withdrawing almost as suddenly as they had entered the war. Captured Chinese soldiers provided detailed information about China's forces in Korea. On November 8, the CIA reported that there were between 30,000 and 40,000 Chinese troops now in Korea and 700,000 more on China's border with Korea. Moscow radio warned on November 19 that a Chinese and North Korean counteroffensive was imminent.[1]

During the UN march northward, the Joint Chiefs of Staff also had expressed reservations about advancing to the Yalu River. They suggested to MacArthur that it might instead be better to establish a defensive line along the waist of Korea. But also believing MacArthur should have the flexibility needed to destroy the enemy, seduced by the prospect of total military victory in Korea, and reluctant, in any case, to challenge a certified war hero venerated by much of the American public, they deferred to MacArthur, who insisted on liberating all of Korea. Furthermore, most diplomats believed that China would not attack without the approval of the Soviet Union, and that Moscow did not want to escalate the war in Korea. As a result, on the eve of the Chinese offensive there was still not anyone with sufficient rank to challenge MacArthur's assertion that the war would be over by Christmas. Indeed, on November 24, the general launched his "home by Christmas" offensive, and for the first two days of the offensive, UN troops advancing northward met little opposition. But on November 26, the Chinese counter-attacked.

When the Chinese launched their massive assault that day, UN troops were divided into two major commands, the Eighth Army under the command of General Walton Walker on the west, and the X Corps consisting of the 1st Marine Division and the Army's 7th Infantry Division led by Major General Edward M. Almond on the east. A number of military analysts would later claim that the separation of these two forces by the high Taebek Mountains that cut through the center of North Korea was the major reason for the humiliating defeat the Chinese were able to inflict on UN forces; that they were able to exploit this gap to outflank both forces. More recently, however, Roy Appleman, a retired Marine colonel and military historian, has successfully shown that this mountainous spine of North Korea was impenetrable by communist as well as by UN forces. At the same time, though, Appleman argues that the separation of command between the Eighth Army and X Corps was a mistake, making any kind of coordinated military response to the Chinese invasion virtually impossible.[2]

The Chinese offensive began on the night of November 26. Hardened by just having won the Chinese Civil War, China's troops were also experienced and well-disciplined. Although they were still a guerrilla army outfitted largely with captured light infantry weapons and no artillery when they attacked, they met an enemy, many of whom had thrown away their helmets, bayonets, blankets, and spare ammunition, so certain were they that the Korean conflict would soon be over. The sheer numbers and the ferocity of the Chinese attack were enough to drive the surprised UN forces back. Two separate armies struck against the UN Eighth Army in the west and the X Corps in the east. Their objective was to pin down enemy troops along Korea's two coasts and then to move other divisions southward to make contact with large concentrations of guerrilla forces operating behind UN lines.

In the west, the 2nd Infantry Division was cut to pieces, losing all its guns. The ROK II Corps also came under fire and was virtually destroyed, leaving the right flank of the Eighth Army exposed. At a meeting in Tokyo that MacArthur called on November 29 with his two military commanders, General Walker and Almond, MacArthur instructed Walker to hold Pyongyang as long as he could. Instead, Walker began a hasty withdrawal southward. Huge stockpiles of supplies, including 1,600 tons of ammunition and winter clothing for American forces, which had been unloaded at the port of Chinnampo thirty-five miles southwest of the North Korean capital, were destroyed. According to Appleman, the "failure of the UN forces to make a defensive stand at Pyongyang was probably one of the most important tactical mistakes of the war."[3] As Walker must have known, the Chinese had nearly exhausted their ammunition and food, were lightly armed, and were spent physically, having been on the offensive for five days and nights. With proper armor and air support, the Eighth Army should have been able to defend along Korea's narrow waist.

In the east, the 1st Marine Division was trapped at the Chosin Reservoir near the town of Hagaru-ri. A common Chinese military tactic was to concentrate their forces at a particular point until it was penetrated or destroyed and then to strike at the flanks or rear of the enemy with a barrage of small-arms fire and grenade attacks. This was the tactic they used in the fighting around the Chosin Reservoir. For a time, it seemed that they might destroy the Marines and other UN forces in the east before they could secure their lines of supply and reinforcements. This did not happen. Resupplied from the air, aided by repeated air strikes against the Chinese, and using their heavy artillery, UN forces were able to resist long enough to allow most troops to escape the trap the Chinese had set for them. In one of the most heroic episodes in the annals of American military history, the 10,000 beleaguered Marines at the Chosin Reservoir braved 60,000 Chinese troops, brutal winds, and temperatures of minus twenty degrees to break out of their trap at Chosin and withdraw seventy miles to the coastal town of Hungnam, where they were then evacuated to Pusan. General O. P. Smith, who commanded the 1st Marine Division, captured headlines at home when he remarked to correspondents, "Gentlemen, we are not retreating. We are merely advancing in another direction."[4] For many Americans, Smith's comments merely underscored the heroism of American forces fighting in Korea. Nevertheless, the evacuation of the X Corps from northeast Korea was the largest retreat in U.S. military history. In all, 105,000 soldiers, 17,500 vehicles, and 350,000 tons of cargo were removed to safe haven. Approximately 4,400 UN troops were killed, wounded, or listed as missing in action. One estimate placed Chinese losses at the Chosin Reservoir at 37,500.[5]

Nevertheless, UN forces were in full retreat along the entire front. Indeed, the Chinese abandoned their strategy of attacking only at night despite suffering heavy losses from the air. From Tokyo, MacArthur reported that he was fighting an entirely new war in Korea. He asked for reinforcements, and he repeated a request he had made several times earlier that he be allowed to employ Chinese Nationalist forces in Korea. Secretary of State Dean Acheson remarked that the Chinese intervention had moved the United States closer to a general war. On December 16, Truman declared a state of national emergency. Truman and Acheson were angered over how badly MacArthur had misjudged the capacity and willingness of China to enter the war. Yet the administration remained convinced that the Soviet Union had incited the Chinese to enter the war, and the CIA warned that the Soviets would give the Chinese maximum support.

The United States's European allies were even more dismayed by the sudden turn of events in Korea. Having always been concerned that MacArthur wanted to expand the war in Korea into a major Asiatic war, they now feared that the Chinese intervention might give the general the opportunity he wanted. When President Truman refused at a press conference to eliminate the possibility that the United States might even use the atomic bomb against the Chinese. Europeans responded with shock and outrage. Under pressure from both public opinion and the Conservative opposition in Britain, British Prime Minister Clement Attlee flew to Washington to make clear Europe's opposition to the use of nuclear weapons. He also made clear Britain's strong opposition to an all-out war with China, which, he pointed out, would threaten British interests in Hong Kong, Singapore, and Malaya.

Attlee failed to gain what he wanted from Truman—a pledge not to use atomic weapons against the Chinese. Both the State Department and the Department of Defense were against restricting U.S. freedom of action in Korea. There was also growing support in the United States to use the atomic bomb if that would bring an end to the war. But the worldwide reaction to the president's press conference was so strong that Truman felt that he could not let Attlee return home empty-handed. He told the prime minister, therefore, that the United States was not actively considering the use of atomic weapons in Asia, and he promised not to employ the nuclear option without first consulting the British.

Meanwhile the Chinese offensive continued. Moving in close formation and striking in overwhelming numbers, the Chinese recaptured Seoul on January 4 and then proceeded to take other major South Korean towns, including the important railway center of Wonju in the east. Not until January 24, when UN forces had withdrawn to defensive positions roughly along the 37th parallel, did the Chinese stop their attack. By this time, the Eighth Army had retreated more than three hundred miles.

Notwithstanding the great success of the Chinese offensive, however, it had come at a heavy cost. By the second week of December, the Chinese IX Army Group were estimated to have suffered more than 40,000 killed in battle with many thousands more wounded or suffering from frostbite. As the Chinese continued on the offensive, their primitive supply lines, based to a considerable extent on human and animal labor, were stretched to the breaking point. What trucks they had fell victim time and again to American air power. Radio communication was so poor that the Chinese were unable to

coordinate their large-scale operations effectively. Had the Chinese continued their attack in force after taking Seoul, they might have been able to
drive UN forces all the way back to the Pusan perimeter. But logistical problems made that impossible.

Chinese clothing was also ill suited for the harshness of the Korean winter. Although they wore several layers of underclothing, heavy quilted coats,
and wool or fur-lined hats, their "boots" were actually nothing more than
tennis shoes made of rubber and canvas, and they often lacked gloves. Captured Chinese reported that as much as 50 percent of China's combat forces
were suffering from frostbite. Morale became a growing problem as the war
stretched into a series of forced marches, missed meals, and recurrent skir-
mishes. "We quickly got used to American biscuits and rice," one Chinese
combat officer later wrote, "but we never cared for tomato juice. . . . Without
the American sleeping bags and overcoats that we captured, I am not sure
we could have gone on."[6] Replacements for the hardened troops killed or
wounded in action were often raw recruits with less than three weeks of
training, some of whom were still unable to fire a rifle.

In contrast, UN forces were being honed into an effective fighting force.
On December 23, the commander of the Eighth Army, General Walker, was
killed in a freak traffic accident. Replacing him was the Eighth Army's deputy chief of staff, Lieutenant General Matthew Ridgway who already had
gained a considerable reputation in military circles for his command of airborne troops during World War II. The failure of the Chinese to press the
Eighth Army hard after taking Seoul allowed it time to regroup and be resupplied. It also gave Ridgway the time he needed to restore the morale and esprit of his forces.

Hard driving and always demanding precision from his staff, the general
was known for his trademark of a single grenade and first-aid kit that he wore
over his trench coat. Given complete charge of military operations by
MacArthur, his only orders were to defend his positions, inflict maximum
damage on the enemy, and maintain major units intact. Arriving in Korea on
December 26, Ridgway was immediately struck by the low morale and lack
of discipline among American troops. He was also upset that the Eighth
Army had not made adequate preparations to try to hold onto Seoul. "I had
discovered," he later wrote, "that our forces were simply not mentally and
spiritually ready for the sort of action I had been planning."[7] Believing that
the system of divided command between the Eighth Army and X Corps was
a mistake, he placed the entire UN force under his command. Rejecting the
sense of defeatism that had become pervasive even among his field officers,
he instilled a new fighting spirit among the troops.

Although UN forces continued to retreat after Ridgway took over, they did so in orderly fashion and at a heavy cost to enemy forces. In the middle of January, the U.S. 2nd Division, aided by French and Dutch battalions, even carried out the first counterattack since the fall of Seoul, briefly fighting their way into the town of Wonju before retreating under small-arms fire. When Army Chief of Staff J. Lawton Collins and Air Force General Hoyt Vandenberg visited Korea in order to determine whether the Eighth Army should stay in Korea, they were pleasantly surprised to find that the military situation in Korea was much better than General MacArthur had led Washington to believe. Henceforth, the Pentagon and the White House would maintain direct contact with Ridgway in Korea rather than following military protocol by going through MacArthur in Japan, who increasingly became a figurehead isolated from the realities of the war.

Finally, on January 25, UN forces launched "Operation Thunderbolt," originally a reconnaissance mission in force, which turned into a major counteroffensive after the Chinese committed seven divisions to the fighting. Thunderbolt lasted for three months. By February 10, Ridgway's forces had recaptured Kimpo and Inchon and neutralized Seoul. Adopting what Ridgway referred to as a "meat grinder" strategy of seeking out the enemy and then striking him repeatedly with tanks and artillery, the Eighth Army had lost forty men killed in the operation compared to an estimated 4,000 Chinese dead. Some estimates of total Chinese casualties between January 25 and February 10 (killed, wounded, or suffering from frostbite) ran as high as 80,000. Meanwhile UN forces had advanced forty to fifty miles north.[8]

On February 11, the Chinese launched a counterattack, their fourth offensive, striking at the weak center of UN lines and forcing Ridgway's forces to retreat once more to below Wonju. But the counteroffensive was short-lived. Chinese General Peng Dehuai, the commander of communist forces, noted the disadvantages the Chinese faced even as they launched their attack and the military mistakes they had made in their past offensives. "The battle begins under unfavorable conditions," he wrote "Our period of rest is interrupted and now, when we are not yet ready to fight the 4th phase is underway." He also conceded that in their earlier operations, the Chinese had failed "to pursue the enemy quickly" because the main force of the enemy still remained intact. "If we had pursued the enemy immediately," he concluded, "we might have gained complete victory, but we lacked mobile equipment to do so."[9]

Using their traditional military tactic of striking at weak points along the main line of defense while engaging simultaneously in flanking operations, the Chinese enjoyed some initial success, eliminating three regiments of

ROK forces and cutting through American support forces. Within forty-eight hours they had advanced fifteen miles against the X Corps. But almost as soon as they launched their new offensive, their forces came under enormous firepower both on the ground and from the air. Ridgway was a strong supporter of close air support for ground troops and used it effectively against the enemy. In the key battle of the offensive, UN forces retook the town of Chipyong-ni, twenty air miles north of Wonju, where the Chinese had surrounded an American regiment and French battalion. Chipyong-ni was strategically important because five major roads leading south and west passed through it. But after a hard-fought battle, UN forces broke through the Chinese encirclement, rescuing the French and Americans and holding on to Chipyong-ni's vital transportation and communication arteries. The effect of Chipyong-ni on morale was as important as the town was strategically. "The myth of the magical millions of the Chinese in Korea has been exploded," wrote one British observer. "In the last United Nations offensive, the Americans have learned how easy it is to kill the Chinese, and their morale has greatly increased thereby."[10] Within less than a week, the Chinese offensive had run out of steam and been contained at a cost to the communists of 33,000 casualties. By week's end, UN forces were once more advancing northward. "We have defeated the Communist counter-offensive in the central sector," Ridgway told reporters. "The Communists have taken a fearful beating, and have disengaged."[11]

Having seized the initiative from the chinese, Ridgway launched "Operation Killer" on February 21. Within a week, he had wiped out almost all pockets of resistance below the Han River. On March 7, the U.S. 25th Division crossed the Han River once more, taking 213 prisoners, the largest number captured in a single day by an American division on the offensive. On that same day, Operation Killer was replaced by "Operation Ripper," one of whose purposes was to recapture Seoul. The enemy put up heavy resistance, but the city was taken again on March 16, the fourth and last time it was to change hands during the war. For the first time since the Chinese invasion, UN forces were beginning to prevail over the communists. Intelligence reported that the North Korean and Chinese were carrying out a well-organized withdrawal north of the 38th parallel. There were also reports of a major outbreak among the Chinese, and especially the North Koreans, of typhoid, smallpox, and whooping cough. That same intelligence also reported, however, that the Chinese were sending fresh troops and supplies into Korea and were preparing to launch a new offensive.

Considerable soul-searching followed in Washington over whether UN forces should again cross the 38th parallel. Few officials gave serious consideration any longer to reunifying Korea, the directive under which UN forces had been operating since October 5. The Chinese intervention and Europe's strong opposition to expanding the war precluded that possibility. State Department officials were even reluctant to send American troops into North Korea. But the Pentagon argued successfully that a limited move into North Korea was necessary in order to prevent giving the communists time for rebuilding and planning another attack into South Korea in March. Ridgway was given orders that left the decision to cross into North Korea up to him, but only for limited military purposes. His orders also made clear that there would be no forceful attempt to unify Korea.

Not entirely happy with the restrictions imposed on his command, Ridgway, nevertheless, at the end of March ordered his troops to cross into North Korea. In fact, some American and ROK units had moved already across the 38th parallel even before they received their orders. By April 22, UN forces had established a new defensive line—Wyoming—which, in the center, reached almost to the "Iron Triangle," a heavily defended area and the logistical center of enemy operations in central Korea with a concentration of rail lines and highways coming from the north. At its northern point, the "Iron Triangle" encompassed Pyonggang (not to be confused with the capital city of Pyongyang), at its northern point, Chorwon at its left point, and Kumhwa at its right point.

On April 22, however, the Chinese launched yet another offensive against UN forces. Begun with a four-hour artillery barrage whose intensity surprised American intelligence officers, it also turned out to be their greatest military effort of the conflict. But Ridgway—who was summoned to Tokyo on April 11 to replace MacArthur as Supreme Commander of UN forces following President Harry Truman's firing of MacArthur—had anticipated and prepared for the offensive, establishing a series of defensive lines around Seoul, each of which was to be defended in succession with mines, barbed wire, interlocking machine gun fire, heavy artillery, and air strikes. In this way, he intended to throw the Chinese off balance and destroy their will and ability to continue offensive operations.

At first, the sheer magnitude of the Chinese attack sent UN forces reeling back. The heaviest fighting was just south of the Imjin River, about twenty-five miles northwest of Seoul. In one of the more well-known and heroic military efforts of the war, ranking in this respect with the December retreat of the 1st Marine Division from the Chosin Reservoir, the heavily outnumbered British Twenty-Ninth Infantry Brigade and a small contingent of other forces held off enemy forces for three days before they were forced to retreat. By the time the battle ended, the Twenty-ninth had suffered more than a thousand casualties. Of the 622 men comprising its famed Gloucester Regiment, only thirty-nine officers and men were left. In the east, two ROK artillery units were overrun and their equipment captured. The new commander of the Eighth Army, General James Van Fleet, ordered his forces to withdraw twenty miles to a new line, "No Name," running roughly from Seoul along the north bank of the Han River.

The withdrawal, however, was orderly, and Ridgway's earlier plans to destroy the Chinese will to continue by inflicting heavy casualties on them as they advanced southward worked. By the end of April, the Chinese had again exhausted themselves. Efforts to outflank Seoul miscarried. On April 29, UN air power broke up a final Chinese attempt to ferry 6,000 troops across the Han Estuary to advance on Seoul from the west. Low on ammunition and food and demoralized by the heavy casualties they had suffered—an estimated 70,000 casualties as opposed to 7,000 for UN forces— they withdrew their forces out of range of UN artillery. Less than three weeks later, they launched what they referred to as the "second phase" of their offensive. The mission of the 175,000 troops they sent southward was to destroy six ROK army divisions along the eastern flank of the Eighth Army. But this offensive also failed, and for the same reasons as their initial attack; although two of the ROK divisions gave way, the Chinese simply lacked the wherewithal to move against the enormous firepower of UN forces. They were also short of food, and many troops were suffering from dysentery. Soldiers were even reported to be eating grass.[12] The carnage was the worst of the war. In the last week of their offensive, between May 17 and May 23, the Chinese had lost 90,000 troops. Estimates of total losses for both phases of the offensive ran as high as 200,000. Ten thousand Chinese had been taken as prisoners of war (POWs).

Instead of having his men dig in, moreover, Van Fleet went on the offensive, driving the Chinese across the 38th parallel along every military sector. How far Van Fleet might have advanced northward had he been allowed to do so is open to some question. The Chinese, who had to endure the mental, as well as physical, anguish of the heaviest artillery attacks of the war (or of any war), were disorganized and demoralized. The Eighth Army claimed that in the second phase of their offensive, the Chinese and North Koreans had suffered a total of 105,000 casualties of which 17,000 had been killed in action and 10,000 taken prisoner.[13] For the first time in the war, large numbers of Chinese were being taken as POWs. Certainly, Van Fleet was upset when he was instructed to advance no farther than line Wyoming. "[W]e had the Chinese whipped," Van Fleet later remarked. "They were definitely gone. They were in awful shape."[14]

Yet it is far from clear just how far into the Iron Triangle Van Fleet's forces could have advanced. Contrary to his belief, the Chinese were far from a defeated enemy. More than one million Chinese remained in North Korea, and they put up increasingly stiff resistance as UN forces moved north toward the Iron Triangle. Many of the Chinese forces were holed up in bunkers and dugouts protected with eight or ten feet of logs and earth, which the North Koreans had built before they invaded South Korea. The Chinese also laid down some of the heaviest artillery barrages of the war using captured American guns and artillery supplied to them by the Soviet Union. A move into the Iron Triangle would have meant enormous casualties. Finally, the Chinese were far along in developing a considerable air force equipped with MIG-15 jets operating from bases in Manchuria. Depending on how far northward UN forces advanced, China's planes could have made life miserable for UN ground troops.[15]

It was political, rather than military, considerations, however, that led to the decision to limit Van Fleet's advance into North Korea. Opposition remained strong throughout Europe and in the United States to prolonging the war. Believing that he could negotiate from a position of military strength, President Truman wanted to test the chances for peace despite the fact that even some of his own White House advisors told him that the enemy had given no indication that it was willing to sit down at the negotiating table or that it had changed its military and political objectives in Korea.

The president's decision to limit the UN advance to the area around the Iron Triangle was a fateful one. Although two more years of combat would follow before the war ended, and some of the conflict's heaviest fighting still lay ahead, the remainder of the war was largely one of stalemate, as both sides dug in and built elaborate fortifications that made a major military offensive either by UN or Chinese forces increasingly unlikely. Indeed, UN forces adopted a military policy known as the active defensive, sending our heavily outfitted reconnaisance missions and patrols to test the Chinese and keep them off balance, but never embarking on a major military offensive to drive the communist forces much beyond the Iron Triangle. Indeed, the military line that was established by the spring of 1951, which had UN forces about ten miles above the 38th parallel for most of the line except in the extreme west where it cut below the 38th parallel, was largely the line that would constitute the armistice line at the war's end two years later.

What had happened during the first year of the war, then, was that UN forces had attempted to "roll back" the North Koreans to the Yalu River and reunify Korea under UN auspices. This had led to the entry of the Chinese into the war (although there is strong evidence that the Chinese had decided to enter the conflict as early as August 1951, before UN forces had even entered North Korea). Enjoying enormous initial success, the Chinese engaged in their own efforts at "roll back," driving UN forces well below the 38th parallel and, for a short time, even raising the specter again of a communist military victory in Korea. However, China's lack of technology and sophisticated military equipment and its primitive lines of communication limited what China could achieve on the battlefield, especially when compared to the modern technology and heavy firepower of UN forces. What followed as a result were two years of largely military stalemate as the focus of the war shifted from the battlefield to the negotiating table.

That the morale of American forces remained relatively high under such conditions was a remarkable achievement. Mostly poorly educated and poorly paid conscripts fighting a war whose purpose they came less and less to understand and to which Americans at home grew increasingly indifferent, they had few of the amenities that even soldiers fighting in Vietnam, perhaps the nation's most unpopular war, would later have. The historian Max Hastings has described the bleak conditions that faced American forces in Korea: "There were no officers' clubs or bars, no drugs or movies or diversion. There were only the mountain ridges, surmounted by the defenses which both sides now dug with extraordinary care and caution." To this could be added Siberian winters, monsoon rains in the spring, South Korean forces American troops came to disdain, persistent patrolling, enemy infiltrations at night, constant shelling, mounting lists of casualties, and the daily grind of living in wet foxholes and bunkers fully aware that military victory was no longer the war's aim.

That UN forces were able to survive and then recover from the Chinese onslaught following their invasion of Korea in November 1950 can be attributed in large measure to the pluck, sheer tenacity, and military brilliance of Matthew Ridgway, who took over command of the Eighth Army at a critical juncture in the war and remolded UN forces into an effective fighting team. "It was for the most part a solo performance," Roy Appleman writes of Ridgway, "he had no help from the army staff and its men. One man, a leader with high resolve, made the difference. In the end his cautious turnaround gained momentum when the officers and men saw that the enemy was vulnerable and overextended and that victories could be won."[16] That seems a fair assessment of what took place under Ridgway's command.

NOTES

1. Roy E. Appleman, *Disaster in Korea: The Chinese Confront MacArthur* (College Station, TX: Texas A&M University Press, 1989), 14.

2. Appleman, *Disaster in Korea*, xiii–xiv, 14–15.

3. Ibid., 305–14, 332–53.

4. Roy E. Appleman, *Escaping the Trap: The U.S. Army X Corps in Northeast Korea, 1950* (College Station, TX: Texas A&M University Press, 1900), 64–74, 286–342

5. Ibid.

6. Hastings, *The Korean War* (New York: Simon and Schuster, 1987), 172.

7. Matthew B. Ridgway, *The Korean War* (Garden City, NY: Doubleday, 1967), 86.

8. Roy E. Appleman, *Ridgway Duels for Korea* (College Station, TX: Texas A&M University Press, 1990), 175–92.

9. Ibid., 218.

10. Quoted in Hastings, *The Korean War*, 196.

11. *Time* 57 (February 26, 1951): 28.

12. Appleman, *Ridgway Duels for Korea*, 509.

13. Ibid., 550–52.

14. *Life* 30 (June 11, 1951): 43.

15. Some of the Chinese planes were flown by Soviet pilots who had been secretly flying over North Korea since September 1950.

16. Appleman, *Ridgway Duels for Korea*, 479–80.

5

Prisoners of War Issue

Except for the issue of repatriating Chinese and North Korean prisoners of war (POWs), an armistice ending the Korean War might have been achieved as early as 1951, two years before an agreement was finally reached. Indeed, after 1951, it was the only issue holding back the signing of a truce agreement. The irony was that at the time armistice negotiations began in July 1951, no one expected that repatriation of POWs would be that much of a problem. Furthermore, the cause of the delay was the unwillingness of President Harry Truman to agree to repatriate POWs against their will even though the Geneva Conference of 1949 specifically required that all POWs be repatriated regardless of their consent. But for Truman, repatriation of unwilling POWs became a moral issue, and he held firm to his position irrespective of the pressures on him to change his mind. And by the time Dwight Eisenhower became president, the policy had become such a matter of principle that the new president could not have adopted a different policy even had he wished to, which he did not.

Following the end of World War II in 1945, tens of thousands of German and Japanese soldiers taken prisoners by the Soviet Union were kept captive in order to help in the country's massive reconstruction effort. In order to prevent this from happening again, Article 118 of the Geneva Convention of 1949 provided for the quick and compulsory return of all POWs at the end of a war; it did not provide for POWs who did not want to be repatriated. In fact, a proposed Austrian amendment to the convention, which would have allowed exceptions to the rule and which was supported by the Soviets, was rejected overwhelmingly by the Convention. Although the United States did not sign the Convention until 1951, it announced very early in the Korean War that it would abide by its provisions, as did North and South Korea.[1]

As UN forces began to capture large numbers of Chinese and North Korean troops during the first year of the war, some American officials began to argue against what was already being referred to as "forced repatriation,"claiming that former prisoners might be executed if they were forced to return to China and North Korea against their will. Indeed, after World War II, many Soviet citizens and troops who had defected to, or been taken captive by, the Axis powers and did not want to return home because of fear of reprisals, were executed or exiled to Siberia by their leaders. Perhaps with this in mind, the U.S. Army's chief of psychological warfare, General Robert A. McClure, proposed to General J. Lawton Collins that Chinese POWs who were former Nationalists be allowed to go to Formosa. "Inducements to surrender will be meaningless [in the future]," McClure warned, "[if it] results in the prisoner's death or slavery."[2] Collins approved the idea, maintaining that this would not be a violation of the Geneva Convention because even Beijing considered Formosa part of China.

Nevertheless, the majority view in Washington war that, at the time of an armistice, all Chinese and North Koreans should be returned home. To do otherwise, it was argued, would not only violate the Geneva Convention, it might put in jeopardy the swift return of UN POWs held by the Chinese and North Koreans. The Joint Chiefs of Staff had gone back and forth on the POW issue, at one time flavoring the forced repatriation of prisoners to get American POWs returned as quickly as possible, at another time ordering General Matthew Ridgway to prepare a proposal for the return of POWs based on voluntary repatriation, but then reversing course again and flavoring the prompt repatriation of all prisoners on the basis of the Geneva Convention. Within the State Department, Secretary of State Dean Acheson flirted with the idea of releasing shortly before an armistice those prisoners who feared for their safety, a deed that he thought also would have considerable propaganda value. But in August, he concluded that the United States was obligated to abide by the terms of the Geneva Convention. Other State Department officials felt the same way, even pointing out the immorality of leaving Americans prisoners of war while trying to get the communists to agree to something they were almost certain to find unacceptable. The UN negotiators at Panmunjom also believed that the fastest way to return UN prisoners home was to agree to an all-for-all-exchange and that voluntary repatriation would violate the Geneva Convention. Because of the strong support in favor of forced repatriation at the Pentagon, the State Department, and the negotiating tents in Panmunjom, few Americans anticipated that the return of POWs would be a problem when the issue was first brought up at Panmunjom in December 1951.

Although President Harry Truman did not entirely rule out returning POWs on an all-for-all basis (all UN POWs in exchange for all communist POWs), he had serious reservations about adopting such a policy. In the first place, he believed that the POW issue should be settled as part of a larger package that included major, unspecified concessions from the enemy. Even more important, he felt it would be morally wrong to force POWs to be repatriated against their will. "He did not want to send back those prisoners who surrendered and have cooperated with us," Acting Secretary of State James Webb commented in October 1951, "because he believes they [would] be immediately done away with."[3]

Complicating matters were the small number of UN POWs the communists claimed to be holding, the imbalance between that number and the number of POWs held by the UN Command, and the mix of enemy POWs. Unwilling at first even to exchange lists of POWs or allow the Red Cross to visit its POW camps, the Chinese and North Koreans finally provided the names of approximately 11,500 UN POWs, including 7,142 South Koreans and 3,198 Americans. What disturbed the UN Command and administration officials in Washington was the fact that the enemy had claimed to have captured 65,000 prisoners and that 88,000 South Koreans and 11,500 Americans were reported missing in action (MIAs). Although many of the MIAs could be attributed to desertions and battlefield deaths, it seemed improbable that all could be accounted for in this way; more likely, an indeterminate number of MIAs had been killed after capture or were being held prisoners by the communists. As for the POWs held by the UN, they numbered 132,000, excluding 37,000 former South Koreans who had been forced into the North Korean army at gunpoint and who had been reclassified as "civilian detainees." The 132,000 POWs consisted not only of North Korean and Chinese communists but an unspecified number of Chinese Nationalist soldiers and officers who had been impressed into the People's Liberation Army (PLA).[4]

What all this meant to a growing number of public commentators and administration officials, including the president, was that the communists could not be trusted to return all UN POWs even on the basis of forced repatriation, that involuntary repatriation would benefit the enemy because of the imbalance in the number of prisoners being held by both sides, and that forced repatriation would amount to turning over to the enemy Chinese Nationalists who had been forced to fight against their will. Furthermore, the likelihood that a large number of these prisoners would reject repatriation to the communists would be a propaganda victory for the West.

Accordingly, the negotiators at Panmunjom were instructed in January to insist on the voluntary repatriation of POWs. Against their better judgment, the UN negotiators carried out their orders by proposing the establishment of a neutral agency to interview all POWs on both sides to determine which of them wanted to be repatriated. The Chinese responded furiously, calling the theory of voluntary repatriation "a gigantic trap" and insisting that the proposal was a ploy meant to strengthen the Nationalist forces in Formosa by sending alleged nonrepatriates to serve in Chiang Kai-shek's army. For weeks, the talks on POWs remained deadlocked while the UN negotiators endured increasingly vituperative language from their communist counterparts.

Yet it was not until February that the administration firmly and finally committed itself against forced repatriation. Quite clearly, the White House was moving in that direction. But for all its qualms about the immorality of forced repatriation, the administration was still unwilling to commit itself irrevocably against that policy. Aware of the political fallout that the failure to end the war was already causing at home, it was concerned about public reaction to a delay in settling the POW question because of an insistence on voluntary repatriation. Accordingly, the Pentagon instructed Ridgway not to be rigid on the POW issue.

That changed in February, when the administration instructed UN negotiators to offer a plan it had worked out according to which the communists would agree to voluntary repatriation in return for concessions on the rehabilitation of airfields in Korea. (In response to the buildup of Chinese air power, the United States had earlier taken the position that there should be no construction or rebuilding of airfields in the war-torn peninsula; now it was willing to concede that point to the enemy.) If the Chinese refused the offer, then Ridgway was instructed to screen all the prisoners held by the UN and to remove from the POW lists those prisoners who expressed fear that they would be killed or harmed if repatriated. The UN negotiators would then offer to return the remaining prisoners to the communists in an all-for-all exchange.

Speaking to the American people, President Truman explained his policy. "To agree to forced repatriation," he said, "would be repugnant to the most fundamental moral and humanitarian principles which underlie our action in Korea." Secretary of State Acheson also took a strong stand against forced repatriation. "My colleagues and I were moved," he later wrote, "by humanitarian reasons and by the effect upon our own and Asian people of the forcible repatriation of prisoners whose lives would be jeopardized. We were also aware of the deterrent effect upon the Communists of the escape offered to their soldiers by falling into our hands."[5]

General Ridgway opposed the newest plan, believing that it would be rejected at Panmunjom and that the communists would punish American POWs in response to the release of UN-held prisoners who did not wish to be repatriated. As he predicted, the Chinese and North Koreans rejected this plan and another one like it that would have deleted restrictions on airfield reconstruction and established a four-member neutral armistice commission in exchange for agreement on voluntary repatriation. They also turned down a proposal to allow prisoners not willing to be repatriated to be removed from the lists of POWs, which would have allowed for the repatriation of the other prisoners without the communists having to agree to voluntary repatriation.

Nevertheless, the communists did agree to have both sides screen POWs in order to determine how many wanted to be repatriated. UN negotiators told the Chinese and North Koreans that they thought 116,000 would agree to repatriation, and the communists indicated that anything over 100,000 would be acceptable to them. Thus, a widespread feeling developed both in Washington and in Korea that what had become a major stumbling block to an armistice might soon be resolved. Unfortunately, when the screening of Chinese and North Korean POWs was carried out in April, only 70,000 said they wanted to be returned home. This figure not only surprised Ridgway and the head of the UN negotiating team, Admiral C. Turner Joy, it startled the communist negotiators, who charged that the prisoners were being pressured into renouncing repatriation. In response, they suspended the armistice talks for almost a week.

There was some truth to the Chinese accusations. Most of the Chinese and North Koreans taken prisoner by UN forces were housed in compounds located on the island of Koje-do off the southeast cost of Korea. They lived in badly overcrowded barracks under unruly conditions. Many of the compounds were actually controlled by the prisoners themselves, who were divided into pro and anticommunist factions. Some Chinese POWs had even allowed themselves to be captured so that they could organize their cadres in the camps. But both groups enforced their own discipline in the compounds they controlled. Pro-communist factions were also brutalized by the prison guards, most of whom were South Korean; there were even some Chinese Nationalists from Formosa. Even the UN's chief negotiator, Admiral Joy, noted in his diary reliable reports he had received of Chinese POWs being "beaten black and blue or killed" after stating their desire to be repatriated. Ambassador John Muccio referred to them as "Gestapos." In May, following months of clashes between guards and prisoners, militants seized the compounds and took captive the commander of the island, General Francis T. Dodd.

Dodd was not released until General Charles T. Colson, who had taken command of Koje-do, made a statement "confessing" to the killing or wounding of Chinese and North Korean POWs. Although the statement was obviously made under duress and was soon repudiated by Colson, when the United States concluded a rescreening of POWs in July, the number of those seeking repatriation climbed to around 83,000. However, the administration would not permit the UN negotiators to use that number fearing that it would bring into question the integrity of its original poll or make it appear that the UN Command was willing to negotiate with the numbers. Even if it had revealed the new number, it is doubtful that the communists would have considered the figure acceptable.

Meanwhile, less than a week after suspending the negotiations at Panmunjom, the communist negotiators returned to the bargaining table. But they held fast to the position that nothing short of the return of at least 100,000 Chinese POWs would be acceptable to them. For its part, the Truman administration stuck to its insistence on voluntary repatriation, although it was willing to consider a package deal in which an armistice would be achieved based on the points already agreed to at Panmunjom in exchange for a communist concession on the POW issue. In October, after months of negotiations without any progress and after the communist negotiators rejected the UN's latest proposal, the new UN chief negotiator, General William K. Harris, suspended the talks indefinitely. The administration decided, instead, to rely on increased military pressure, mainly stepped-up bombing of North Korea, to end the war.

This was the situation when newly elected President Dwight Eisenhower took office in January 1953. During his presidential campaign, Eisenhower had made it clear that he would never permit the return of POWs against their will. Following his election, he agreed to a statement, made at the Truman administration's behest, backing the White House position on voluntary repatriation and reiterating that there would be no change in that policy once he took office. Although Eisenhower was determined to take new initiatives to end the war, including the possible use of nuclear weapons, he remained steadfastly committed to the principle of voluntary repatriation. With neither side offering any new proposals to resolve the POW question, the truce tent at Panmunjom stayed empty.

In March, however, a major breakthrough occurred when the Chinese and North Korean negotiators agreed to a proposal from the International Red

Cross in Switzerland made in December and accepted by the UN commander, Mark Clark, for an exchange of sick and wounded POWs. Clark agreed to the proposal after conferring with Washington, not because he thought the Chinese and North Koreans would accept it, but because he believed UN acceptance would have a favorable impact on world opinion. Much to his surprise, however, the Chinese and North Koreans not only agreed to the exchange, they even suggested that the negotiations be resumed at Panmunjom. Two days later, China's premier, Zhou En-lai, delivered a radio broadcast in which he offered to have all nonrepatriates turned over to a neutral state "so as to ensure a just solution to the question of their repatriation."[6]

Why the communists accepted the UN proposal several months after it had first been offered is not entirely clear. But undoubtedly the death in March of Soviet leader Joseph Stalin and the desire of the new regime in Moscow, headed by Georgi Malenkov, to improve relations with the West was a factor. Pursuing what some political observers called Soviet peace offensive," fearful that the war could escalate into a global conflict, and more confident about its own military capability now that they had their own nuclear arsenal, the Soviets most likely applied pressure on China and North Korea to end the war.

But the Chinese were also probably anxious to end the conflict, which they could claim as a victory, because they had driven UN forces from the Yalu River back to a military front approximating the 38th parallel, but which had become stalemated and increasingly costly to them. Estimates of Chinese losses were placed as high as 900,000 men, and the Chinese badly needed to rebuild a nation that had been ravaged by thirty years of civil war. As for the North Koreans, they had lost in excess of 500,000 military personnel, and civilian casualties were estimated as high as 1 million.[7] The country was also suffering from food shortages and widespread hunger. Even if North Korea's leader, Kim Il Sung, was not as anxious to end the war as his communist allies (and this is not clear), he was hardly in a position to continue the struggle alone.

As soon as the Chinese announced their agreement to exchange sick and wounded POWs and to modify their position on the POW issue, tremendous pressure was placed on the United States by its allies to resume negotiations immediately, to be flexible, and to bring the war to an end. British Foreign Secretary Anthony Eden wrote U.S. Secretary of State, John Foster Dulles, stating that the UN should not even insist upon the actual exchange of sick and wounded POWs before returning to Panmunjom. "We should retain flexibility so as to appear to exploit developments to our advantage," he told the secretary of state.[8]

Nevertheless, both Dulles and Eisenhower remained suspicious about communist intentions and insisted that China first had to make good on its promise to swap the prisoners before they would agree to go back to the bargaining table. Indeed, Dulles thought that China's latest offer was a sign of weakness, which should be exploited by insisting on an armistice line along the narrow waist of the Korean peninsula, about ninety miles north of the existing front. Eisenhower vetoed the idea, believing that the American people would never countenance what Dulles was proposing. Instead, he instructed his secretary of state to take the Chinese offer seriously. At the same time, however, he agreed to a National Security Council statement to the effect that the United States reserved the right to void any armistice agreement that would not lead to a political settlement in Korea.

In an operation known as "Little Switch," which began on April 20 and was concluded on May 3, the communists handed over to the UN Command 684 POWs in exchange for 6,670 POWs held by the United Nations Command, thereby making good on their promise to swap sick and wounded prisoners. With growing optimism now that peace might finally be at hand, the UNC reopened negotiations at Panmunjom. But a number of difficult questions still had to be resolved, such as which neutral nation would assume responsibility for those POWs who did not want to be repatriated, whether the prisoners would remain in Korea or be sent to that custodial country, and what Zhou En-lai meant when he talked in his radio address about a "just solution" to the POW question. Furthermore, the United States had to deal with the recalcitrant leader of South Korea. Syngman Rhee, who did want the war to end until Korea had been unified under his leadership.

Once the talks were resumed at Panmunjom, it became clear just how far apart the Chinese and UN negotiators were on the specifics of a prisoner exchange. The Chinese and North Koreans insisted that nonrepatriates be sent to a neutral nation, where agents from their governments would have up to six months to try to persuade them to return home. Those who still refused repatriation would be held prisoner indefinitely or until a postwar political conference could decide their fate. These proposals were completely unacceptable to the UN negotiators who insisted on a limit as to how long nonrepatriates could be held before being released.

On May 7, however, the Chinese and North Koreans made another major concession by no longer insisting that the fate of remaining nonrepatriates ultimately be settled at a postwar political conference. They also agreed to a maximum of 120 days for nonrepatriates to be retained, the first ninety days of which were to be used to try to persuade the nonrepatriates to change their minds. And they suggested that in lieu of a single neutral nation serving as the custodian of the nonrepatriates, that responsibility be given to a Neutral Nations Repatriation Commission (NNRC). The UN negotiators counteroffered with a proposal that would have established a five-member NNRC and provide for the eventual release of nonrepatriates within five months after an armistice. They also insisted that all decisions by the NNRC be unanimous.

As the two sides at Panmunjom drew closer to an agreement on the POW issue, Syngman Rhee sought to undermine the talks by releasing 25,000 North Koreans under his custody. Rhee's action infuriated the Chinese and North Korean negotiators who demanded to know whether the United States would be able to control its South Korean ally should an armistice be reached. But even though Rhee's action gave the communists justification to suspend negotiations, they did not do so. Instead, they launched a military offensive against South Korean forces as a warning of the military power they could employ against the government in Seoul if it tried to sabotage an armistice agreement.

Finally, on June 4, the Chinese and North Koreans accepted the UN counteroffer with only minor changes, the most important of which was a 4-1, rather than a unanimous, voting rule for the NNRC. Indeed, in some respects—for example, the formula for releasing nonrepatriates to civilian status—the communist proposals exceeded the administration's most optimistic expectations. Within thirty days after a post-armistice political conference, those prisoners still refusing repatriation and for whom no other disposition had been agreed to would be released from prisoner status. The NNRC would then have another thirty days to help relocate the nonrepatriates, after which it would be disbanded. Although there were still many issues that had to be resolved before the war was ended and an agreement finally signed at Panmunjon on July 27, including getting the Rhee government to accept an armistice agreement, the most insuperable issue of the war had finally been resolved. Of the 22,604 enemy nonrepatriates (including 14,704 Chinese), 628 eventually decided to go home. Of the others, 86 went to India, 51 escaped or died in captivity, and 21, 389 were sent back to the UNC and released. Of 359 UNC nonrepatriates, 2 of 23 Americans and 8 Koreans changed their minds and returned home. Two Koreans went to India, and 347 stayed with the communists.

NOTES

1. On World War II POWs, see Richard Whalen, *Drawing the Line: The Korean War, 1950–1953* (Boston: Little, Brown and Co., 1990), 331.

2. Barton J. Bernstein, "The Struggle over the Korean Armistice: Prisoners or Repatriation," in Bruce Cumings, ed. *Child of Conflict: The Korean-American Relationship, 1943–1953* (Seattle: University of Washington Press, 1983), 276.

3. Quoted in Rosemary Foot, *A Substitute for Victory: The Politics of Peacemaking at the Korean Armistice Talks* (Ithaca, NY: Cornell University Press, 1990), 88–89.

4. Walter G. Hermes, *Truce Tent and Fighting Front* (Washington, DC: Government Printing Office, 1961), 175–78.

5. Briefing of Foreign Government Representatives in Korea, January 8 and 18, 1952, Box 3, Selected Records Relating to the Korean War, Truman Library.

6. Hermes, *Truce Tent and Fighting Front*, 411–14.

7. Robert R. Simmons, *The Strained Alliance: Peking, Pyongyang, Moscow, and the Politics of the Korean Civil War* (New York: Free Press, 1975), 213.

8. Memorandum for the President, April 1, 1953, Box 9, Subject Series, John Foster Dulles Papers, Dwight D. Eisenhower Library, Abilene, KS.

6

Meaning and Implications of the Korean Conflict

The Korean Conflict was the natural extension of the policy of containment that the United States had adopted as its strategy for fighting the Cold War. Essentially this policy rested on the assumption of an implacable foe—the Soviet Union—whose ultimate aims were the expansion of communism and world domination. Prior to 1950, however, American officials in Washington perceived the immediate Soviet menace as being directed primarily against western Europe and, to a lesser extent, a northern tier of Near East countries that included Greece, Turkey, and Iran. In their view, moreover, Moscow sought to achieve its ambitions not through acts of overt military aggression but through subversion of economically destitute governments. Accordingly, their chosen weapons in the battle against Soviet expansion were economic assistance as embraced in the Marshall Plan of 1948 and collective security as embodied in the formation of the North Atlantic Treaty Organization (NATO) in 1949.

The Korean Conflict dramatically changed American perceptions of the world scene and the U.S. strategy for dealing with the communist threat. No longer was the danger viewed as one directed primarily against western Europe or the countries of the northern tier. Nor was economic assistance always enough to contain the communist threat. Military assistance and even intervention might also be required. President Harry S Truman put it best when he commented soon after the North Korean invasion of South Korea that "the attack upon Korea makes it plain beyond all doubt that Communism has passed beyond the use of subversion to conquer independent nations and will now use armed invasion and war."[1]

Indeed, there was a direct link between the U.S. military intervention in Korea in 1950 and its later military involvement in Vietnam in the 1960s. As a result of the Korean Conflict, the United States increased its military assistance to the French fighting communist forces, known as the Vietminh, in Indochina, so that by 1954 the United States was underwriting about 80 percent of the cost of the war. At the same time, a widespread conviction existed in the United States that the communists, have failed to achieve their original objective of subjugating South Korea, had made Vietnam their next target of opportunity. Accordingly, Americans might be called upon to continue the struggle against communist expansion in that part of the world. A defeat in Indochina, the National Security Council even determined in 1954, would greatly damage "the security of the U.S."[2]

Yet the Korean War made the United States hesitant in the 1950s to fight another limited war, such as the one being fought in Indochina. In 1953 Secretary of State Dean Acheson warned Truman that committing troops in Indochina would be "futile" and a "mistake." We "could not have another Korea, we could not put ground forces into Indochina," he told the president.[3] Eisenhower shared Acheson's views. In 1954 the French were on the brink of defeat at their outpost of Dien Bien Phu in the northwest corner of Vietnam. The fall of Dien Bien Phu would almost certainly mean the end of the French war against the Vietminh. But despite widespread calls for American intervention to save the French, including even the use of tactical nuclear weapons, Eisenhower refused to intervene without the support of Congress and the Allies, an unlikely possibility. "[I]f the United States were unilaterally, to permit its forces to be drawn into conflict in Indochina and in a succession of Asian wars," he remarked, "the end result would be to drain off our resources and to weaken our over-all defensive position."[4]

U.S. military leaders generally felt the same way. In fact, many of them found themselves on the horns of a dilemma as a result of the Korean Conflict. Although the conflict made clear the futility of fighting a limited war, it also underscored the unlikelihood of fighting any other kind of conflict. Former General Matthew Ridgway thus wrote in 1967:

Before Korea, all our military planning envisioned a war that would involve the world and in which the defense of a distant and indefensible peninsula would be folly. But Korea taught us that all warfare from this time forth must be limited. It could no longer be a question of whether to fight a limited war, but of how to avoid fighting any other kind.[5]

Other leaders drew different conclusions. For President Lyndon Johnson, who, in 1965, was about to begin the buildup of U.S. military forces in Vietnam, the North Korean invasion of June 1950 was a lesson in the dangers of not meeting military responsibilities abroad. "I could never forget the with-drawal of our forces from South Korea," he later wrote, "and then our imme-diate reaction to the Communist aggression of June 1950."[6] Testifying before the Senate Foreign Relations Committee in 1965, Assistant Secretary of State William P. Bundy drew three lessons from the Korean War. The first was to recognize that aggression must be met "head-on" or else it would in-tensify and be harder to contain. The second was that a defense line in Asia limited to an island perimeter, such as existed before Korea, did not ade-quately define America's vital interests in that region of the world and that what happened on the Asian mainland would bear directly on these interests. The third lesson of the Korean Conflict was that "a power vacuum was an in-vitation to aggression" and that in such cases "there must be a demonstrated willingness of major external powers both to assist and to intervene if re-quired."[7] Thus the war in Korea failed to prevent the United States from en-gaging in another limited war in Vietnam in the 1960s.

Were there, in fact, lessons from the Korean War that might have bene-fited American forces fighting in Vietnam a decade later? The answer would seem to be that there were, but in responding to this question, the major dif-ferences between the two conflicts also need to be taken into account. For one thing, there was no Korean equivalent of Laos and Cambodia through which the enemy could be supplied; supplies had to flow directly from the north. This led General MacArthur to make a major strategic and tactical er-ror. Although Korea was a peninsula linked to Communist China and the So-viet Union and not an island, MacArthur believed that he could use the Seventh Fleet in the Formosa Straits and strategic air power to isolate the Chinese communists, cut them and their supply lines off from the mainland, and force them into submission, just as he had done to the Japanese in the South Pacific during World War II. But MacArthur's reliance on strategic air power in the Korean Conflict proved as disappointing as it had during World War II. The communists made brilliant use of the rugged and uncharted ter-rain, moving at night to diminish the chances of air interdiction, hiding their troops and supplies, and ambushing and enveloping UN forces and supply lines dependent on Korea's poor road system.

Another major difference between the Korean and Vietnam Wars was the influence of television. Although both conflicts were highly unpopular at home, there was no antiwar campaign in the United States during the Korean War comparable to the antiwar crusade against Vietnam in the 1960s and early 1970s. Undoubtedly one reason for this was that television was still in its infancy in the 1950s, and the horrors of war were not brought home to the American people in quite the same way they were in the 1960s. In contrast to television news coverage in the 1960s, when every major broadcasting company had thirty-minute newscasts in the evening and a variety of other news programming, the only televised evening news in the early 1950s was a fifteen-minute program on NBC. Moreover, only ten million Americans owned television sets, and newsreels from the battlefront were in black and white and of very poor quality because of poor lighting. As a result, television coverage of the Korean Conflict did not present the same problem for Truman that television coverage of the Vietnam War presented for Johnson.[8]

Finally, resistance to the two wars came from different elements of the political spectrum. In the case of the Korean Conflict, the opposition came from the political right in the United States because of what it perceived as the White House's bungling and no-win policy. In the case of the Vietnam conflict, opponents of the war were generally from the political left who were outraged at what they considered to be the moral depravity of American foreign policy.

Even more striking than these differences between the Korean and Vietnam Wars are the parallels between them, which suggest that the United States might very well have profited in Vietnam from a better understanding of its earlier military venture in Korea. Both wars were limited wars whose object was less than total victory. Truman had gone to war in 1950 because he believed that the world was in a state of crisis and because he was concerned with maintaining the international credibility of the United States and his own credibility at home. Because the war followed on the heels of the communist victory in China and the Soviet Union's successful testing of an atomic bomb, much of the world seemed to the Truman administration in danger of falling to the communists. The possibility of an atomic war also loomed large in their minds. Complicating matters even more was the fact that the president was confronted with a domestic "Red Scare" and charges that he was "soft on communism"; together they posed the threat of unraveling his administration. Faced with such an international and domestic crisis, Truman concluded that he had no alternative other than to respond to what he regarded as naked aggression in Korea sponsored and directed from Moscow. Like Truman in 1950, Lyndon Johnson looked at the world in 1965 from the myopic perspective of the Cold War and believed that U.S. credibility in resisting communist aggression was at issue in Vietnam.

In committing American forces to Korea in 1950 and in greatly expanding the U.S. war effort in Vietnam after 1965, both Truman and Johnson also failed to grasp the civil nature of the conflicts being fought in these two countries. Indeed, it would take the Vietnam War to educate Americans about the differences between nationalist movement with leftist (even communist) orientations and Soviet efforts at global expansion. Even intelligence officers before and during the Korean Conflict failed to understand the indigenous forces of change taking place in Korea. In all the thousands of reports and assessment emanating from the war, in fact, only a depressingly small number commented on the needs and concerns of the Korean people. "Korea," the military historian Max Hastings has commented, "merely chanced to be a battlefield upon which the struggle against the international Communist conspiracy was being waged."[9] Similarly, American troops on the battlefield were high critical, even contemptuous, of their erstwhile comrades-in-arms, the Republic of Korea army.

Finally, American leaders during both the Korean and Vietnam conflicts had much the same ends in mind, although they used different terminology. Presidents Harry Truman and Dwight Eisenhower in the 1950s and Presidents Lyndon Johnson and Richard Nixon in the 1960s and 1970s sought to extricate themselves from an unpopular and costly conflict but in a way that preserved American honor and denied the communists a military—and political—victory. In essence, the Munich syndrome of the Korean War (appeasement leads to further acts of aggression) and the domino theory of the Vietnam War period (if Vietnam falls to the communists, then the rest of Southeast Asia would fall like a row of dominoes) were products of the same Cold War mentality.

What Korea might have taught both the military and civilians who were responsible for the conduct of the war in Vietnam were some of the problems of waging a limited war, particularly the unique problems of command. For example, Korea might have made abundantly clear the difficulty in sustaining public support for a war in which total victory (the complete destruction of the enemy) was not the aim and in having constantly to reassure America's own allies of its limited purpose in the war. One of General Douglas MacArthur's problems as commander was his inability or unwillingness to appreciate the constraints under which Truman operated because of the pressures imposed on the United States by its allies. Although the president was able for the most part to get the British and other U.S. allies to cooperate with the administration in Korea and at the United Nations, this had to involve political—and military—compromises on the part of the United States. MacArthur never fully grasped this fact.

At the same time, the administration often lacked appreciation of the military implications of its political decisions. As a result, seemingly contradictory orders were sometimes given to MacArthur and his successors, Generals Ridgway and Clark. This included their general instructions, irrespective of any consideration about the safety and security of their forces, to maintain maximum military pressure on the enemy without doing anything that might escalate the war into a larger conflict. This mistake on the administration part to comprehend fully the military implications of its political actions had tragic consequences later. As the historian, D. Clayton James, later commented, it was "one of the key factors that would lead the United States into its tragic entanglement in Vietnam."[10]

The Joint Chiefs of Staff themselves must bear a good part of the responsibility for the White House's failure to understand fully the military imperatives of fighting a war. Instead of making the administration aware of the nation's military capabilities and limitations in Korea, it played a generally passive role in formulating political *and military* policy in Korea. The decision to limit the war in Korea after the Chinese invasion was essentially a political one reached without much input from the Joint Chiefs. Much the same was true of the military strategy—the active defense—that was subsequently followed notwithstanding calls from the field for a general offensive above the 38th parallel. Throughout most of the war, the Pentagon allowed political decisions to be made without much reference to battlefield conditions.

Had UN forces been allowed to maintain greater military pressure against the Chinese and North Koreans after negotiations started in July 1951, it is quite possible that a settlement of the war might have been reached much earlier, well before Eisenhower warned of the possibility of atomic warfare. But the longer the war continued, the more dangerous a general offensive became and the more difficult it was to follow any military strategy other than the active defense. As General Maxwell Taylor, who in 1953 succeeded General James Van Fleet as commander of the Eighth Army, later commented, "Our unwillingness to keep military pressure on the enemy during the negotiations had been a mistake, I was sure, but by 1953 it was established policy, and it was too late to try to change."[11]

As it was, the Chinese were able to hold their own against American forces. Had the Chinese been more a modern military force and less of a primitive army lacking equipment and hampered by poor communications and lines of supply, in fact, they may very well have been able to drive UN troops from Korea before they had an opportunity to regroup and take the military offensive. Even though the Chinese failed to do this, they were still able to fight a more modern and better equipped force to a virtual draw. As a result, they gained international stature and became a major player in the global political arena.

At the same time, though, the manpower costs to China of fighting a technologically far superior military machine were huge. Although Mao Zedong continued to insist on human wave assaults, other Chinese military leaders concluded that revolutionary armies without sophisticated military equipment should never engage Western armies on their own terms; instead, they should probe for weaknesses, attacking when Western resources and technology were of least value and depending on Western impatience with extended war to bring about ultimate victory.

Unfortunately, the American military reached just the opposite conclusion. As Max Hastings has also commented, "The American Army emerged from Korea convinced that its vastly superior firepower and equipment could always defeat a poorly equipped army if it was provided with the opportunity to deploy them."[12] It failed to realize that because the Chinese relied heavily on human and animal labor for supplies, they did not need to rely, as the Americans did, on Korea's road system. This gave them a flexibility denied to UN forces and accounted for much of their success in attacking American supply lines and engaging in flanking operations and roadblocks. The United States would later pay a heavy price in Vietnam for relying so heavily on military technology and underestimating the enemy's ability to fight in an unconventional manner.

Nevertheless, the Korean War remains one of the most decisive events of recent American history. As one writer has remarked, "In many ways Korea did for the [C]old War what Pearl Harbor had done for World War II." It "globalized" the Cold War.[13] Prior to Korea, the only American political or military commitment outside the Western Hemisphere had been the North Atlantic Treaty, but by 1955 the United States had about 450 bases in thirty-six countries and was linked by political and military pacts with some twenty countries outside Latin America. Also, the U.S. foreign aid program, appropriately named "the mutual security program," no longer had as its purpose economic and social reconstruction but military support for recipient countries. Most important, the communist menace was now perceived in Washington in broad global terms rather than in terms of Europe alone, as had largely been the case prior to 1950.

Indeed, as European politics stabilized and the communist threat diminished over the next ten years, the United States became increasingly concerned with events in Southeast Asia. Ironically, two Democratic presidents, John F. Kennedy and Lyndon B. Johnson, came to share the view Douglas MacArthur had promulgated during the Korean War—that the battlefield of the Cold War would be Asia rather than Europe. The result was the Vietnam tragedy of the 1960s and 1970s.

Yet the Korean Conflict had not been fought in vain insofar as the United States—and many South Koreans—were concerned. Although Washington failed to achieve the political reunification of Korea, which had become its objective after the Inchon invasion of 1950, it had prevented South Korea from falling to the communists. This, in turn, allowed South Korea eventually to become one of Asia's major economic and industrial powers and for its citizens to enjoy one of the continent's highest standards of living. Although South Korea was to be governed over the next forty years by authoritarian leaders who greatly restricted democratic political processes, they escaped falling under the control of the far more totalitarian regime of North Korea. Notwithstanding the undeniably repressive regime of the Seoul government, therefore, it is not unreasonable to conclude that the major beneficiaries of the Korean Conflict were the South Koreans themselves.

But the United States also benefited from the war. In the first place, the conflict provided assurances to Japan's fledging democracy, just emerging from America's military occupation, that it could look to the United States for political and military support. The war also jump-started the Japanese economy, beginning the process of turning Japan into an economic colossus and a model for other East Asian nations to emulate, including South Korea. Despite the Vietnam War, therefore, the United States achieved its post–World War II policy for the Far East, based as it was on an economically strong Japan tied closely to the West. In contrast, Moscow's lackluster support for China emerged as a strong rival to the Soviet Union within the communist bloc and especially among Third World countries, which admired and identified with China's successful resistance to what they viewed as "Western imperialism." In geopolitical terms, therefore, the biggest loser of the Korean conflict might have been the nonbelligerent Soviet Union.

Perhaps as important as any consequence of the Korean Conflict, however, is its legacy in terms of the use of nuclear weapons to fight a war. Korea was the first conflict the United States fought in the nuclear age. Both Presidents Truman and Eisenhower had considered the nuclear operation on several occasions. The threat of nuclear warfare was also basic to the Eisenhower-Dulles doctrine of massive retaliation. Yet the very existence of atomic weapons had dictated a limited war in Korea. And as the first war the United States had fought since the advent of nuclear weapons, Korea confronted American leaders with the relative powerlessness of a weapon that, in the final analysis, was too terrible to be used.

NOTES

1. Harry S Truman, *Memoirs: Years of Trial and Hope* (Garden City, NY: Signet, 1956), 338–39.

2. The quote is from Robert J. Donovan, *Nemesis: Truman and Johnson in the Coils of War in Asia* (New York: St. Martin's Press, 1984), 24.

3. The quotes are from George C. Herring, *America's Longest War: The United States and Vietnam, 1950–1975*, 3rd ed. (New York: McGraw Hill, 1996), 2.

4. Dwight D. Eisenhower, *Mandate for Change* (Garden City, NY: Doubleday, 1963), 354. See also Norman Podhoretz, *Why We Were in Vietnam* (New York: Simon & Schuster, 1982), 34–35, 51.

5. Matthew P. Ridgway, *The Korean War* (Garden City, NY: Doubleday, 1976), vi.

6. Lyndon Baines Johnson, *The Vantage Point: Perspectives of the Presidency* (New York: Holt, Rinehart and Winston, 1971), 152.

7. The quote is from Russell H. Fifield, *Americans in South East Asia: The Roots of Commitment* (New York: Crowell, 1973), 150–51.

8. Alonzo L. Hamby, "Public Opinion, Korea and Vietnam," *Wilson Quarterly* 2 (Summer 1978): 137–41.

9. Max Hastings, *The Korean War* (New York: Simon and Schuster, 1987), 338–39.

10. D. Clayton James, *Refighting the Last War: Command and Crisis in Korea, 1950–1953* (New York: The Free Press, 1993), 6.

11. Maxwell D. Taylor, *Swords and Plowshares* (New York: Norton, 1972), 137.

12. Hastings, *The Korean War*, 334.

13. Lisle A. Rose, *Roots of Tragedy: The United States and the Struggle for Asia, 1945–1953* (Westport, CT: Greenwood Press, 1976), 239–44.

Two army privates operating a bazooka, July 17, 1950. Library of Congress

Soldiers returning from patrol, September 26, 1950. Library of Congress

Truman presents MacArthur with medal at Wake Islands, October 14, 1950. Library of Congress

South Korean marines hold North Korean captives. National Archives

Typical mixed uniform of Chinese Communist soldier, January 1951. National Archives

Three bearded GIs, March 8, 1951. Library of Congress

Three U.S. tankmen. Library of Congress

General Douglas MacArthur's farewell address before a Joint Session of Congress, April 19, 1951. Library of Congress

UN forces advance under cover of machine guns, July 1951. Library of Congress

Biographies: The Personalities Behind the Korean Conflict

Dean G. Acheson (1893–1971)

Dean Acheson was secretary of state during the Korean Conflict. His statement before the National Press Club in January 1950 excluding Korea from the defense perimeter of the United States in the Far Pacific has often been cited by historians as one of the major reasons why North Korea decided to attack South Korea the following June.

Acheson was born on April 11, 1893, in Middletown, Connecticut. After graduating from Yale University in 1915 and Harvard Law School in 1918, he served for two years as private secretary to Associate Justice Louis D. Brandeis. During the period between World Wars I and II, he practiced corporate and international law and served briefly (1933) as undersecretary of the treasury under President Franklin D. Roosevelt. In 1941, he returned to public service, serving as assistant secretary of state (1941–1945), undersecretary of state (1945–1947), and secretary of state (1949–1953) under President Harry Truman.

Believing that the United States's most vital interests were tied to the reconstruction of Europe after the war and the development of a strong Atlantic alliance, he helped implement the Marshall Plan and served as the U.S. negotiator in the talks leading to the formation of NATO in 1949. Following the communist victory in China in 1949, he came under increasing criticism from the right-wing of the Republican Party and from others who believed that U.S. policy should be oriented more towards Asia for allowing China to "fall" to the communists. His clipped speech and aristocratic demeanor made him an easy target for many of these same persons who also resented what they considered to be the wrong-headed control of the nation's foreign policy by a small coterie of eastern intellectual liberals.

During the Korean Conflict, Acheson was a strong supporter of Truman's policies, including his decision to intervene militarily in Korea, to carry the war into North Korea, and then to fight a limited war. He also supported Truman's decision in April 1951 to relieve General Douglas MacArthur of all his commands because of insubordination. During congressional hearings in the spring of 1951 on MacArthur's firing, the secretary of state delivered a three-hour statement on America's China policy that amounted to a diplomatic history of Sino-American relations since before World War II.

In 1953 Acheson returned to his private law practice. But he continued to be consulted on foreign policy issues, and in 1962 he was part of the Executive Committee (EXCOM) that advised President John F. Kennedy during the Cuban missile crisis. He also published several books, including *Present at the Creation: My Years in the State Department* (1969), for which he received the Pulitzer Prize in history. He died on October 12, 1971.

Clement Attlee (1883–1967)

Clement Attlee was British prime minister from July 1945 to October 1951. Born on January 23, 1883, he had headed the Labour Party in Britain since 1935. He became prime minister in 1945 following the defeat of the Conservative Party. As prime minister, he nationalized basic industry in Britain, extended social services, and instituted a national health service. Nevertheless, he was widely regarded as a moderate in a badly divided party, and he generally supported U.S. policy during the Korean conflict. But he wanted the United States to recognize the Beijing government of China and to begin early negotiations with the Chinese after they entered the war in November 1950. Like most European leaders, he also was horrified by the remarks of President Harry S Truman the next month that he had not ruled out the use of nuclear weapons in the war and that a decision on their use would be left to the military commanders in the field. Flying to the United States, he got Truman to state that he hoped the use of nuclear weapons would not be necessary, that only the president would make the decision on their use, and that he would keep the prime minister informed if developments in Korea warranted a change of policy. But he failed to get Truman to commit himself to a partnership with Britain on the conduct of the war or to an unconditional promise against using atomic weapons.

In October 1951, the Labour Party was swept out of office in elections that returned the Conservative Party, headed by Winston Churchill, to power. But Attlee was able to remain head of his party until 1955 when ill health forced him to resign his leadership post. He died on October 8, 1967.

Winston Churchill (1874–1965)

Widely regarded as one of the world's great figures of the twentieth century, Winston Churchill was leader of Britain's Conservative Party during the Korean War and British prime minister from October 1952 until the end of the Korean War in July 1953. Born on November 30, 1874, into a family with a long lineage of famous political and military leaders, Churchill was a graduate of the Royal Military Academy at Sandhurst (1895). In 1899, after a short career as an army officer and part-time war correspondent, he resigned his commission to become a full-time correspondent covering the Boer War. Following his capture by the Boers and a daring escape, he began his long political career by being elected a Conservative member of Parliament.

Over the next forty years, Churchill distinguished himself by changing political parties several times and by holding a number of high government positions, including president of the Board of Trade (1908–1910), first lord of the admiralty (1911–1915), minister of ammunitions and secretary of war (1917–1922) and chancellor of the exchequer (1924–1929). For most of the 1930s, however, he did not hold any office. Regarded as something of a renegade because of his opposition to self-rule for India, his complaints about Britain's failure to rearm, and his strong opposition to the Munich Agreement that Prime Minister Neville Chamberlain had reached with Adolf Hitler in 1938, he was denied a position in Chamberlain's cabinet. But when Britain declared war on Germany in 1939, Chamberlain was forced to appoint him again as first lord of the admiralty. When Chamberlain fell during the dark days of the 1940s, Churchill, who had warned of an impending war with Germany, was named to replace him.

A master of rhetoric and prose, Churchill rallied the British people to carry on the conflict against the Axis powers even during the dark hours of 1940 and 1941. Indeed, a number of historians of the war have maintained that Churchill's oratory was one of Britain's strongest weapons in the war. During the fighting, Churchill, whose mother had been an American citizen, worked very closely with President Franklin Roosevelt and with Soviet leader Joseph Stalin as part of the Grand Coalition that led the Allied armies to victory over the Axis powers.

In elections held after the victory in Europe, however, Churchill's Conservative Party lost to the Labour Party, headed by Clement Attlee. In 1946 Churchill visited the United States in which he delivered one of his most famous talks at Westminster College in Missouri. In his address, Churchill talked about an "Iron Curtain" descending over eastern Europe and warned of the danger of Soviet aggression. But until 1951, when his Conservative Party was returned to power. Churchill spent most of his time in relative seclusion.

By the time Churchill, as leader of the Conservatives, returned as prime minister, he was old and in ill health. As a result, he was no longer the dynamic leader that he had been during the war. Even among Conservatives, there was a growing sense that he should step down from office. Nevertheless, Churchill gave his strong support to UN military operations in Korea, although, like other British leaders, he strongly opposed expanding the war, was concerned about calls among right-wing elements in the United States to expand the war against China, and favored a *quid pro quo* in which the United States would recognize communist China in return for an end to the war. He brought up many of these issues with President Harry S Truman and Secretary of State Dean Acheson during a visit to Washington in January 1952. Although his visit resulted in no significant change in American policies, his trip represented a personal triumph for the British leader and reinvigorated, at least for the moment, the Anglo-American alliance that had been under growing stress not only in Korea but also in other parts of the world.

Upon Churchill's return to London, Labourites in Parliament, led by Aneurin Bevan, introduced a motion of censure against the elder statesman because he endorsed the "greater sanction" policy of the United States, which called for retaliation against China should it agree to, and then break, an armistice agreement. But taking to the floor of Parliament, Churchill showed some of the flair he had displayed as prime minister during World War II. In a brilliant performance, he turned the motion of censure against the Bevanites by pointing out that the Labour government before him had secretly made the same commitments they now accused him of making.

Still, Churchill was disappointed by the slow progress in the peace talks at Panmunjom, and he berated the United States for its unwillingness to meet with Soviet leaders, especially following the death of Joseph Stalin in 1953. Indeed, he continued to attack Washington's lack of flexibility in dealing with the communists for the remainder of the war, leading some American officials to accuse Britain of blackmail and nettlesome interference in America's internal affairs.

Churchill finally retired as prime minister in 1955. He remained one of the world's most venerated figures until his death on January 24, 1965, at the age of 90. He was accorded the rare privilege of a state funeral.

Mark W. Clark (1896–1984)

Mark W. Clark replaced Matthew Ridgway as Commander of U.S. forces in the Far East and Supreme Commander of UN forces in Korea on May 7, 1952, following President Harry Truman's appointment of Ridgway as the new NATO commander. Clark was a tough field commander who during

World War II had been nicknamed "the American Eagle" by British Prime Minister Winston Churchill. Clark was born on May 1, 1896, at Madison Barracks, New York. The son of an Army officer, Clark attended the United States Military Academy (West Point), where he graduated in 1917. During World War I he saw action at St. Mihiel and in the Meuse-Argonne offensive and was awarded the Purple Heart for wounds received in battle. Between World Wars I and II he served at various posts in the United States and was a graduate of both the Command and General Staff College (1935) and the Army War College (1940). At the time the United States entered World War II in 1941, he was an instructor at the War College assigned to the staff of General Headquarters. In April 1942, he was given the temporary rank of major general.

Trained as an infantry officer, Clark was appointed the next month as chief of staff of the Army Ground Forces, and in July he was given command of all American ground forces in the European Theater of Operations. Believing in strict discipline and tough training under conditions that simulated real battle conditions, he helped plan the North African campaign and served as deputy to General Dwight D. Eisenhower during the invasion of North Africa (Operation Torch) in November 1942. Promoted to lieutenant general in November at age forty-six, making him the youngest three-star general in the Army, Clark commanded 5th Army Operations at Anzio during the Allied invasion of Italy in 1943. Believing in what he called "the calculated risk," he later received considerable criticism for his leadership of the 5th Army, which suffered heavy casualties at the Rapido River battles in early 1944.

Accusations that Clark unnecessarily endangered the lives of soldiers under his command followed Clark through the rest of his military career and was heard among American troops after he assumed command of UN forces in Korea. But it did not harm his military career. In June 1944, the 5th Army marched into Rome after bitter fighting against German defenders of the city. For the remainder of World War II, Clark commanded all Allied forces in Italy as they advanced up the peninsula. On May 2, 1945, he accepted the surrender of German forces in Italy. Promoted to full general, Clark headed the American occupation of Austria after the war. He also commanded the 6th Army before being given the assignment of leading UN forces in Korea.

Clark's immediate task upon arriving in Korea was to deal with a constitutional crisis that had developed in South Korea following President Syngman Rhee's effort to force the National Assembly to change the Korean constitution in order to provide for the election of a president by popular vote rather than by the Assembly; this would allow Rhee to seek a second term as president. Although Rhee was able to cower the Assembly into submission, at the height of the crisis Clark prepared plans for a coup against Rhee should he try to dissolve the government.

Like Generals Douglas MacArthur and Ridgway before him, Clark chafed at the restrictions on military operations in Korea placed upon him. He believed that an expansion of the war to include air attacks on Manchuria was necessary to achieve a military victory, and much to the chagrin of most U.S. allies, he stepped up bombing of North Korean oil refineries and chemical and power plants along the Yalu River. He also ordered the bombing of dams in North Korea in order to destroy its food crops. Believing that he lacked sufficient manpower to fight a war in Korea and defend Japan at the same time, he requested that two divisions of Chinese Nationalist forces be sent to Korea. Although the Pentagon ultimately agreed to the proposal, newly elected President Eisenhower vetoed the idea.

Thoroughly distrustful of the communists, Clark also recommended that the UN command agree to a proposal from the International Red Cross for an exchange of sick and wounded prisoners of war (POWs). He was persuaded that the Chinese and North Koreans would never agree to such a swap but that the offer would make a favorable impression on world opinion. When the communists, in fact, accepted the offer, Clark presided over the exchange, known as "Little Switch." At the same time, he pressed unsuccessfully for the release of all nonrepatriated North Korean POWs and strongly objected to the White House's decision at the beginning of May to turn all nonrepatriated POWs over to a Neutral Nations Repatriation Commission (NNRC).

As the negotiators at Panmunjom drew closer to a final armistice agreement in May, Clark's attention turned back to President Rhee. Worried that the South Korean leader might try to sabotage an agreement, the administration instructed General Clark and Ambassador Ellis Briggs to warn Rhee not to impede the peace process. In no uncertain terms, Clark told Rhee that American military assistance to Korea after the war depended on Rhee's acceptance of the peace agreement. He even indicated that the United States might try to replace Rhee should he attempt to undermine the agreement. At the same time, Clark helped persuade the administration to agree to a mutual defense pact with South Korea as a way of molifying the South Koreans.

Despite these blandishments and promises, Rhee released North Korean POWs on June 18. Clark and special envoy, Walter Robertson, then spent the rest of June and beginning of July in private talks with Rhee, listening to the South Korean's leaders harangues against the United States but also trying to get him to agree to accept the armistice agreement worked out at Panmunjom. Finally, after the Chinese inflicted heavy casualties in a final attack against ROK forces, Rhee agreed to go along with the armistice but not to sign it. Clark himself refused to be present at the final signing ceremonies at Panmunjom on July 27, leaving that task to the chief UN negotiator, General William K. Harrison. Although he later countersigned the agreement at his headquarters, he was angered that he was the first U.S. Army commander in history to sign an armistice agreement without victory in a war which, he always believed, could have been won militarily. After the armistice went into effect, he advocated using nuclear weapons should the communists break it.

Following the war, Clark retired from the Army. From 1954 until 1966, he served as president of the Citadel, a military college in Charleston, South Carolina. In 1954 he published his memoirs *From the Danube to the Yalu* in which he criticized the United States for lacking the will to win in Korea. In a magazine article, he was also critical of efforts during the war to integrate black soldiers into white squadrons, maintaining that blacks generally performed poorly. He died on April 16, 1984.

John Foster Dulles (1888–1959)

John Foster Dulles was a leading Republican spokesman on foreign policy and secretary of state from 1953 until his death in 1959. Dulles was born on February 25, 1888, the grandson of John W. Foster, secretary of state under Benjamin Harrison, and the nephew of Robert Lansing, secretary of state under Woodrow Wilson. A graduate of Princeton University (1908) and George Washington University Law School (1911), Dulles combined a career as a partner in one of the nation's leading law firms with that of an experienced diplomat. Following World War II, President Harry Truman named him to serve as a consultant at several international conferences. In 1951 Truman appointed him to negotiate the U.S. peace treaty with Japan. Two years later, President Dwight Eisenhower asked him to be his secretary of state.

Dulles is best known for the policy of "brinkmanship," which threatened the use of nuclear weapons at a place and time of the United States's own choosing (a willingness, in other words, to go the "brink" of a nuclear war) in response to communist aggression; this policy also has been referred to as "massive retaliation." During Eisenhower's administration and for at least a decade thereafter, Dulles was commonly believed by historians to have been in almost total control of Eisenhower's foreign policy. Historians now generally recognize that although Dulles had great influence within the administration, it was Eisenhower who determined his own foreign policy and that, like the president, Dulles shared a more sophisticated and nuanced view of foreign policy than "brinkmanship" or "massive retaliation" might suggest. For example, he campaigned actively for the establishment of a European Defense Community (EDC) as a means of containing Soviet aggression, and he played a major role in the formation in 1954 of the Southeast Asia Treaty Organization (SEATO) and in 1955 of the Baghdad Pact in the Middle East, both also intended to contain the communist threat.

Nevertheless, Dulles did raise the possibility of using nuclear weapons during the Korean War, and his fervent anticommunism and frequent bellicose remarks sometimes scared the United States's European allies, who regarded the secretary of state as reckless and irresponsible and thought the administration might escalate rather than search for a peaceful resolution of the war. In addition, they were taken back by Dulles's talk in 1953 of "liberating" eastern Europe from the Soviets at a time when British Prime Minister Winston Churchill was promoting a Big Four meeting with Soviet, British, and French leaders to settle world problems. Because they thought Dulles was dictating Eisenhower's foreign policy, the United States's Western allies concluded that it was necessary to press even harder for an end to the Korean War.

Dulles died on May 24, 1959, following a lengthy bout with cancer.

Dwight D. Eisenhower (1890–1969)

Dwight D. Eisenhower was elected president of the United States in 1952 and reelected in 1956. He presided over the last six months of the Korean War. Born in Denison, Texas, on October 14, 1890, Eisenhower grew up in Abilene, Kansas, before entering the U.S. Military Academy (West Point) in 1911. Graduating four years later after an undistinguished career as a cadet, he failed to see combat during World War I and spent most of the next twenty-five years in relative obscurity in the army. As late as 1941, he only held the rank of lieutenant colonel. But in 1926 he attended the prestigious Command and General Staff School at Fort Leavenworth, where he graduated first in his class. During the 1930s, he served as personal assistant to Army Chief of Staff General Douglas MacArthur, and later accompanied him to the Philippine Islands.

Eisenhower's meteoric rise in military rank began in 1941 when he was promoted to colonel. During maneuvers in Louisiana that year, he displayed tactical skills that won him promotion to brigadier general and brought him to the attention of Army Chief of Staff George Marshall. Following the Japanese bombing of Pearl Harbor in December, Marshall ordered him to Washington to head the Operations Division. In March 1942, he was promoted to major general. In June he was given a third star and sent to Europe to command U.S. forces in the European Theater of Operations and to help develop plans for the invasion of Europe and with British Prime Minister Winston Churchill and other British leaders. His tact and diplomacy in dealing with Churchill and these other senior officials won for him command of the Allied invasion of North Africa (Operation Torch) in 1942. In 1944 he was given the plum assignment to head the invasion of Europe (Operation Overlord).

The successful invasion of Europe and the victory over Germany less than a year later turned "Ike" into a world celebrity. In 1945 he was appointed Army Chief of Staff. In 1948 he retired from the army to become president of Columbia University. Unhappy in that position, he assumed command in 1950 of NATO forces in Europe. By this time, a movement was underway in both major parties to draft Eisenhower for president. In 1952 he was persuaded by a group of moderate Republicans to head the Republican ticket.

Prior to becoming a candidate for president, Eisenhower had said or written very little about the Korean Conflict other than to express support for Truman's decision to intervene militarily after North Korea invaded South Korea in 1950. Although he continued to be strongly supportive of the UN action in Korea, most of his attention as NATO commander during the first two years of the war was centered on building the Atlantic alliance. Indeed, he later claimed that if the leading contender for the Republican presidential nomination in 1952, Senator Robert Taft of Ohio, had supported collective security, he might have withdrawn his own name as a candidate for president.

Privately, however, Eisenhower thought that the administration was not doing enough to marshal the nation's forces against communist aggression in Korea. In meetings with President Harry Truman and Defense Secretary George Marshall, he maintained that the administration needed to begin a rapid rearmament program. This enabled him to argue later that he had urged the White House to do more in Korea but had been ignored.

Not until Eisenhower formally announced his candidacy for president in a speech and news conference in his boyhood home of Abilene in June 1952 did he begin to speak out publicly on the Korean War. In his remarks, he once more seemed to express support for the administration's policy. In contrast to his rival for the Republican nomination, Senator Taft, who bitterly attacked the administration and called for a decisive victory in Korea, Eisenhower said he had no easy prescription for ending the war.

Once Eisenhower won the Republican nomination, however, he began to lash out at the White House for what he called its failed policies in Korea and its defeatist policies in general. In one speech, he even claimed that the United States was in Korea because the administration had abandoned China to the communists. Those who had welcomed Eisenhower's nomination, including most of the United States's West European allies, because they thought he was an internationalist and a moderate, were shocked by the Republican candidate's increasingly shrill attacks against the White House. More and more, they feared that he had become a captive of Republican right-wingers who wanted to expand the war to include attacks against the Chinese mainland.

Elections are won at home and not abroad, however, and the combination of President Harry Truman's unpopularity, Adlai Stevenson's ineffective campaign, and Eisenhower's status as a hero of World War II almost certainly would have assured victory in November. But a pledge that Eisenhower made toward the end of the campaign to go to Korea if he were elected, with the implicit promise of ending what had become an extremely unpopular war, resonated with the voters and contributed to the size of his victory over Stevenson.

Once elected president, Eisenhower kept his promise to go to Korea. In December, he visited American troops along the front and met with South Korea's president Syngman Rhee, who had hoped to turn Eisenhower's visit into a major celebration. But to Rhee's disappointment, Eisenhower purposely kept a low profile and said nothing to indicate that he intended to pursue the war more vigorously than his Democratic predecessor. As president-elect, Eisenhower also paid a courtesy visit to his former superior, General MacArthur, who said he had a secret plan for ending the war. But MacArthur's plan turned out to be nothing more than the atomic bombing of enemy military concentrations and installations in North Korea and the sowing of a nuclear shield along the Yalu River to prevent the flow of enemy supplies from China to North Korea. Eisenhower listened politely to what MacArthur had to say, but remained noncommittal. Privately, he dismissed MacArthur's proposal out-of-hand.

In assuming the presidency in January, however, Eisenhower was determined to bring the Korean Conflict to a speedy conclusion. He had returned from Korea convinced that a military action of considerable magnitude was warranted. He also thought that the military strategy being pursued in Korea, known as the "active defense," was nothing more than a prescription for a military deadlock. Furthermore, although he and his secretary of state, John Foster Dulles, generally accepted the basic tenets of containment, which had guided American foreign policy since it was first developed in 1946 by the diplomat and expert on the Soviet Union, George Kennan, they were convinced the way containment was being executed left the initiative to the enemy. Instead of responding to military aggression at the point it took place, they maintained that aggression could be avoided by making clear to the enemy that it would be met with an American response at a place, and with weapons, of its own choosing, including even atomic weapons.

This policy, sometimes referred to as "massive retaliation" or the "New Look," helped shape Eisenhower's approach to the Korean War. At a meeting of the National Security Council (NSC), less than a month after taking office, the new president himself raised the nuclear option, saying that the United States needed to pursue a different approach to fighting the war. Its self-respect and that of its allies was at stake. Although Eisenhower realized that the allies, in fact, would object strongly to the use of atomic weapons, he raised that possibility again at another meeting of the NSC at the end of March.

There is some controversy over whether Eisenhower actually ever threatened the Chinese directly with the use of nuclear weapons. According to one view, Secretary of State Dulles was supposed to have delivered a nuclear ultimatum to the Chinese through the government of India. There is no hard evidence to substantiate this claim. But Eisenhower did not have to give the Chinese such an ultimatum. Almost certainly they understood that his patience was wearing thin, that he was determined to end the Korean War quickly; that he did not feel restricted by the previous administration with respect to any military operation, including the use of nuclear weapons; and that the United States had nuclear weapons on Okinawa. The president, in other words, did not have to present such an ultimatum to Beijing—peace or atomic bombs—because he was thinking along these lines anyway.

In response to—or in spite of—the threat of nuclear weapons. Eisenhower was able to achieve an end to the war within six months after assuming office, an objective that his predecessor, Truman, had not been able to achieve in more than two years. On June 4, the communist negotiators in Panmunjom agreed to the United Nations's position on prisoners of war (POWs), which provided for the return of prisoners on a voluntary basis only. With the issue settled, the armistice was signed on July 27, 1953.

The end of the Korean War contributed to making Eisenhower one of the most popular presidents of the post–World War II period. In 1956 he was reelected to a second term by an even greater margin than in 1952. In 1961 he retired to his farm in Gettysburg, Pennsylvania, the only home that he and his wife, Mamie, had ever owned. Before leaving office he delivered a "farewell address" in which he warned against the dangers of a "military-industrial establishment" that he feared was developing in the United States.

In retirement, Eisenhower continued to be consulted on foreign policy questions by his Democratic successors, John F. Kennedy and Lyndon Johnson. He also appears to have become politically more conservative during the last years of his life, and he continued to advocate a strong anticommunist policy. On March 28, 1969, he died of heart failure.

Kim Il Sung (1912–1994)

Kim Il Sung was the leader of the People's Republic of Korea (North Korea) during the Korean War and remained in absolute control of that country, first as prime minister (1948–1972) and then as president (1972–1994) until his death in 1994. He was also one of the last of the hard-line communist leaders. Little is known about Kim prior to the establishment of North Korea in 1948. He was born near Pyongyang in 1912. In 1919 his family moved to a town in Manchuria near the Korean border. As a teenager, he was thrown into prison for anti-Japanese activities. In 1932, after Japan invaded Manchuria, he founded the Korean People's Revolutionary Army, which waged a long struggle against the Japanese. During World War II, he received military training in the Soviet Union and, in 1945, he returned to Soviet-occupied North Korea. Widely acclaimed in Korea as a war hero, he was awarded the Order of Lenin by Soviet Premier Joseph Stalin. When efforts to reunify the Korean peninsula fell victim to the Cold War, the Soviets established the People's Republic of Korea in 1948 and named Kim to head its government.

A nationalist dedicated to the reunification of Korea under his leadership as well as a communist, Kim built up his military forces with substantial assistance from Moscow. He also supported guerrilla activity against the government of Syngman Rhee in South Korea. Although both Stalin and communist China's leader, Mao Zedong, were reluctant to chance war with the United States over Korea, he won their approval in 1950 for the June 25 invasion of South Korea. Though North Korean forces enjoyed initial success in the conflict, seizing almost all of Korea except for a small perimeter around the port city of Pusan, General Douglas MacArthur's amphibious operation at Inchon in September changed the whole complexion of the war. By November, when the Chinese communists entered the conflict in massive numbers, North Korea's army had been pushed back to the Yalu River separating Korea from China. Although the Chinese were able to rescue Kim from defeat, and the war eventually ended in a military stalemate roughly along the 38th parallel, Kim was forced to subordinate his activities during the war to China's military leaders.

At the same time, Kim's own leadership of North Korea remained intact. After the conflict, he helped rebuild the war-torn nation's economy through nationalization and collectivization of the nation's industries and farms. But

North Korea remained a poor country, especially when its economy was contrasted to the vibrant and growing economy of South Korea. North Korea also remained cut off from most of the rest of the noncommunist world. Even Kim's relations with his wartime benefactors, the Soviet Union and China, soured, as Kim resisted de-Stalinization efforts begun by the Soviet leader Nikita Khrushchev in the mid-1950s, and as he strove for complete political autonomy. Indeed, during the period from the end of the Korean Conflict in 1953 until his death in 1994, his own authority over North Korea became absolute. He ruthlessly suppressed dissent, carried out purges, and executed his political enemies. A cult of personality developed around him, with thousands of museums, monuments, and statues built around the country in his honor.

At the same time, Kim continued, unsuccessfully, to seek the reunification of Korea. In the 1970s, he even began a series of talks with South Korean negotiators. But frequent clashes between North Korean forces and South Korean and American troops along the heavily guarded 38th parallel and a failed effort in 1968 to assassinate South Korea's president, Chung Hee Park, made a diplomatic solution to the division of Korea extremely difficult. In fact, at the time of Kim's death on July 8, 1994, North Korea remained something of a pariah for much of the international community.

Douglas MacArthur (1845–1964)

General Douglas MacArthur was Commander of U.S. Forces in the Far East and Supreme Commander of UN Forces in Korea from July 14, 1950, to April 11, 1951. He was a handsome and imposing figure with angular facial features, a jutting jaw, and a majestic countenance who was known for his trademarks of a corncob pipe, sunglasses, open collar, and a bashed-in-cap. He was also brilliant and articulate with an ability to hone rich and euphonious language that flowed from a voice that was both deep and commanding; rarely did he even read from a prepared text. At the same time, he was the supreme egotist—arrogant, self-promoting, and possessed of a sense of superiority and mission that led him to ignore or disregard higher authority or opposing opinion and that would lead to his firing in 1951 by President Harry Truman.

MacArthur was born in Little Rock, Arkansas, on January 26, 1880, the son of Mary Pinkney Hardy and General Arthur MacArthur, who had won the Congressional Medal of Honor during the Civil War and would later serve as military commander of the Philippine Islands. In 1897 MacArthur entered the United States Military Academy (West Point). He was first in his class academically, receiving the highest grades ever recorded there. He also was named first captain, the highest honor in the cadet corps. Following his graduation in 1903, he quickly rose in rank after a series of choice assignments that included serving as aide to President Theodore Roosevelt, participating in the seizure of Vera Cruz in 1914, and working on the general staff in Washington, DC. After the United States entered World War I in 1917, he commanded the famed Rainbow Division's 84th Infantry Brigade that saw action in the St. Mihiel, Meuse-Argonne, and Sedan offensives. As a field commander, he was both daring and dashing, often risking his own life by leading his forces into no-man's land. According to Secretary of War Newton Baker, he was the best frontline officer fighting in France. Only thirty-eight years old at the end of the war, he already had achieved the rank of brigadier general.

Military cutbacks following the end of a war normally diminish the chances for rapid military promotion for career officers. But this did not happen to MacArthur. After a few months serving in the office of chief of staff in Washington, DC, he was named in 1919 as superintendent of West Point, the youngest officer ever to hold that post. As superintendent, he modernized the West Point curriculum, requiring cadets to take more courses in the humanities and social sciences. In 1922 he married a wealthy divorcee, Henrietta Louise Cromwell Brooks. During the 1920s, he also served two tours of duty in the Philippines, the first from 1922 to 1925 and the second from 1929 to 1930 as commanding general of the Philippine Department. Louise, who had hated the hot and damp climate of the Philippines during his first tour, refused to return with him to the Philippine. Theirs, in fact, had been a poor union, a socialite who loved the glamorous life and a self-possessed genius who intimidated Louise's friends. In 1939 they were divorced.

In 1930 MacArthur was named by President Herbert Hoover as chief of staff of the army with the rank of full general (four stars). At age fifty, he had achieved the highest military post in the United States. But he would later be criticized by historians for the harsh manner in which he dispersed the Bonus Army, a group of World War I veterans who had come to Washington in the summer of 1932 to collect war bonuses that were not due to be paid until 1945. Personally taking command of his troops, he used tanks and cavalry to break up the rag-tag group of protesters who has set up camp on Anacostia Flats.

As chief of staff, MacArthur was also later criticized for not recognizing the increased role that armored warfare and strategic bombing would play in future wars. Instead of a separate mechanized force, he wanted tanks integrated with horses in the cavalry, which would be responsible for developing new combat vehicles. And instead of a balanced air force of fighters and bombers, he thought in terms of a single prototype that could perform both functions. Yet he understood that tanks, planes, and submarines would be the decisive weapons of the next war, and he reintegrated the Air Corps with the Army from which it had been removed in 1926.

In 1935 MacArthur was asked by President Manuel Quezon of the newly established Philippine Commonwealth to serve as his military advisor. His responsibility was to develop a military force able to defend the Philippine Islands once it received its independence from the United States in 1946. MacArthur accepted the financially attractive offer, and, two years later, he retired from the U.S. Army. During that same year, he married Jean Faircloth, a woman much younger than he, whom he had met in Manila. In 1938 she gave birth to Arthur MacArthur, their only child.

On July 26, 1941, as war in the Pacific became imminent, President Franklin Roosevelt issued an executive order inducting the small Philippine army into the United States Army. He also recalled MacArthur to military service, placing him in command of U.S. Army Forces in the Pacific. MacArthur maintained that the Philippine Islands was the key to American defenses in the Pacific. But he did not prepare his small force as well as he might have for a Japanese attack, underestimating the chances of a Japanese invasion of the Philippines. Following the outbreak of war between Japan and the United States on December 7, 1941, the Japanese were easily able to overrun most of the Philippines, forcing MacArthur to retreat to the peninsula of Bataan, where he established his command on the island fortress of Corregidor that guarded Manila Harbor. Although MacArthur hesitated to leave his forces, when it became clear that Bataan's fall was imminent, he was ordered by President Franklin Roosevelt on February 22 to leave for Australia. Nine days later, he, his wife, and their son executed a daring escape to Australia on a PT boat that might very well have been intercepted by the Japanese.

From Australia, MacArthur, who had been named Supreme Commander of the Southwest Pacific Area, planned the defeat of the Japanese and his return to the Philippines. The strategy that he adopted was a combination of amphibious landings and "leapfrogging" across the coast of New Guinea and the Dutch East Indies, thereby bypassing large concentrations of Japanese and cutting them off from their supply lines. Meanwhile Admiral Chester Nimitz followed a similar policy of "island hopping" across the central Pacific. On October 20, 1944, MacArthur's forces began the invasion of the Philippines, fulfilling a promise the general had made in 1942 that he would return to the islands. A photograph showing him leaving an amphibious landing craft to wade ashore on Leyte, south of the main island of Luzon, in order to greet the invasion force remains one of the most famous snapshots of the war. By this time, MacArthur had become a living legend, and in December he was awarded his fifth star. According to polls, he was the second-most-admired hero, second only to General Dwight D. Eisenhower who had led Allied forces to victory against Germany.

On September 2, 1945, MacArthur presided over the formal surrender of Japan on board the USS *Missouri* anchored in Tokyo Bay. Appointed by President Truman as Supreme Commander of the Allied Powers (SCAP) in Japan, he ran the defeated nation benevolently but autocratically, seeking little advice even from Washington. Among his accomplishments as Supreme Commander were the preparation of a new and democratic constitution, reduction in the power of the *zaibatsu* (the eleven great industrial families of Japan), introduction of collective bargaining, extension of civil liberties and the suffrage to women who had hitherto been treated as inferior beings, and land reform. He also allowed the deified emperor of Japan, Hirohito, to remain as emperor, but as a symbol of the state rather than as a divine being. In all, he treated Japan with kindness and generosity and was widely admired by the Japanese people.

He also continued to be widely admired in the United States, and in 1948 his name was touted as a possible Republican candidate for president. Although he was never an official candidate, he allowed his name to appear on primary ballots in Wisconsin and Nebraska. He was keenly disappointed at his poor showing in these states and, later, at the Republican convention in Philadelphia.

Having spent a good part of his adult life in Asia, MacArthur was convinced that the Cold War would be won or lost in that part of the world. North Korea's invasion of South Korea on June 25, 1950, and the subsequent withdrawal of UN forces to a small perimeter around the southern port city of Pusan represented for him a military challenge to the noncommunist world of the highest order. Victory or defeat in Korea might very well determine the outcome of the Cold War. At stake was not only Korea but Formosa, which he regarded as a unique strategic asset because of its geopolitical location and potential as an air base. At the end of July, he visited Formosa and, acting on his own, virtually promoted an alliance with Chinese Nationalist leader Chiang Kai-shek. A month later, he sent a message to the Veterans of Foreign Wars, again without any clearance from Washington, in which he demeaned as appeasers those who opposed extending the U.S. military shield to include Formosa. This was an obvious slap at the administration, which, at the beginning of the Korean Conflict, had imposed the Seventh Fleet between Formosa and mainland China but had no intention of committing U.S. forces to Formosa's defense. The White House responded by ordering the general to withdraw his statement, which he did. But by then his remarks had received national media attention.

From the beginning of the war, MacArthur had planned an amphibious operation well behind enemy lines similar to the amphibious operations he had conducted during World War II. Despite major reservations about its feasibility by most military planners, including the Joint Chiefs of Staff, he carried out the maneuver on September 15 at Inchon, about twenty-five miles west of Seoul. It was brilliantly executed and coordinated with a breakout of UN forces from the Pusan perimeter. Although the pincer operation failed to entrap the North Koreans, it forced them to retreat north of the 38th parallel.

Now a decision had to be made about whether to send MacArthur's forces into North Korea, thereby risking the possible expansion of the conflict to include communist China and even the Soviet Union, but also offering the prospect of rolling back communist aggression. MacArthur never doubted what that decision should be. At Wake Island in October, the general assured President Truman that communist China would not enter the war even if UN forces crossed the 38th parallel and advanced toward the Yalu River separating the Korean peninsula from China. He also apologized for his statement in August to the Veterans of Foreign Wars and promised an end to the war by Christmas. Once he was given approval to cross into North Korea, he dismissed warnings from Beijing that it would enter the war if his forces approached the Yalu. Even as the Chinese began to cross into North Korea in massive numbers on November 24, he began his "home by Christmas" offensive convinced that the war would soon be over.

The offensive proved disastrous. By December UN forces had again been pushed back below the 38th parallel. Even though it had become clear by this time that the Korean conflict had entered a new phase, MacArthur refused to contemplate anything short of total victory. Rather, he insisted that he be allowed to bomb China, establish air bases on Formosa, and permit the use of Chinese Nationalist forces in Korea (something he had lobbied unsuccessfully for since the beginning of the conflict). In March, he undermined an initiative by the White House to begin negotiations on ending the war by depicting China as an overrated military power on the brink of being annihilated unless it was willing to negotiate a settlement of the conflict. Exasperated by orders that prohibited him from expanding the war, he publicly questioned the administration's policies. After the Republican Minority Leader in the House of Representatives, Joseph Martin of Massachusetts, read a letter to the House from MacArthur in which he again questioned the administration's policy in Korea, stating that there was no "substitute for victory," the president decided that he had no choice but to dismiss him from his commands, which he did on April 11.

The backlash against Truman was enormous, and MacArthur, returning to the United States for the first time in almost fifteen years, was greeted with a hero's welcome wherever he went. In New York City, he was given a ticker-tape parade that was watched by an estimated 7.5 million onlookers, nearly twice as many as had greeted General Dwight Eisenhower in 1945 after his victory in Europe. In a rare tribute, MacArthur was invited to speak to a joint session of Congress and then to be the first witness in special congressional hearings called to review the administration's policy in the Far East. But even Republican opponents of the administration sensed that MacArthur had exceeded his authority by publicly challenging the president's policy. Although he was greeted warmly in a tour he made of a number of American cities and was the keynote speaker at the Republican national convention in 1952, he soon became yesterday's news. He spent most of the remainder of his life in quiet retirement, residing until his death on April 5, 1964, at the Waldorf Astoria Hotel in New York City.

Mao Zedong (1893–1976)

Chairman of China's Communist party and undisputed leader of the People's Republic of China (PRC) from its inception in 1949 until his death in 1976 Mao Zedong (Mao-Tse-tung) was a zealous revolutionary who made the decision, perhaps as early as August 1950, for China to send massive numbers of "volunteers" into Korea in October and November 1950. One of the giant figures of the twentieth century, Mao was born in the village of Shao Shan in central China on December 26, 1893. From a relatively comfortable farm family, he rebelled against the authoritarianism of his father, who treated his family and servants badly. After graduating from a teacher's college, he worked as a school teacher and library assistant. In 1922 he attended the first party Congress of China's Communist party, which met in Shanghai. Helping to organize the peasantry, he came to recognize its potential revolutionary power, thereby breaking with traditional Marxist theory, which emphasized revolution by the working-class proletariat. In 1927 he began his long civil war with the Chinese Nationalists headed by Chiang Kai-shek, who, at one time, had been an ally in the Koumintang, a nationalist organization formed in 1907 to overthrow foreign rule. But Mao broke with Chiang after the latter succeeded Sun Yat-sen as leader of the Kuomintang following Sun's death in 1925 and then proceeded to rid the Kuomintang of communists and Russian advisors.

During the first years of the civil war, the conflict went badly for the communists, who were forced to go underground. In the summer of 1931, Chiang scored a major victory over the communist insurgency in the north. A year later, as many as 10,000 communists died as Chiang stepped up his campaign against them. But at the end of 1934, Mao, who had been in hiding, ordered his followers to march 6,000 miles from Kiangsi Province to Yenan. During the legendary long march through hostile territory, Mao spread his message for the peasants to rise up against their oppressors.

In 1936 Mao called for a united front with the Kuomintang against the Japanese, who had invaded Manchuria in 1931. Over the next fourteen years, Chiang, whose regime had become increasingly corrupt, fought the communists more than the Japanese while Mao pursued the opposite course. As a result, when the war ended, the communists found themselves in a strong position. Efforts by the United States after the war to unite the communists and Kuomintang failed, and the power of the communists among China's millions of peasants continued to grow. On April 21, 1949, communist armies crossed the Yangtse River, bringing an end to Kuomintang rule and forcing Chiang and his remaining forces to flee to the island of Formosa. On October 1, 1949, Mao was elected chairman of the new People's Republic of China (PRC). Although he voluntarily relinquished that position in 1959 to concentrate his attention on questions of Marxist-Leninist theory, he remained the undisputed leader of China until his death in 1976.

Having placed the peasantry rather than the proletariat in the vanguard of world revolution, he came to despise the United States, which he regarded as the greatest threat to his own regime and to the world revolutionary movement he advocated. His determination to be a leader in the Third World struggle against capitalist imperialism, rather than concern about China's security, may have been the primary reason why he decided, perhaps as early as August 1950, to enter the Korean War against UN forces led by the United States. Although he signed a thirty-year mutual assistance agreement with the Soviet Union in February 1950, he distrusted the Soviets because of their lackluster support in his civil war against the Kuomintang and because of territorial disputes with Moscow.

Beginning in 1952, Mao sought to restructure the whole of Chinese society by instituting a series of five-year plans that called for the elimination of the landholding classes in China and the collectivization of agriculture. As many as 800,000 former property holders may have been liquidated in a reign of terror that he instituted; by 1956 over 80 percent of all Chinese peasants were living on collective farms. By this time, too, Mao had firmly established his reputation as the ideological leader of the communist world. In

1966 his reputation was sullied by the "Cultural Revolution," during which he tried to revive China's revolutionary zeal by the elimination or reindoctrination of China's intelligentsia and other Chinese accused of bourgeois reactionary thinking. The major effect of the Cultural Revolution, however, was to destroy much of China's leadership class and to reverse the country's economic development.

Although Mao remained a lifelong revolutionary, he mellowed somewhat in his senior years, turning over more of his authority to his subordinates and even posing for pictures with President Richard Nixon during Nixon's historic visit to China in 1972. In declining health for years, Mao died on September 9, 1976, still regarded as China's political and spiritual leader and one of the great figures of the century.

George C. Marshall (1880–1959)

George C. Marshall was secretary of defense from September 1950 until September 1951. Although he had a distinguished career as Army chief of staff during World War II and as secretary of state from 1947 to 1949 and was immensely popular in Washington, he also became a target of right-wing Republicans, who held him responsible for the loss of China to the communists in 1949.

Born in Uniontown, Pennsylvania, on December 31, 1880, Marshall graduated from the Virginia Military Institute in 1901. During World War I, he gained a considerable reputation as a staff officer in the St. Mihiel and Meuse-Argonne operations. After the war, he was as an aide to Army Chief of Staff John Pershing, who also became a personal friend. During the 1920s and 1930s, he served in various posts in the United States and China. In 1936 he was promoted to brigadier general. In 1939, following Germany's invasion of Poland, President Franklin Roosevelt named him chief of staff with the responsibility of expanding the nation's armed forces. Following the United States's entry into World War II in December 1941, he was put in overall charge of U.S. military operations and was responsible for naming Dwight D. Eisenhower to lead the Allied invasion of Normandy in 1944. A quiet and generally unassuming leader, he, nevertheless, commanded great loyalty and respect from those who worked for him because of his dignified bearing, sound judgment, reasoned arguments, and good common sense.

Following the end of World War II, Truman appointed Marshall as a special envoy to China in an effort to mediate a settlement of the Chinese Civil War. He remained in China until 1947 but failed to end the conflict. Returning to the United States, he was named in 1947 as secretary of state, a position he held until 1949. The following year, about the same time that UN forces were preparing to go on the offensive in Korea, Truman asked Marshall to be his secretary of defense.

His appointment was not without opposition on Capitol Hill. As secretary of state, Marshall had carried out the U.S. policy of containment against the Soviet Union and was responsible for the European Recovery Plan (or what became known as the Marshall Plan because Marshall had first proposed the plan during a commencement address at Harvard University in 1947). In 1953 he received the Nobel Peace Prize for his efforts in behalf of European recovery. But because Marshall had been Truman's representative to China after the war and then his secretary of state, Marshall was considered by the China lobby and right-wing Republicans as one of the architects of the policy that had led to the communist victory in China in 1949. There were also objections to his nomination on the grounds that the National Security Act of 1947 prohibited military officers from serving as defense secretary.

Still, Marshall's appointment was generally a popular one both in the United States and in Europe, where the prevailing view was that Marshall would be a restraining force at the Pentagon and would work closely with Secretary of State Dean Acheson in carrying out defense policy. This was correct on both accounts, and during congressional hearings in 1951 on the firing of General Douglas MacArthur by President Truman, Marshall refuted charges that MacArthur had made to the effect that the Joint Chiefs of Staff (JCS) had approved his recommendations for an escalation of the war to include an economic and naval blockade of China, the end of restrictions on air reconnaissance of China's coastal areas and of Manchuria, and the end of restrictions on the operations of the Chinese Nationalist forces against the Chinese Communists. As Marshall pointed out, these proposals were only part of a series of options considered by the JCS but never adopted.

Marshall retired from public service in 1951. He died in Washington, DC, on October 16, 1959.

Joseph R. McCarthy (1908–1957)

Joseph R. McCarthy was a U.S. senator from Wisconsin whose charges of an internal communist conspiracy were a major political issue during the Korean Conflict. Born on November 14, 1908, he was a graduate of Marquette University Law School (1935). After practicing law, he was elected a circuit judge in 1939. During World War II he served as a Marine intelligence officer in the South Pacific. In 1946 he surprised political pundits by beating Robert M. LaFollette, Jr., in the Republican primary for the U.S. Senate and then winning the Senate seat in the general elections in November. A genial but ambitious and unscrupulous lawmaker, McCarthy did not attract much national attention until 1950 when, in a speech in Wheeling, West Virginia, he claimed to have a list of 205 known communists working for the State Department. In fact, no such list existed, and he never "uncovered" a single communist in the State Department. Nevertheless, his charges of an internal communist conspiracy reaching to the highest levels of government came at a time when a climate of fear and crisis was already gripping the nation. A series of events in 1949 and 1950, including the successful Soviet testing of an atomic bomb in September 1949, several years ahead of schedule, the "loss" of China to the communists a month later, the perjury conviction in January 1950 of Alger Hiss, a former State Department official, who, under oath, had denied charges that he had been a communist in the 1930s, and the confession about the same time in Britain of Klaus Fuchs, a high-level atomic scientist, that he had given atomic secrets to the Soviet Union lent credence to McCarthy's accusations, and he quickly became one of the most well-known—and feared—figures in Washington.

During the Korean Conflict, the Wisconsin senator even accused Defense Secretary George Marshall of taking part in an immense conspiracy against the United States. He also denounced the State and Defense Departments for not pursuing a policy of victory in Korea. He was finally brought down after televised hearings in 1954 resulting from charges he had made that the Army had promoted a dentist, Irving Peress, who was a known communist, and countercharges by the Army that he had sought special treatment for one of his associates, G. David Schine, who had been drafted into the Army. In December 1954, the Senate censured him for actions unbecoming a U.S. Senator. Discredited, he died on May 2, 1957. But by then a new word, "McCarthyism," had been introduced into the language to describe unsupported accusations of disloyalty and demagoguery.

Syngman Rhee (1875–1965)

As the first president of the Republic of Korea, Syngman Rhee was the leader of South Korea during the Korean Conflict. He remained president until 1960 when he was forced to leave the country following a military coup.

Born on April 26, 1875, in Hwang-hae province, Rhee was educated at an American missionary school, where he learned to speak English. In 1896 he joined the Independence Club, whose purpose was to reform the monarchy system and remove Japanese influence in Korea. Thrown into prison the next year for his political activity, he was converted to Christianity. Released from prison in 1904, he went to the United States, where, in 1905, he received a B.A. degree from George Washington University and, in 1910, a

Ph.D. in international law from Princeton University. During this time, he also became an outspoken advocate of Korean independence from Japanese domination. At the Portsmouth Conference of 1905, which ended the Russo-Japanese War and made Korea a Japanese protectorate, he petitioned unsuccessfully on behalf of Korea.

Following his graduation from Princeton in 1910, the same year that Japan formally annexed Korea, Rhee returned to his native country, where he worked briefly for the Y.M.C.A. But fearing arrest because of his outspoken opposition to Japanese annexation, he fled the country two years later. Returning to the United States, he spent most of the next thirty-five years promoting Korean nationalism and independence from Japan. In 1912 he met the Democratic candidate for president and his former teacher, Woodrow Wilson, in an effort to gain his support for Korea, but Wilson told Rhee that international intervention to free Korea from Japan was inappropriate. This was much the same message he was to hear for the next thirty-five years.

By 1919 Rhee was identified so closely with the cause of Korean nationalism that he was named by other Korean exiles and advocates of Korean independence as president of the Korean Provisional government, which had been formed that year in Shanghai. Although the Provisional government never gained any official recognition from the international community, for the remainder of the Japanese occupation, Rhee traveled throughout the United States speaking and promoting the cause of Korean independence. The large sums of money needed to finance his travel and activities he raised from Koreans in the United States and from American businessmen to whom he promised lavish concessions once Korea was freed from Japanese control. A proud obstinate, and obstreperous person, as well as an avowed anticommunist, Rhee came to represent, more than anyone else, the cause of Korean nationalism.

In 1945 Rhee returned to Korea after his long exile abroad. By this time, Korea had been divided into two zones, a Soviet zone north of the 38th parallel and an American zone south of the parallel. By this time, too, Korea was in the midst of political chaos as rightist and leftists vied for political power. At first, the United States sought to avoid involvement in the maelstrom by refusing to recognize any group as the legitimate government of Korea. Officials in the State Department distrusted Rhee, believing that he was an extremist who did not represent the Korean people. At one point, American military authorities even tried unsuccessfully to establish a consensus government that excluded Rhee. But as the political fighting intensified and as the division of Korea into northern and southern zones became permanent, Washington found itself increasingly committed to the South Korean leader because of his anticommunist credentials and support among many Koreans. After efforts to form a coalition government for a united Korea failed in 1947, the United States threw its full support behind Rhee. In 1948 he was elected president of the Republic of Korea (ROK).

As president, Rhee quickly became a thorn in the side of Washington as he sought large amounts of military equipment, including airplanes, combat ships, and arms to equip 100,000 troops, in order to prevent what he warned would be a North Korean invasion of South Korea but also to invade North Korea in order to reestablish a united country. The United States was willing to help train ROK forces and to provide limited military assistance for South Korea's defense. But it had no intention of giving Rhee the equipment he needed to invade North Korea, especially because it considered Korea to be of limited military or strategic value and regarded the Korean leader as an extremist. For his part, Rhee made caustic remarks about the insufficiency of American aid and demanded American guarantees of protection for his country.

Once war broke out in Korea in 1950, Rhee held steadfastly to the view, even after the Chinese intervention in the conflict in November 1950 and the opening of armistice negotiations in July 1951, that there could be no end to the fighting short of complete victory over the communists and the reunification of Korea. This embroiled him with the White House, which had dropped Korean reunification as a war objective. By the end of February 1952, Rhee had become such a problem for the administration that President Truman warned him that he would lose American support if he did not become less obstreperous. Administration officials also were disturbed by the despotic manner in which he ran the government and by the growing unpopularity of his regime, especially when, in the spring of 1952, he forced through the National Assembly a change in the Korean constitution allowing him to run for a second term as president. In response, the new commander of UN forces in Korea, Mark Clark, even prepared plans for a coup against the South Korean leader, which he filed for future use if needed.

Rhee's most provocative act, however, came on June 18, when, just as UN and communist negotiators were nearing completion of an armistice agreement, Rhee tried to undermine the agreement by releasing 25,000 North Korean prisoners of war (POWs). Although his action failed to derail the agreement, Rhee was able, by his persistent opposition to an armistice, to win some major concessions from the United States, including a mutual defense pact and a sizable package of economic and military assistance. In return, the South Korean leader promised not to disrupt the armistice, which went into effect on July 27, although he refused to become a party to the agreement.

Following the end of the Korean Conflict, Rhee continued to serve as president of South Korea. He also remained committed to the eventual unification of the two Koreas, by arms if necessary. But the increasingly authoritarian nature of his regime and widespread government corruption led to his overthrow in 1960. Fleeing the country he loved so much, he went to Hawaii, where he died on July 19, 1965.

Matthew B. Ridgway (1895–1993)

General Matthew B. Ridgway was Commander of U.S. Forces in the Far East and Supreme Commander of UN Forces in Korea from 1951 to 1952. A tough field commander who had led the 82nd Airborne Division during World War II and had jumped with the division at Normandy and later with XVII Corps at Nijmegan and the Ardennes, Ridgway was known for his trademark of carrying a single grenade and first-aid kit hooked to a web harness that he wore over his trench coat. A protégé of General George Marshall, Ridgway was also an intellectual who read widely and was thoughtful and deliberate in making decisions.

Appointed to head the Eighth Army in December 1950 after the death of its commander General Walton Walker in a freak accident, Ridgway is generally given credit for stopping the Chinese communist offensive during the darkest days of the Korean War and then, through a series of military operations, forcing the communists to retreat to a line roughly following what became the armistice line in 1953. In April 1951, following the firing of General Douglas MacArthur from his commands, President Harry Truman named Ridgway to replace MacArthur at the rank of full general. A year later, Ridgway succeeded General Dwight Eisenhower as supreme allied commander in Europe. In 1953 he was named chief of staff of the Army.

Ridgway was born on March 3, 1895, in Fort Monroe, Virginia. After graduating from the U.S. Military Academy (West Point) in 1917, he was assigned to the Infantry School at Fort Benning, Georgia. Between World Wars I and II, he served in a variety of staff positions in the United States, China, Nicaragua, the Panama Canal Zone, and the Philippines. He also spent a year (1937) at the Army War College.

In 1942 Ridgway was appointed commander of the 82nd Infantry Division, which was converted into the 82nd Airborne Division. During World War II, Ridgway developed his reputation as a "soldier's soldier," jumping with his men and leading them into action. In 1944 he was given command of the 18th Airborne Command, which saw action in France, Belgium, the

Netherlands, and Germany and played an important role in stopping the German offensive during the Battle of the Bulge.

Following the end of World War II, Ridgway served in the Philippines and Mediterranean and at the newly organized United Nations. In 1949 he was brought into the Pentagon as deputy chief of staff, and at the time of his appointment to replace General Walker in 1951, he was widely regarded as a likely candidate for Army chief of staff. A demanding administrator, he insisted on precision from his staff and became infuriated when someone gave him an evasive answer. These were qualities he would carry with him to Korea.

Ridgway arrived in Korea on December 26 after receiving a short briefing in Tokyo from General Douglas MacArthur. Rejecting the defeatist view that had become widespread in the ranks and even at the Pentagon following the Chinese offensive and the United States's longest retreat in its history, Ridgway set about to clean house, rebuild his forces, and make the Chinese pay heavily for their advance. He was eminently successful in all these respects. On orders from the Pentagon, the X Corps was merged into the Eighth Army under his command. Believing that the most serious problem he faced was the low morale of his troops, Ridgway sought to restore their confidence and fighting vigor through stern discipline, tough training, and a sense of esprit de corps. He also adopted a "meat grinder" strategy, seeking out the enemy and striking at him repeatedly while making maximum use of tanks and firepower. By mid-January, he had stopped the enemy offensive. Between January 25 and February 10 alone, his troops inflicted an estimated 80,000 casualties on the enemy.

The success Ridgway had on the battlefield played an important role in undermining MacArthur's influence in Washington. A team from the Pentagon that had been sent to Korea in mid-January to assess the morale of UN forces after MacArthur had described it as dismal was encouraged by what they found. The Eighth Army, they reported, was now prepared to launch its own counteroffensive. Henceforth, the Pentagon and President Truman increasingly circumvented Tokyo, choosing instead to deal directly with Ridgway. On February 21, Ridgway launched "Operation Killer." this was followed the next month by "Operation Ripper." By March 24, his forces had retaken Seoul. By April 22, when the Chinese launched their spring offensive, UN forces had established a defensive line, "Line Wyoming," which again took them above the 38th parallel.

By this time, Ridgway had been appointed to succeed General MacArthur in Tokyo. Following the opening of armistice negotiations in July, Ridgway was forced to limit his military operations largely to the existing line of demarcation between UN and enemy forces. Although some heavy fighting took place at Bloody Ridge and Heartbreak Ridge, in an area known as the Punchbowl, neither UN nor Chinese forces launched any major new offensive. In November, Ridgway was instructed by the Joint Chiefs of Staff (JCS) to accept the present line of contact as the demarcation line for a demilitarized zone. Although the JCS also stated that the line would be renegotiated if the armistice talks at Panmunjom were not successfully concluded within a reasonable time (a month or so), for the rest of the war Ridgway had to confine his military operations largely to that line. This allowed the Chinese to build extensive fortifications behind the line, thereby making a major offensive by UN forces increasingly difficult even if Ridgway had been authorized to launch such an offensive.

The UN commander became almost as frustrated with his orders from Washington as MacArthur had been. He objected to what amounted to a military stalemate. Forced to assume what he referred to as "an active defense," limiting offensive operations largely to the seizure of ground necessary to protect his position, he wanted instead to increase military pressure against the Chinese. He also found his orders from the Pentagon to be vacillating and indecisive, and he strongly opposed a proposal in April 1952 that the UN negotiators at Panmunjom agree to allow the communists to rebuild airfields in North Korea in return for the enemy's agreement to voluntary repatriation of POWs, something that he also opposed because he feared that it might lead to communist retaliation against UN POWs.

Although Ridgway shared many of MacArthur's frustrations about fighting a limited war, he did not speak out against the Truman administration's policies, as his predecessor had done. Indeed, he thought MacArthur should have been relieved of his commands as early as December 1950 for violating his orders not to question publicly White House policy. Accordingly, unlike MacArthur, he was not relieved of his commands in humiliation but, instead, was appointed in April 1952 to replace General Eisenhower as supreme allied commander in Europe following Eisenhower's decision to run for president. The next year, he was named Army chief of staff, a position he held until his retirement in 1955.

Following his return to civilian life, Ridgway was named chairman of the board of trustees of the Mellon Institute for Industrial Research. In 1956 he published his memoirs *Soldier*. This was followed in 1967 by *The Korean War*, in which he wrote about the problems of fighting a limited war but made clear, at the same time, that in the nuclear age it was no longer a question of fighting a limited war but of avoiding fighting any other kind. In 1986

Ridgway received the Presidential Medal of Freedom and, in 1991, he was awarded the Congressional Gold Medal. He died on July 26, 1993.

Joseph Vissarionovich Stalin (1879–1953)

Joseph Stalin was the leader of the Soviet Union from 1924 to 1953. Born in Georgi, Georgia, on December 21, 1879, he came to power in 1924 following the death of Vladimir I. Lenin. One of the most ruthless tyrants of the twentieth century, Stalin is reported to have been responsible for the deaths of hundreds of thousands of his adversaries. He, nevertheless, successfully defended the Soviet Union against the German invasion during World War II. Although a member of the Grand Coalition that won the war, he broke with the West over the postwar status of eastern Europe, which he was determined to control but whose governments the United States wanted to be freely elected. The onset of the Cold War meant the permanent division of Korea, and in 1948 Stalin helped install Kim Il Sung as the communist leader of North Korea. Although Stalin was reluctant to approve Kim Il Sung's proposal in 1949 for an invasion of South Korea, he consented to it in the spring of 1950 after being reassured by the North Korean leader that he could quickly defeat South Korea and reunite Korea under communist rule. Stalin also did not think that the United States would enter the war. During the conflict, he continued to provide supplies to communist forces in China, but he distrusted the Chinese, and his major concern was assuring that the limited war in Korea would not become a major world war involving the Soviet Union and the United States. Stalin died on March 5, 1953, after suffering a brain hemorrhage.

Robert A. Taft (1889–1953)

Robert A. Taft was Republican leader of the Senate during the Korean Conflict and one of the leading opponents of President Harry Truman's conduct of the conflict. The son of former President William Howard Taft, Robert was born on September 8, 1889, in Cincinnati, Ohio. From a privileged background, he proved to be a highly able and distinguished politician in his own right. He graduated from Yale in 1910 and from Harvard Law School in 1913, where he was first in his class. After serving in both houses of the Ohio legislature, he was elected to the U.S. Senate in 1938. Representing the more conservative right wing of the Republican party, he was a candidate for the Republican nomination for president in 1940, 1948, and 1952, losing narrowly in 1952 to General Dwight D. Eisenhower, with whom he developed a good working relationship.

Believing that the United States was tied too closely to Europe in its foreign policy and that it had not paid enough attention to developments in the Far East, thereby allowing China to fall to the communists in 1949, he supported President Harry Truman's decision to commit American military forces to Korea. However, he believed that Truman should have asked Congress for a declaration of war before committing the United States militarily in Korea; this was an issue that he continued to raise over the next three years.

Following communist China's entry into the war in November 1950 and the retreat of UN forces below the 38th parallel, he attacked the administration's "defeatist" policy in Korea. When Truman told congressional leaders in December that he was going to declare a state of national emergency and impose price and wage controls, Taft responded that what the country needed was not a state of national emergency but a well-defined program of military preparedness. In the winter of 1951, he denounced, on both constitutional and strategic grounds, Truman's decision to send four military divisions to Europe to bolster NATO and, in April 1951, he bitterly assailed Truman's firing of General Douglas MacArthur.

Over the next eighteen months, Taft continued to lash out at the Truman administration for its conduct of the war and joined with other right-wing Republicans in "red-baiting" the administration (accusing it of harboring communists). During the 1952 campaign, he described the war in Korea as "useless and expensive" and charged that Truman lacked "the guts" to win the war. Following the election of Dwight Eisenhower as president, however, Taft muted his criticisms, although he continued to believe that the war was unconstitutional and that it represented the failure of U.S. foreign policy in the Far East. Taft died of cancer on July 31, 1953. Despite his strident anti-communism and "red-baiting." Taft has been widely acknowledged by historians to have been one of the nation's most able and respected senators.

Harry S Truman (1884–1972)

Harry S Truman was President of the United States during the first two and half years of the Korean Conflict. An unassuming man of humble origins and modest abilities, at the time he was Franklin D. Roosevelt's last vice-president and was elevated to the presidency in April 1945 on Roosevelt's death in office. Sometimes, Truman spoke and acted impetuously. He was also feisty and could be petty and vindictive. But as president, he proved to be as crafty as any political leader and made some of the most difficult and important decisions of any modern president. These included his decisions to drop the atomic bomb against Japan in 1945, to issue the Truman Doctrine and go forward with the Marshall Plan in 1947, to respond in 1948 to the Soviet blockade of Berlin with a massive airlift of food and supplies, to commit U.S. military forces to the defense of South Korea in 1950, and to fire General Douglas MacArthur in 1951.

Born in Lamar, Missouri, on May 8, 1884, Truman had held a series of jobs and operated a family farm until 1917, when he served in World War I as an Army captain in France. Following the war, he married his childhood sweetheart, Bess Wallace, the daughter of a local farmer, and opened a haberdashery shop in Kansas City. In 1924 Bess gave birth to the Truman's only child, Mary Margaret, now a well-known author.

Although Truman's business failed, he became good friends with the local political boss, Tom Pendergast, and with Pendergast's backing he was made a county judge in 1922 (the equivalent of a county commissioner). Swept out of office in 1924, he was elected two years later as Presiding Judge of the County Court of Jackson (the equivalent of a county executive); this was an important position because Jackson County included Kansas City. He remained in that post until 1934 when he was elected to the U.S. Senate by a plurality of 262,000 votes over his nearest opponent. After narrowly winning re-election in 1940, he gained national attention by heading a committee investigating defense spending and exposing considerable mismanagement and malfeasance in the defense industries. When President Franklin Roosevelt decided in 1944 to dump his controversial vice-president, Henry Wallace, in his bid for a fourth term in office, he turned to the Missouri senator because Truman did not offend any of the fractious wings of the Democratic party. Yet Roosevelt failed to take his new vice president into his confidence and rarely consulted with him. Indeed, when Truman assumed the presidency on April 12, 1945, following Roosevelt's sudden death from a cerebral hemorrhage, he did not even know about the Manhattan Project, the program underway to develop an atomic bomb. He was informed of the project by Secretary of War Henry Stimson. Clearly, Truman had good reason to feel unprepared to assume the tremendous responsibilities that were suddenly thrust upon him by Roosevelt's death.

Immediately facing Truman was the postwar settlement of Europe. Although he sought to carry out Roosevelt's plans for the postwar world, which were predicated on maintaining the wartime coalition, he was heavily influenced by the anti-Soviet views of the State Department, which were in accord with his own loathing of communism. At a meeting in April with Soviet Foreign Minister Vyacheslav Molotov, he berated the Soviets for not honoring a pledge they had made at the Yalta Conference of February 1945 to hold free elections in eastern Europe after the war.

Truman's most important decision in his first six months in office, however, was to use the atomic bomb against Japan. Although the war in Europe ended in May, the Japanese continued to fight tenaciously. In the battle for Okinawa, more than 11,000 Americans were killed before the island was taken. The planned invasion of the Japanese island was expected to result in enormous additional casualties. Nevertheless, critics of Truman's decision to drop two atomic bombs on Japan, the first at Hiroshima on August 6 and the second at Nagasaki three days later, have argued that the war could have been ended without the use of nuclear weapons. They also have offered various scenarios on how this might have happened, ranging from a naval blockade of the Japanese islands to the dropping of a bomb on a deserted island in order to make the Japanese aware of its devastating impact. Whatever the legitimacy of these arguments, Truman approved the use of the atomic bomb against Japan because he thought it was the quickest way to end the war and to prevent further American casualties.

Although Truman used the bomb to force Japan into surrendering, he believed that a combination of the United States's atomic monopoly and the Soviet Union's need for American economic assistance after the war would persuade Soviet leaders to behave as they had promised at Yalta. But this did not happen. Instead, Moscow and Washington locked horns in a series of escalating crises in what became known as the Cold War. In 1946 the United States clashed with the Soviet Union after Moscow refused to withdraw its troops from northern Iran. Not until Washington sent a strong note to Moscow demanding immediate withdrawal and the Iranians agreed to establish a joint company to exploit the oil resources of the region (in a treaty later rejected by Parliament) did the Soviets agree to pull out their forces.

In 1947 Britain announced that it could no longer be the defender of Western interests in the Mediterranean region. The president responded with the Truman Doctrine, which provided $400 million in economic and military assistance to Greece and Turkey and included an open-ended pledge to protect friendly nations from subversion and aggression. In June, Secretary of State George C. Marshall proposed the Marshall Plan for the economic reconstruction of Western Europe. That same month George Kennan, a high State Department official, published an article signed "X" in the American journal *Foreign Affairs*, in which he outlined the doctrine of containment, America's strategy for waging the Cold War. In 1948 Truman ordered an airlift of supplies to Berlin after the Soviets imposed a blockade on that city. In 1949 he extended diplomatic recognition to West Germany (the Federal Republic of Germany) and approved American membership in NATO.

The most serious foreign policy crisis that Truman faced as president, however, was the Korean Conflict. Although the administration had not included Korea within the U.S. defense perimeter in the Far East because it thought it lacked any strategic value, he committed American troops to the defense of South Korea because he believed that U.S. credibility abroad and his own credibility at home were at issue in the conflict. Like many Americans who remembered the Munich Agreement of 1938, in which British Prime Minister Neville Chamberlain sacrificed part of Czechoslovakia to Adolf Hitler's Germany in the name of peace, he also concluded that appeasement would only lead to further aggression.

Once the tide of battle had turned in September 1950, Truman agreed to sending UN forces above the 38th parallel because, like others in his administration, he saw an opportunity to roll back communism. But from the start of the war, he was determined not to escalate it into a military confrontation with the Soviet Union. When communist China entered the conflict in November 1950 and drove UN forces below the 38th parallel, he changed back the conflict's objective from rollback to its original one of containing communist aggression.

At times during the war, the president acted precipitously, such as during his news conference in December 1950 when he stated that he had not ruled out the use of nuclear weapons in Korea and implied that a decision to use such weapons would be left to the field commanders. The furor that caused in Europe forced Truman to make it clear that a decision on employing atomic weapons would be his alone and that he would consult with his allies before making that decision. Truman also ruminated in his diary on the possibility of dropping atomic bombs on the major cities of the Soviet Union and China if the enemy did not agree to a negotiated settlement of the war. But once China entered the war, he never wavered from his determination to limit the war to one of containment.

Given General Douglas MacArthur's huge popularity and the president's own growing unpopularity, in good measure a result of the recent turn of events in Korea, Truman's decision in April 1951 to relieve MacArthur of his commands for publicly questioning the administration's policy was also one of the most politically courageous decisions of any modern American president. The firing of the five-star general even led to calls on Capitol Hill for Truman's impeachment. But by his action, Truman reaffirmed the role of the president as commander in chief. Similarly, he established the authority of the presidency in foreign policy at a time when the United States was thrust into the role of leader of the noncommunist world. As president, this may have been his greatest legacy. The president's steadfast opposition to the forced repatriation of enemy prisoners of war, even though repatriation was called for by the Geneva Convention of 1949, and his stand on the issue probably delayed an end to the war by eighteen months, also indicated Truman's commitment to principle regardless of the consequences.

Because the Korean Conflict continued without the kind of complete victory Americans were used to winning and without an end in sight, it cost Truman heavily in public opinion polls; there seems little doubt that Dwight D. Eisenhower's promise to end the war if he were elected president in 1952 contributed to the size of the Republican candidate's victory over the Democratic candidate, Adlai Stevenson, although Eisenhower would probably have won without that pledge. By the time Truman left office in January 1953, he had become one of the nation's most unpopular presidents. According to one poll, only 31 percent of Americans approved of his performance in office—in large part due to frustrations over the stalemate in Korea, but also due to Truman's inability to control post–World War II inflation, his pro-civil rights stand, and a rightward shift generally in American political sentiment.

After leaving the presidency, Truman returned to his home in Independence, Missouri. Although he would live another twenty years, he occupied most of his time in quiet retirement, occasionally advising his successors and giving talks to college students, but mostly reading history, especially military history (something he had always enjoyed), watching over the construction of the Truman Library that he came to love dearly, and when it was finished, meeting visitors and working in his office at the Library. He died on December 26, 1972.

Walton H. Walker (1889–1950)

Walton H. Walker was a lieutenant general and commander of the Eighth Army in Korea from June 1950 until his accidental death in December 1950. Born in Belton, Texas, on December 3, 1889, he graduated from the United States Military Academy (West Point) in 1912. During World War I, he saw action at St. Mihiel and in the Meuse-Argonne. An artillery officer, he served in various posts during the 1920s and 1930s and was a graduate of both the Command and General Staff School (1926) and the Army War College (1936). During World War II, he served with General George Patton in Europe and won considerable distinction for his drive across France and Germany as commander of Patton's Twentieth Corps. By the end of the war, he had been promoted to lieutenant general (temporary) and received numerous decorations, including the Distinguished Service Cross.

After serving for three years as commander of the Fifth Army Area in the United States (1945–1948), he was appointed in 1948 as commanding general of the Far East Command's Eighth Army. Following the outbreak of hostilities in Korea in June 1950, the Eighth Army was sent from Japan to Korea. Forced to retreat to a perimeter around Pusan, he gained fame for his frequent visits to the battlefront and for his order to "stand or die." Following the amphibious invasion of Inchon in September, Walker led the Eighth Army's breakout from Pusan and by the end of the month his forces had linked up with X Corps advancing from the Northwest. Shortly thereafter, he led the advance of the Eighth Army into North Korea and then the drive toward the Yalu River. But following the entrance of the Chinese into the war at the end of November, he began the long retreat of his forces below the 38th parallel. As he retreated, he adopted a "scorched-earth" policy destroying bridges, transportation facilities, and supply depots to slow down the enemy advance and to prevent equipment and supplies from falling into their hands.

On December 23, 1950, Walker was killed in a freak jeep accident while his forces were still retreating. Though praised for his dogged defense of the Pusan perimeter during the first two months of the war, he has since been criticized by some military officers and historians for not putting up more resistance to the advancing enemy after the Chinese entered the conflict, especially at the narrow waist of the Korean peninsula above Pyongyang in the west and Wonson in the east, and for his demolition policy, which later hampered UN forces after they halted the communist advance and began moving northward once more. Even during the war, the term "bugout" was used to describe the Eighth Army's rapid retreat southward.

Primary Documents
of the Korean Conflict

The opening, in recent years, of archives from the former Soviet Union reveal the reluctance of the Soviet Union—and the People's Republic of China—to support an invasion of South Korea by North Korea at least through the winter of 1950. Although North Korean leader Kim Il Sung proposed in the fall of 1949 only an attack on the Ongjin Peninsula, on the western coast of Korea extending both above and below the 38th parallel, Soviet leader Joseph Stalin understood that such an attack could result in a full-scale war that might involve the United States; this he was anxious to avoid at all costs. Kim also argued that partisans in South Korea were waiting for the opportunity to overthrow its leader, Syngman Rhee, and he even seemed to suggest that the Chinese would support him even if the Soviets did not. But the Soviet leader had doubts that a popular uprising against Rhee would happen without more support of the partisans in the south or that Kim could defeat South Korea in short order as he promised. Stalin also raised questions about the military superiority of North Korean over South Korean forces. At the same time, however, he never excluded entirely the possibility of a North Korean invasion, and he promised military assistance in order to build up Kim Il Sung's forces. What is also striking in the documents that follow—all from the Soviet Foreign Ministry Archives—is the economic and political dependence of North Korea on the Soviet Union. Kim made it clear that he would not act without Stalin's approval, and the Soviet leader virtually ordered the North Koreans in January 1950 to supply 25,000 tons of lead to the Soviet Union in return for Soviet technical assistance.

Document 1
CIPHERED TELEGRAM FROM [T.F.] SHTYKOV
[SOVIET AMBASSADOR TO DEMOCRATIC PEOPLE'S
REPUBLIC OF KOREA] TO [A.IA] VYSHINSKY [SOVIET
MINISTER OF FOREIGN AFFAIRS], SEPTEMBER 3, 1949

On September 3, the personal secretary of Kim Il Sung, Mun Il (A Soviet Korean), came to me and at the commission of Kim Il Sung reported that they had received reliable information that in the near future the southerners intend to seize the part of the Ongjin peninsula which is located to the north of the 38th parallel, and also to bombard the cement plant in the city of Kaisiu.

In connection with this, Mun Il said, Kim Il Sung asks permission to begin military operations against the south, with the goal of seizing the Ongjin peninsula and part of the territory of South Korea to the east of the Ongjin peninsula, approximately to Kaesong, so as to shorten the line of defense.

Kim Il Sung considers, Mun said, that if the international situation permits, they are ready to move further to the south. Kim Il Sung is convinced that they are in a position to seize South Korea in the course of two weeks, maximum 2 months.

I asked [Mun] to transmit to Kim Il Sung that this question is very large and serious, it is necessary to think it through carefully and that I therefore urgently recommend to Kim Il Sung not to be in a hurry and not to take [any measures] while there is no decision on this question.

Kim Il Sung will probably raise this question again soon.

It has been established that the [North Koreans] truly did seize an order to the commander of troops on the Ongjin Peninsula to begin artillery fire on the cement plant in Kaisiu on September 2 at 8:00 and to destroy it. From the order, it is clear that the southerners consider this plant to be military. The period indicated in the order has past but so far there has been no shelling. The northerners have taken the necessary measures in case of firing on the plant.

Regarding the intentions of the southerners to seize part of the Ongjin peninsula to the north of the 38th parallel, we have only indications [of this] from deserters from the south.

There have not been any serious incidents at the 38th parallel since August 15. Small exchanges of fire have taken place, [there have been] instances of artillery firing on the territory of North Korea on the Ongjin peninsula, trespassing of the parallel. The southerners are carrying on defensive work at the 38th parallel at a faster tempo. I ask your order. [Grigori] Tunkin [charge d'affairs of the Soviet embassy in Pyongyang].

Document 2
CIPHERED TELEGRAM FROM GROMYKO TO
TUNKIN, SEPTEMBER 11, 1949

You must meet with Kim Il Sung as soon as possible and try to illuminate from him the following additional questions:

1. How do they evaluate the South Korean army, [its] numbers, arms and fighting capacity?

2. The condition of the partisan movement in the south of Korea and what real help they think they will receive from the partisans.

3. How do the society and people regard the fact that northerners will be the first to begin an attack? What kind of real aid can be given by the population of the south to the army of the north?

4. Are there American troops in the south of Korea? What kind of measures, in the opinion of Kim Il Sung, can the Americans take in case of an attack by the northerners?

5. How do the northerners evaluate their possibilities, i.e., the condition of the army. Its supplies and fighting capacity?

6. Give your evaluation of the situation and of how real and advisable is the proposal of our friends.

Document 3
CIPHERED TELEGRAM FROM TUNKIN TO SOVIET
FOREIGN MINISTRY (IN REPLY TO TELEGRAM OF
SEPTEMBER 11), SEPTEMBER 14, 1949

Kim thinks they should not count on substantial help from the partisans, but Pak Honyong [Foreign Minister of the Democratic People's Republic of Korea] has a different opinion. He thinks the help [from partisans] will be significant. At any rate, they hope that the partisans will help in actions against the communications of the enemy and that they will occupy the main ports of South Korea, though they will not be able to do this at the beginning of the campaign.

3. With regard to the question of how the population will regard the fact that the northerners will begin a civil war, Kim Il Sung oscillates. During the conversation on September 12 he definitely stated that if the northerners begin military actions, this will produce a negative impression in the people and that it is politically disadvantageous to them to begin it. In connection with this he recollected that during the conversation between Mao Zedong and the Korean representative Kim Il [Chief of the Political Administration of the North Korean Army] in the spring of this year Mao stated that in his

opinion the northerners should not begin military action now, since in the first place, it is politically disadvantageous and in the second place, the Chinese friends are occupied at home and cannot give them serious help. The thinking of Kim Il Sung amounts to waiting until the conclusion of the main [military] operation in China.

In the conversation on September 13 Kim Il Sung . . . declared that the people will welcome an armed attack by the northerners and that if they begin military actions they will not lose politically because of this. Later in the course of the conversation Kim Il Sung stated that if a civil war is drawn out, then they will be in a politically disadvantageous position. And since under present conditions it is impossible to count on a rapid victory, he does not propose to begin a civil war, but only to secure the Ongjin peninsula and a portion of the territory of South Korea to the east of this peninsula. . . .

They consider that in case of a civil war the population of South Korea will be sympathetic toward the northern army and will help it. In the case of successful military actions they hope to organize a number of uprisings in South Korea.

4. According to official data, there are 500 American military advisers and instructors in South Korea. According to secret service information, which needs confirmation, there are 900 American military advisers and instructors and 1500 soldiers and security officers in South Korea. In case of a civil war in Korea, the Americans, in the opinion of Kim Il Sung and Pak Honyong, can: send Japanese and Chinese [soldiers] to the aid of the southerners; support [the South Koreans] from the sea and air with their own means; American instructors will take immediate part in organizing military actions.

5. The North Korean army numbers 97,500 men (including the air force and coastal defense units). The army has 64 tanks, 59 armored cars, 75 airplanes. The police force in the north numbers 23,200 men. Kim considers that the northern army is superior to the southern army in its technical equipment (tanks, artillery, planes), its discipline, the training of the officers and troops and also its moral-political relations.

In the northern army there are a number of insufficiencies: insufficient number and weak preparation of pilots, insufficient number of ships, large caliber arms are unprepared for military operations, insufficient military supplies.

The proposal of Kim Il Sung amounts to the following: at the beginning to strike the South Korean Army on the Ongjin peninsula, to destroy the two regiments located there, to occupy the territory of the peninsula and the territory to the east of it . . . and then to see what to do further. After this blow, the

South Korean army may have become demoralized. In this case move further to the south. If the South Korean army is not demoralized as a result of the Ongjin operation, to seal the borders seized, to shorten in that way the line of defense approximately by one third.

It is not possible to hurry with the operation on the Ongjin peninsula. [It is necessary] to wait until additional arms arrive from the Soviet Union. Meanwhile [we must] consolidate the defenses on the remaining portions of the 38th parallel.

Kim Il Sung admits the possibility of the Ongjin operation turning into a civil war, but he hopes that this does not happen, since the southerners, in his opinion, do not dare to attack other portions of the 38th parallel.

Our formulations.

The partial operation outlined by Kim Il Sung can and will probably turn into a civil war between north and south. There are more than a few supporters of civil war in the leading circles of both the north and the south. Therefore, in beginning this partial operation it is necessary to calculate that it might be the beginning of a civil war. Is it advisable to the north to begin a civil war now? We propose that this is not advisable.

The northern army is insufficiently strong to carry out successful and rapid operations against the south. Even taking into account the help which will be rendered to the northern army by the partisans and the population of South Korea, it is impossible to count on a rapid victory. Moreover, a drawn out civil war is disadvantageous for the north both militarily and politically. In the first place, a drawn out war gives the possibility to the Americans to render corresponding aid to Syngmann [sic] Rhee. After their lack of success in China, the Americans probably will intervene in Korean affairs more decisively than they did in China and, it goes without saying, apply all their strength to save Syngmann [sic] Rhee. Further, in case of a drawn out civil war the military casualties, suffering and adversity may elicit in the population a negative mood toward the one that began the war.

Moreover, a drawn out war in Korea could be used by the Americans for purposes of agitation against the Soviet Union and for further inflaming war hysteria. Therefore, it is inadvisable that the north begin a civil war now. Given the present internal and external situation a decision about an attack on the South would be correct only in such cases as the northerners could count on ending the war quickly; the preconditions for it are not there.

But if the indicated partial operations were crowned with success and did not lead to civil war, then in this case the northerners, while having won strategically, would lose politically in many regards. Such an operation would be used to accuse the northerners of trying to inflame a fratricidal war. It would also be used for the purpose of further increasing American and international interference in Korean affairs in the interests of the south.

We propose that under the indicated conditions to begin the partial operation conceived by Kim Il Sung is advisable.

Document 4
POLITBURO DECISION TO CONFIRM THE FOLLOWING DIRECTIVE TO THE SOVIET AMBASSADOR IN KOREA, SEPTEMBER 24, 1949

Commission Comrade Shtykov to meet with Kim Il Sung and Pak Hon-yong and, strictly adhering to the text given below, to declare the following:

In connection with the questions raised by you in conversations with me on August 12 of this year, I received an order to transmit to you the opinion of Moscow on the question touched on by you. . . .

From the military side it is impossible to consider that the People's Army is prepared for such an attack. If not prepared for in the necessary manner, the attack can turn into a prolonged military operation, which not only will not lead to the defeat of the enemy but will also create significant political and economic difficulties for North Korea, which, finally, cannot be permitted. Since at present North Korea does not have the necessary superiority of military forces in comparison with South Korea, it is impossible to acknowledge that a military attack on the south is now completely prepared for and therefore from the military point of view it is not allowed.

From the political side, a military attack on the south by you is also not prepared for. We, of course, agree with you that the people are waiting for the unification of the country and in the south they, moreover, are waiting for liberation from the yoke of the reactionary regime. However, until now very little has been done to raise the broad masses of South Koreans to an active struggle, to develop the partisan movement in all of South Korea, to create there liberated regions and to organize forces for a general uprising. . . .

As concerns a partial operation to seize Ongjin peninsula and the region of Kaesong, as a result of which the borders of North Korea would be moved almost to Seoul itself, it is impossible to view this operation other than as the beginning of a war between North and South Korea, for which North Korea is not prepared either militarily or politically, as has been indicated above.

Moreover, it is necessary to consider that if military actions begin at the initiative of the North and acquire a prolonged character, then this can give to the Americans cause for any kind of interference in Korean affairs.

In view of all that has been stated it is necessary to acknowledge that at the present the tasks of the struggle for the unification of Korea demand a concentration of a maximum effort, in the first place, to the development of the partisan movement, the creation of liberated regions and the preparation of a general armed uprising in South Korea in order to overthrow the reactionary regime and successfully resolve the task of unifying all Korea, and secondly, to further strengthen in every way the Peoples' Army of Korea.

Document 5
CIPHERED TELEGRAM FROM SHTYKOV TO VISHINSKY, JANUARY 19, 1950

Strictly secret, I report about the frame of mind expressed by Kim Il Sung during a luncheon at the Ministry of Foreign Affairs of the DPRK. On January 17, the minister of foreign affairs of the DPRK Pak Hon-yong held a lunch attended by a small circle of persons, on the occasion of the departure of the Korean ambassador Yi Chu-Yon to the Chinese Peoples Republic. At the luncheon from the Korean side were Kim Tubong, Kim Il Sung, Pak Hon-yong, deputy minister of foreign affairs Pak Chong-jo, [and] Yi Chu-Yon. The trade representative of the PRC Vyn Shi Chzhen attended the luncheon. On our side in attendance were myself and the advisers of the embassy, Ignatiev and Pelishenko. The luncheon took place in a friendly, warm atmosphere. . . .

During the luncheon Kim Il Sung and the Chinese trade representative, who was sitting next to him, many times enthusiastically conversed with each other in Chinese. From individual phrases it was possible to understand that they were speaking about the victory in China and about the situation in Korea. After the luncheon, in the reception room Kim Il Sung gave advice and orders to his ambassador to China Yi Chu-Yon about his work in China, and moreover, while speaking in Korean, Kim several times said phrases in Russian about how Yi would act boldly in China, since Mao Zedong is his friend and will always help Korea.

Then, after Yi Chu-Yon left, Kim, addressing the advisers Ignatiev and Pelishenko in an excited manner, began to speak about how now, when China is completing its liberation, the liberation of the Korean people in the south of the country is next in line. In connection with this he said:

"The people of the southern portion of Korea trust me and rely on our armed might. Partisans will not decide the question. The people of the south know that we have a good army. Lately I do not sleep at night, thinking about how to resolve the question of the unification of the whole country. If the matter of the liberation of the people of the southern portion of Korea and the unification of the country is drawn out, then I can lose the trust of the people of Korea." Further Kim stated that when he was in Moscow, Comrade Stalin said to him that it was not necessary to attack the south, in case of an attack on the north of the country by the army of Rhee Syngmann [*sic*], then it is possible to go on the counteroffensive to the south of Korea. But since Rhee Syngmann [*sic*] is still not instigating an attack, it means that the liberation of the people of the southern part of the country and the unification of the country are being drawn out, that he (Kim Il Sung) thinks that he needs again to visit Comrade Stalin and receive an order and permission for offensive action by the People's Army for the purpose of the liberation of the people of Southern Korea. Further Kim said that he himself cannot begin an attack, because he is a communist, a disciplined person and for him the order of Comrade Stalin is law. Then he stated that if it is now possible to meet with Comrade Stalin, then he will try to meet with Mao Zedong, after his return from Moscow. Kim underscored that Mao Zedong promised to render him assistance after the conclusion of the war in China . (Apparently Kim Il Sung has in mind the conversation of his representative Kim Il with Mao Zedong in June 1949, about which I reported by ciphered telegram.) Kim said that he also has other questions for Mao Zedong, in particular the question of the possibility of the creation of an eastern bureau of the Cominform. He further stated that on all these questions, he will try to meet with Comrade Shtykov and to secure through him a meeting with Comrade Stalin.

The advisers of the embassy Ignatiev and Pelishenko, avoiding discussing these questions, tried to switch the discussion to a general theme, then Kim Il-Sung came toward me, took me aside and began the following conversation: can he meet with Comrade Stalin and discuss the question of the position in the south and the question of aggressive actions against the army of Rhee Syngmann, [since the] people's army now is significantly stronger than the army of Rhee Syngmann. Here he stated that if it is impossible to meet with Comrade Stalin, then he wants to meet with Mao Zedong, since Mao after his visit to Moscow will have orders on all questions.

Then Kim Il Sung placed before me the question, why don't I allow him to attack Ongjin peninsula, which the People's Army could take in three days, and with a general attack the People's Army could be in Seoul in several days.

I answered Kim that he has not raised the question of a meeting with Comrade Stalin and if he raises such a question, then it is possible that Comrade Stalin will receive him. On the question of an attack on the Ongjin peninsula I answered him that it is impossible to do this. Then I tried to conclude the conversation on these questions and, alluding to a later time, proposed to go home. With that the conversation was concluded.

Document 6
CIPHERED TELEGRAM FROM STALIN TO SHTYKOV, JANUARY 30, 1950

1. I received your report. I understand the dissatisfaction of Kim Il Sung, but he must understand that such a large matter in regard to South Korea such as he wants to undertake needs large preparation. The matter must be organized so that there would not be too great a risk. If he wants to discuss this matter with me, then I will always be ready to receive him and discuss with him. Transmit all this to Kim Il Sung and tell him that I am ready to help him in this matter.

2. I have a request for Comrade Kim Il Sung. The Soviet Union is experiencing a great insufficiency in lead. We would like to receive from Korea a yearly minimum of 25,000 tons of lead. Korea would render us a great assistance if it could yearly send to the Soviet Union the indicated amount of lead. I hope that Kim Il Sung will not refuse us in this. It is possible that Kim Il Sung needs our technical assistance and some number of Soviet specialists. We are ready to render this assistance. Transmit this request of mine to comrade Kim Il Sung and ask him for me, to communicate to me his consideration on this matter.

Source: Reprinted from Kathryn Weathersby, "Korea, 1949–1950: To Attack or Not to Attack: Stalin, Kim Il Sung, and the Prelude to War," in Woodrow Wilson International Center for Scholars, *Cold War International History Project Bulletin*, Issue 5 (Spring 1995): 4–9

Many historians believe that Secretary of State Dean Acheson's failure, in a speech he gave at the National Press Club on January 12, 1950, to include Korea within the U.S. defense perimeter in the Far East, was a signal to North Korea that it could invade South Korea without fear of an American military response. But as Acheson later stated in defending his remarks, he made clear in his address that the United States had a "direct responsibility" for safeguarding Korea from communist aggression. He was more concerned, however, about internal subversion than about an attack by North Korea. He also thought that the United States could best contribute to South Korea's security through a program of military assistance rather than through the stationing of American forces in Korea. For that reason, he vigorously opposed efforts on Capitol Hill to cut off aid to Korea. Indeed, the secretary carefully distinguished in his address between the northern and southern parts of East Asia, making clear that the United States had a much greater role to play in the northern region, which included Korea, than in the southern part. Acheson's lengthy speech is also interesting because of its harsh remarks about the former government in China of

Chiang Kai-shek and because it provides considerable insight into the Truman administration's Asian policy at the beginning of 1950, shortly after the communists had won the civil war in China and six months before the North Korean invasion of South Korea.

Document 7
CRISIS IN ASIA—AN EXAMINATION OF U.S. POLICY: REMARKS BY SECRETARY OF STATE DEAN ACHESON AT THE NATIONAL PRESS CLUB, JANUARY 12, 1950

This afternoon I should like to discuss with you the relations between the peoples of the United States and the peoples of Asia, and I used the word "relations of the peoples of the United States and the peoples of Asia" advisedly. I am not talking about governments or nations because it seems to me what I want to discuss with you is this feeling of mine that the relations depend upon the attitudes of the people; that there are fundamental attitudes, fundamental interests, fundamental purposes of the people of the United States, 150 million of them, and of the peoples of Asia, unnumbered millions, which determine and out of which grow the relations of our countries and the policies of our governments. Out of these attitudes and interests and purposes grow what we do from day to day. . . .

Now let's consider some of the basic factors which go into the making of the attitudes of the peoples on both sides. I am frequently asked: Has the State Department got an Asian policy? And it seems to me that that discloses such a depth of ignorance that it is very hard to begin to deal with it. The peoples of Asia are so incredibly diverse that how could anyone, even the most utter charlatan[,] believe that he had a uniform policy which would deal with all of them. On the other hand, there are very important similarities in ideas and in problems among the peoples of Asia and so what we come to, after we understand these diversities and these common attitudes of mind, is the fact that there must be certain similarities of approach, and there must be very great dissimilarities in action. . . .

Let's come now to the matters which Asia has in common. There is in this vast area what we might call a developing Asian consciousness and a developing pattern, and this, I think, is based upon two factors which are pretty nearly common to the entire experience of all these Asian people.

One of these factors is a revulsion against the acceptance of misery and poverty as the normal condition of life. Throughout all of this vast area, you have that fundamental revolutionary aspect in mind and belief. The other common aspect that they have is revulsion against foreign domination. Whether that foreign domination takes the form of colonialism or whether it takes the form of imperialism, they are through with it. They have had enough of it, and they want no more.

These two basic ideas which are held so broadly and commonly in Asia tend to fuse in the minds of many Asian peoples and many of them tend to believe that if you could get rid of foreign domination, if you could gain independence, then the relief from poverty and misery would follow almost in course. It is easy to point out that that is not true, and of course, they are discovering that it is not true. But underneath that belief, there was a very profound understanding of a basic truth and it is the basic truth which underlies all our democratic belief and all our democratic concept. The truth is that just as no man and no government is wise enough or disinterested enough to direct the thinking and the action of another individual, so no nation and no people are wise enough and disinterested enough very long to assume the responsibility for another people or to control another people's opportunities.

The great truth they have sensed and on that great truth they are acting. They say and they believe that from now on they are on their own. They will make their own decisions. . . .

. . . Resignation is no longer the typical emotion of Asia. It has given way to hope, to a sense of effort, and in many cases, to a real sense of anger.

Now, may I suggest to you that much of the bewilderment which has seized the minds of many of us about recent developments in China comes from a failure to understand this basic revolutionary force which is loose in Asia. The reasons for the fall of the Nationalist Government in China are preoccupying many people. All sorts of reasons have been attributed to it. Most commonly, it is said in various speeches and publications that it is the result of American bungling, that we are incompetent, that we did not understand that American aid was too little, that we did the wrong thing at the wrong time.

Nobody, I think, says that the Nationalist Government fell because it was confronted by overwhelming military force which it could not resist. Certainly no one in his right mind suggests that. . . .

The broad picture is that after the war, Chiang Kai-shek emerged as the undisputed leader of the Chinese people. Only one faction, the Communists, up in the hills, ill-equipped, ragged, a very small military force, was determinedly opposed to his position. He had overwhelming military power, greater military power than any ruler had ever had in the entire history of China. He had tremendous economic and military support and backing from the United States. He had the acceptance of all other foreign countries. . . . Here he was in this position, and 4 years later what do we find? We find that his armies have melted away. His support largely outside the country has melted away, and he is a refugee on a small island off the coast of China with the remnants of his forces.

As I said, no one says that vast armies moved out of the hills and defeated him. To attribute this to the inadequacy of American aid is only to point out the depth and power of the forces which were miscalculated or ignored. What has happened in my judgment is that the almost inexhaustible patience of the Chinese people in their misery ended. They did not bother to over-throw his government. There was really nothing to overthrow. They simply ignored it throughout the country. They took the solution of their immediate village problems into their own hands. . . .

The Communists did not create this. The Communists did not create this condition. They did not create this revolutionary spirit. They did not create a great force which moved out from under Chiang Kai-shek. But they were shrewd and cunning to mount it, to ride this thing into victory and into power.

That, I suggest to you, is an explanation which has certain roots in realism and which does not require all this examination of intricate and perhaps ir-relevant details. So much for the attitude of the peoples of Asia.

Let's consider for a moment another important factor in this relationship. That is the attitude of our own people to Asia. What is that fundamental atti-tude out of which our policy has grown? What is the history of it? Because history is very important, and history furnishes the belief on the one side in the reality and truth of the attitude.

What has our attitude been toward the peoples of Asia? It has been, I sub-mit to you, that we are interested in the peoples of Asia. We are not interested in them as pawns or as subjects for exploitation but just as people. . . .

Through all this period of time also, we had and still have great interest in Asia. But let me point out to you one very important factor about our inter-ests in Asia. That is that our interests have been parallel to the interests of the people of Asia. For 50 years, it has been the fundamental belief of the Ameri-can people—and I am not talking about announcements of a government but I mean a belief of people in little towns and villages and churches and mis-sionary forces and labor unions throughout the United States—it has been their profound belief that the control of China by a foreign power was con-trary to American interests. And so from the time of the announcement of the open door policy through the 9-power treaty to the very latest resolution of the General Assembly of the United Nations, we have stated that principle and we believe it. And similarly in all the rest of Asia—in the Philippines, in India, in Pakistan and Indonesia, and in Korea—for years and years and years, the interests of Americans throughout this country have been in favor of independence. . . .

Now, I stress this, which you may think is a platitude, because of a very important fact: I hear almost every day someone say that the real interest of the United States is to stop the spread of communism. Nothing seems to me to put the cart before the horse more completely than that. Of course we are interested in stopping the spread of communism. But we are interested for a far deeper reason than any conflict between the Soviet Union and the United States. We are interested in stopping the spread of communism because communism is a doctrine that we don't happen to like. Communism is the most subtle instrument of Soviet foreign policy that has ever been devised, and it is really the spearhead of Russian imperialism. . . .

Now, it is fortunate that this point that I made does not represent any real conflict. It is an important point because people will do more damage and create more misrepresentation in the Far East by saying our interest is merely to stop the spread of communism than any other way. Our real interest is in those people as people. It is because communism is hostile to that interest that we want to stop it. . . .

It is important to take this attitude not as a mere negative reaction to communism but as the most positive affirmation of the most affirmative truth that we hold, which is in the dignity and right of every nation, of every people, and of every individual to develop in their own way, making their own mistakes, reaching their own triumphs but acting under their own responsibility. That is what we are pressing for in the Far East, and that is what we must affirm and not get mixed up with purely negative and inconsequential statements.

Now let me come to another underlying and important factor which determines our relations and, in turn, our policy with the peoples of Asia. That is the attitude of the Soviet Union toward Asia, and particularly toward those parts of Asia which are contiguous to the Soviet Union, and with great particularity this afternoon, to north China.

The attitude and interest of the Russians in north China, and in these other areas as well, long antedates communism. This is not something that has come out of communism at all. . . . But the Communist regime has added new methods, new skills, and new concepts to the thrust of Russian imperialism. This Communistic concept and techniques have armed Russian imperialism with a new and most insidious weapon of penetration. Armed with these new powers, what is happening in China is that the Soviet Union is detaching the northern provinces [areas] of China from China and is attaching them to the Soviet Union. This process is complete in outer Mongolia. It is nearly complete in Manchuria, and I am sure that in inner Mongolia and in Sinkiang there are very happy reports coming from Soviet agents in Moscow. This is what is going on. . . .

What does that mean for us? It means something very, very significant. It means that nothing that we do and nothing that we say must be allowed to obscure the reality of this fact. All the efforts of propaganda will not be able to obscure it. The only thing that can obscure it is the folly of ill-conceived adventures on our part which easily could do so, and I urge all who are thinking about these foolish adventures to remember that we must not seize the unenviable position which the Russians have carved out for themselves. We must not undertake to deflect from the Russians to ourselves the righteous anger, and the wrath and the hatred of the Chinese people which must develop. It would be folly to deflect it to ourselves. We must take the position we have always taken—that anyone who violates the integrity of China is the enemy of China and is acting contrary to our own interest. . . .

Now, let's in the light of that consider some of these policies. First of all, let's deal with the question of military security. I deal with it first because it is important and because, having stated our policy in that regard, we must clearly understand that the military menace is not the most immediate.

What is the situation in regard to the military security of the Pacific area, and what is our policy in regard to it?

In the first place, the defeat and the disarmament of Japan has placed upon the United States the necessity of assuming its military defense of Japan so long as that is required, both in the interest of our security and in the interests of the security of the entire Pacific area and, in all honor, in the interest of Japanese security. . . . I can assure you that there is no intention of any sort of abandoning or weakening the defenses of Japan and that whatever arrangements are to be made either through permanent settlement or otherwise, that defense must and shall be maintained.

This defensive perimeter runs along the Aleutians to Japan and then goes to the Ryukyus. We hold important defense positions in the Ryukyu Islands, and those we will continue to hold. In the interest of the population of the Ryukyu Islands, we will at an appropriate time offer to hold these islands under trusteeships of the United Nations. But they are essential parts of the defensive perimeter of the Pacific, and they must and will be held.

The defensive perimeter runs from the Ryukyus to the Philippine Islands. Our relations, our defensive relations with the Philippines are contained in agreements between us. Those agreements are being loyally carried out and will be loyally carried out. Both peoples have learned by bitter experience the vital connections between our mutual defense requirements. We are in no doubt about that, and it is hardly necessary for me to say an attack on the

Philippines could not and would not be tolerated by the United States. But I hasten to add that no one perceives the imminence of any such attack.

So far as the military security of other areas in the Pacific is concerned, it must be clear that no person can guarantee these areas against military attack. But it must also be clear that such a guarantee is hardly sensible or necessary within the realm of practical relationship.

Should such an attack occur—one hesitates to say where such an armed attack could come from—the initial reliance must be on the people attacked to resist it and then upon the commitments of the entire civilized world under the Charter of the United Nations which so far has not proved a weak reed to lean on by any people who are determined to protect their independence against outside aggression. But it is a mistake, I think, in considering Pacific and Far Eastern problems to become obsessed with military considerations. Important as they are, there are other problems that press, and these other problems are not capable of solution through military means. These other problems arise out of the susceptibility of many areas, and many countries in the Pacific area, to subversion and penetration. That cannot be stopped by military means. . . .

Here, then, are the problems in these other areas which require some policy on our part, and I should like to point out two facts to you and then discuss in more detail some of these areas.

The first fact is the great difference between our responsibility and our opportunities in the northern part of the Pacific area and in the southern part of the Pacific area. In the northern, we have direct opportunity to act. The same thing to a lesser degree is true in Korea. There we had direct responsibility, and there we did act, and there we have a greater opportunity to be effective than we have in the more southerly part.

In the southerly part of the area, we are one of the many nations who can do no more than help. The direct responsibility lies with the peoples concerned. . . .

In Korea, we have taken great steps which have ended our military occupation, and in cooperation with the United Nations, we have established an independent and sovereign country recognized by nearly all the rest of the world. We have given that nation great help in getting itself established. We are asking the Congress to continue that help until it is firmly established, and that legislation is now pending before the Congress. The idea that we should scrap all of that, that we should stop half way through the achievement of the establishment of this country, seems to me to be the most utter defeatism and utter madness in our interests in Asia. . . .

So after this survey, what we conclude, I believe, is that there is a new day which has dawned in Asia. It is a day in which the Asian peoples are on their own, and know it, and intend to continue on their own. It is a day in which the old relationships between east and west are gone, relationships which at their worst were exploitation, and which at their best were paternalism. That relationship is over, and the relationship of east and west must now be in the Far East one of mutual respect and mutual helpfulness. We are their friends. Others are their friends. We and those others are willing to help, but we can help only where we are wanted and only where the conditions of help are really sensible and possible. So what we can see is that this new day in Asia, this new day which is dawning, may go on to a glorious noon or it may darken and it may drizzle out. But that decision lies within the countries of Asia and within the power of the Asian people. It is not a decision which a friend or even an enemy from the outside can decide for them.

Source: Department of State, *Bulletin* 22 (January 23, 1950), 111–18.

> Despite the United States's avowed support for the government of South Korea, in the months prior to outbreak of hostilities in Korea, the Truman administration continued to fear that inflation and suppression of legitimate opposition to the authoritarian rule of President Syngman Rhee might lead to the overthrow of his government by communist and other leftist forces. In April, Secretary of State Dean Acheson spelled out these concerns in an aide-mémoire that he presented to Korea's ambassador to the United States, Dr. John M. Chang, as he was about to embark for Seoul. The harsh tone of the aide-mémoire and the threat to cut back economic assistance to South Korea, coupled with the recall of the American ambassador in Seoul, John Muccio, infuriated Rhee, who released the document to the public even before it was released to the American press on April 7. However, the aide-mémoire did succeed in preventing the South Korean leader from postponing elections from May to November as he originally had planned.

Document 8
THE SECRETARY OF STATE TO THE KOREAN AMBASSADOR [DR. JOHN M. CHANG]: AIDE-MÉMOIRE, APRIL 3, 1950

The Secretary of State wishes to take this opportunity to express to His Excellency, the Ambassador of the Republic of Korea, prior to the latter's return to Seoul, the deep concern of this Government over the mounting inflation in Korea. The Secretary of State wishes his Excellency to convey to the

President of the Republic of Korea the view of this Government that the communication of March 4, 1950, from the Korean Prime Minister to the Chief of the Economic Cooperation Mission in Korea, in which the view was expressed that there is no serious problem of inflation in Korea, but rather a threat of deflation, indicates a lack of comprehension on the part of the Korean Government of the seriousness of the problem and an unwillingness to take the drastic measures required to curb the growing inflation.

It is the judgment of this Government that the financial situation in Korea has already reached critical proportions and that, unless this progressive inflation is curbed in the none too distant future, it cannot but seriously impair Korea's ability to utilize effectively the economic assistance provided by the Economic Cooperation Administration. Government expenditures have been vastly expanded by bank overdrafts without reference to limits set by an approved budget. Tax collections have not been increased, aid goods have been under-priced, and governmental subsidies have been expanded. The dangerous practice of voluntary contributions has been used as an inefficient substitute for a sound taxation system. These uneconomic practices have, in turn, served to expand the currency in circulation, unbalance the Korean national budget, and cause a sharp rise in wholesale and retail prices, thereby strengthening the growing forces of inflation.

The Secretary of State must inform His Excellency that, unless the Korean government is able to take satisfactory and effective measures to counter these inflationary forces, it will be necessary to reexamine, and perhaps to make adjustments in, the Economic Cooperation Administration's assistance program in Korea.

The Secretary of State wishes to inform his Excellency in this connection that the American Ambassador in Seoul is being recalled for consultation within the next few days regarding the critical problems arising out of the growing inflation in Korea.

Of equal concern to this Government, are the reported intentions of the Korean Government, as proposed by the President of the Republic of Korea in a message to the National Assembly on March 31, to postpone the general elections from the coming May until sometime in November. The Secretary of State wishes to draw to His Excellency's attention the fact that United States aid, both military and economic, to the Republic of Korea has been predicated upon the existence and growth of democratic institutions within the Republic. Free, popular elections, in accordance with the constitution and other basic laws of the Republic, are the foundation of those democratic institutions. The holding of the elections as scheduled and provided for by the basic laws of the Republic appears to this Government as equally urgent with the taking of necessary measures for the countering of the inflationary forces already discussed.

Source: *Foreign Relations of the United States: 1950.* Volume VII. *Korea* (Washington, DC: Government Printing Office, 1976): 43–44.

In addition to inflation and the repressive nature of the Rhee government, the United States was increasingly worried in the months prior to June about the infiltration of guerrilla forces from North Korea, as the following document indicates. In fact, though, guerrilla activity and clashes along the 38th parallel actually decreased prior to the North Korean invasion of South Korea.

Document 9
THE CHARGÉ IN KOREA [EVERETT DRUMRIGHT] TO THE SECRETARY OF STATE, APRIL 25, 1950

CONFIDENTIAL

During last weekend Korean Army units broke up organized resistance of remaining band of North Korean Guerrillas, numbering more than 600, who had penetrated into Odae Mountain area of Kangwon Province on or about March 25. On April 21 and 22, 70 guerrillas were killed including leader Kim Mu Hyon, 24 captured. Total result of operations against Kim Mu Hyon group, which lasted intermittently for more than three weeks, were 237 killed, 47 captured, and 172 small arms, 12 automatic weapons and 3 mortars seized. Kim Mu Hyon guerrillas were best trained and equipped Korean Army has yet faced. Fierceness of battles which took place in very rugged country, attested by fact Korean Army had 57 killed, 164 wounded and 5 missing. Other large band which had simultaneously crossed parallel in area west of Kangnung was routed and virtually destroyed first week in April. Of more than 600 guerrillas who came across in total operation, it estimated not more than 50–75 remain and these are now scattered in small groups.

It is perhaps significant these guerrillas had been systematically trained for a year, first at Kangdong Academy and later at other centers. They were far and away best equipped guerrillas yet to come south. It seems clear their mission was to join other guerrillas in north Kyongsang with aim of setting up "liberated area." Communist hopes in this direction have, of course, been utterly dashed.

6th and 8th divisions of KA gave very good account of themselves in these operations, especially 8th, which acted with dispatch and efficiency and with small cost to own forces. Leadership of 6th, especially 8th Regi-

ment, was weak and lacked aggressiveness until past week when new colonel was brought to assume overall command.

It is understood another force of 500 guerrillas remains just north of parallel in same area. Thus far they have made no effort to come south. With loss
during past three weeks of about 500 men and several hundred weapons,
North Koreans may be loath to commit more men and equipment to such
adventures.

Drumright

Source: Foreign Relations of the United States: 1950. Volume VII. Korea (Washington, DC:
Government Printing Office, 1976), 47–48.

> Although the North Korean invasion of South Korea almost assured an
> American response, President Truman's first reaction to the invasion,
> the news of which he received from Secretary of State Dean Acheson
> while in his home in Independence, Missouri, was to ask for an emer-
> gency meeting of the United Nations Security Council. The Security
> Council approved an American resolution condemning the invasion
> and calling for a cessation of hostilities. As the situation in Korea dete-
> riorated, the president returned to Washington, D.C., where he met
> with members of his cabinet, other senior members of his administra-
> tion, and the Joint Chiefs of Staff. On the second day of the fighting, he
> approved recommendations by the State Department and the Penta-
> gon to send supplies and a survey team to Korea. But it was not until the
> third day of fighting, June 27, that he released his first public statement
> on the war. In it, he committed the United States to contain commu-
> nism throughout Asia. Although it would not be until the sixth day of
> fighting on June 30 that the president actually approved sending Ameri-
> can military forces in Japan to Korea, the president's statement of June
> 27 marked a real turning point in the Cold War. Having already commit-
> ted the United States to contain communism in western Europe, he
> was, in effect, committing the nation to contain communist expansion
> globally.

Document 10
STATEMENT BY PRESIDENT HARRY S TRUMAN ON THE OUTBREAK OF THE KOREAN CONFLICT, JUNE 27, 1950

In Korea, the Government forces, which were armed to prevent border
raids and to preserve internal security, were attacked by invading forces from
North Korea. The Security Council of the United Nations called upon the invading troops to cease hostilities and to withdraw to the thirty-eighth parallel. This they have not done but, on the contrary, have pressed the attack. The

Security Council called upon all members of the United Nations to render every assistance to the United Nations in the execution of this resolution. In these circumstances I have ordered United States air and sea forces to give the Korean Government troops cover and support.

The attack upon Korea makes it plain beyond all doubt that communism has passed beyond the use of subversion to conquer independent nations and will now use armed invasion and war. It has defied the orders of the Security Council of the United Nations issued to preserve peace and security. In these circumstances the occupation of Formosa by Communist forces would be a direct threat to the security of the Pacific area and to United States forces performing their lawful and necessary functions in that area.

Accordingly, I have ordered the Seventh Fleet to prevent any attack on Formosa. As a corollary of this action, I am calling upon the Chinese Government on Formosa to cease all air and sea operations against the mainland. The Seventh Fleet will see that this is done. The determination of the future status of Formosa must await the restoration of security in the Pacific, a peace settlement with Japan, or consideration by the United Nations.

I have also directed that United States forces in the Philippines be strengthened and that military assistance to the Philippine Government be accelerated.

I have similarly directed acceleration in the furnishing of military assistance to the forces of France and the associated states in Indochina and the dispatch of a military mission to provide close working relations with those forces.

I know that all members of the United Nations will consider carefully the consequences of this latest aggression in Korea in defiance of the Charter of the United Nations. A return to the rule of force in international affairs would have far-reaching effects. The United States will continue to uphold the rule of law.

I have instructed Ambassador [Warren] Austin, as the representative of the United States to the Security Council, to report these steps to the Council.

Source: Department of State, *Bulletin* 23 (July 3, 1950): 5–6.

> By the middle of August 1950, the military situation in Korea had begun to stabilize. Although driven back to a small perimeter around the city of Pusan in southeast Korea, United Nations forces, under the command of General Douglas MacArthur, were able to hold on to the perimeter, and MacArthur already began planning a surprise amphibious operation to trap North Korean forces. A month earlier, the general had visited Formosa, where he held talks with Generalissimo Chiang Kai-shek. After their discussions, Chiang issued a statement in which he said that his discussions with the UN commander had laid the basis

for Sino-American military cooperation. Annoyed that MacArthur had superseded his authority by going to Formosa and strongly opposed to the use of Nationalist forces in Korea, which could bring the Chinese communists into the war, Truman sent the diplomat Averell Harriman to Tokyo to explain the administration's China policy to MacArthur. In response, MacArthur stated that the purpose of his trip had been misunderstood, but he also suggested that those who opposed the use of Nationalist forces in Korea or attacks against the Chinese mainland from Formosa were guilty of defeatism and military appeasement. Irate, Truman issued an order to MacArthur not to authorize any attacks from Formosa against the mainland. Instead of remaining silent, however, the general responded by sending the message which follows to the annual convention of the Veterans of Foreign Wars (VFW). By virtually repudiating the administration's China policy, it represented the first salvo in what was to grow into a major confrontation between the commander in chief and his five-star general. So angered was the president by MacArthur's message to the VFW that he issued a directive ordering the general to withdraw it immediately, which he did. Truman even gave thought to firing MacArthur but, aware of the backlash against the administration that that would cause, he decided to keep him in command.

Document 11
GENERAL DOUGLAS MacARTHUR'S LETTER TO THE VETERANS OF FOREIGN WARS, AUGUST 17, 1950

Your inspiring message of the 17th has moved me deeply and I trust that you will convey to all my comrades in arms of the Veterans of Foreign Wars assembled on the occasion of our Fifty-first Annual National Encampment my assurance that their confidence and support will give this command much added strength to meet the tests of battle which lie immediately ahead.

Tell them that I am happy to report that their successors in arms now engaging the enemy along our battle lines in South Korea are exemplifying that same high standard of devotion, fortitude, and valor which characterized their own march to victory when they themselves engaged in combat in the field.

From senior commanders down through all ranks, their tactical skill, their invincible determination, and their fighting qualities against a fanatical foe, well trained, expertly directed and heavily armed, have upheld our country's finest traditions.

Toward victory, however difficult the road, they are giving an account of themselves which should make every American heart beat with pride and infinite satisfaction.

In view of misconceptions currently being voiced concerning the relationship of Formosa to our strategic potential in the Pacific, I believe it in the public interest to avail myself of this opportunity to state my views to you, all of whom, having fought overseas, understand broad strategic concepts.

To begin with, any appraisal of that strategic potential requires an appreciation of the changes wrought in the course of the past war. Prior thereto the western strategic frontier of the United States lay in the littoral line of the Americas with an exposed island salient extending out through Hawaii, Midway, and Guam to the Philippines.

The salient was not an outpost of strength but an avenue of weakness along which the enemy could and did attack us. The Pacific was a potential area of advancement for any predatory force intent upon striking at the bordering land areas.

All of this was changed by our Pacific victory. Our strategic frontier then shifted to embrace the entire Pacific Ocean, which has become a vast moat to protect us as long as we hold it.

Indeed, it acts as a protective shield to all of the Americas and all free lands of the Pacific Ocean area we control to the shores of Asia by a chain of islands extending in an arc from the Aleutians to the Marianas held by us and our free Allies. From this island chain we can dominate with air power every Asiatic port from Vladivostok to Singapore and prevent any hostile movement into the Pacific.

Any predatory attack from Asia must be an amphibious effort. No amphibious force can be successful with our control of the sea lanes and the air over these lanes in its avenue of advance. With naval and air supremacy and modern ground elements to defend bases, any major attack from continental Asia toward us or our friends of the Pacific would come to failure.

Under such conditions the Pacific no longer represents menacing avenues of approach for a prospective invader—it assumes instead the friendly aspect of a peaceful lake. Our line of defense is a natural one and can be maintained with a minimum of military effort and expense.

It envisions no attack against anyone nor does it provide the bastions essential for offensive operations, but properly maintained would be an invincible defense against aggression. If we hold this line we may have peace—lose it and war is inevitable.

The geographic location of formosa is such that in the hand of a power unfriendly to the United States it constitutes an enemy salient in the very center of this defensive perimeter, 100 to 150 miles closer to the adjacent friendly segments—Okinawa and the Philippines—than any point in continental Asia.

At the present time there is on Formosa a concentration of operational air and naval bases which is potentially greater than any similar concentration of the Asiatic mainland between the Yellow Sea and the Straits of Malacca. Additional bases can be developed in a relatively short time by an aggressive exploitation of all World War II Japanese facilities.

An enemy force utilizing those installations currently available could increase by 100 percent the air effort which could be directed against Okinawa as compared to operations based on the mainland and at the same time could direct damaging air attacks with fighter-type aircraft against friendly installations in the Philippines, which are currently beyond the range of fighters based on the mainland. Our air supremacy at once would become doubtful.

As a result of its geographical location and base potential, utilization of Formosa by a military power hostile to the United States may either counter-balance or overshadow the strategic importance of the central and southern flank of the United States front line position.

Formosa in the hands of such a hostile power could be compared to an unsinkable aircraft carrier and submarine tender ideally located to accomplish offensive strategy and at the same time checkmate defensive or counter-offensive operations by friendly forces based on Okinawa and the Philippines.

The unsinkable carrier-tender has the capacity to operate from ten to twenty air groups of types ranging from jet fighters to B-29 type bombers as well as to provide forward operating facilities for short-range coastal submarines.

In acquiring this forward submarine base, the efficacy of the short-range submarine would be so enormously increased by the additional radius of activity as to threaten completely sea traffic from the south and interdict all sea lanes in the Western Pacific. Submarine blockade by the enemy with all its destructive ramifications would thereby become a virtual certainty.

Should Formosa fall and bases thereafter come into the hands of a potential enemy of the United States, the latter will have acquired an additional "fleet" which will have been obtained and can be maintained at an incomparably lower cost than could its equivalent in aircraft carriers and submarine tenders.

Current estimates of air and submarine resources in the Far East indicate the capability of such a potential enemy to extend his forces southward and still maintain an imposing degree of military strength for employment elsewhere in the Pacific area.

Historically, Formosa has been used as a springboard for just such military aggression directed against areas to the south. The most notable and recent example was the utilization of it by the Japanese in World War II. At the outbreak of the Pacific War in 1941, it played an important part as a staging area and supporting base for the various Japanese invasion convoys. The supporting air forces of Japan's Army and Navy were based on fields situated along southern Formosa.

From 1942 through 1944 Formosa was a vital link in the transportation and communication chain which stretched from Japan through Okinawa and the Philippines to Southeast Asia. As the United States carrier forces advanced into the Western Pacific, the bases on Formosa assumed an increasingly greater role in the Japanese defense scheme.

Should Formosa fall into the hands of a hostile power, history would repeat itself. Its military potential would again be fully exploited as the means to breach and neutralize our Western Pacific defense system and mount a war of conquest against the free nations of the Pacific basin.

Nothing could be more fallacious than the threadbare argument by those who advocate appeasement and defeatism in the Pacific that if we defend Formosa we alienate continental Asia.

Those who speak thus do not understand the Orient. They do not grant that it is in the pattern of the Oriental psychology to respect and follow aggressive, resolute, and dynamic leadership—to quickly turn on leadership characterized by timidity or vacillation—and they underestimate the Oriental mentality. Nothing in the last five years has so inspired the Far East as the American determination to preserve the bulwarks of our Pacific Ocean strategic position from future encroachment, for few of its people fail accurately to appraise the safeguard such determination brings to their free institutions.

To pursue any other course would be to turn over the fruits of our Pacific victory to a potential enemy. It would shift any future battle area 5,000 miles eastward to the coasts of the American continents, our own home coast; it would completely expose our friends in the Philippines, our friends in Australia and New Zealand, our friends in Indonesia, our friends in Japan, and other areas, to the lustful thrusts of those who stand for slavery against liberty, for atheism as against God.

The decision of President Truman on June 27 lighted into flame a lamp of hope throughout Asia that was burning dimly toward extinction. It marked for the Far East, the focal and turning point in this area's struggle for freedom. It swept aside in one great monumental stroke all of the hypocrisy and the sophistry which has confused and deluded so many people distant from the actual scene.

Source: The Military Situation in the Far East: Hearings before the Committee on Armed Services and the Committee on Foreign Relations, U.S. Senate, 82nd Congress, 1st Session (Washington, DC: Government Printing Office, 1951): 3477–80.

Despite General Douglas MacArthur's withdrawal of his August 17, 1950, message to the Veterans of Foreign Wars, U.S. allies in Korea, most notably Britain, were alarmed by what they believed to be the growing political influence of right-wing elements in the United States and by the provocative talk of some of MacArthur's staunchest supporters, who advocated expanding the war to include communist China. Although London had backed U.S. policy in Korea and agreed to commit British forces to the conflict, it had done so reluctantly. Indeed, it had been disturbed from the beginning of the war about Washington's unwillingness to try to reach some kind of accommodation with the People's Republic of China (PRC), which might have involved recognition of the PRC and its seating at the United Nations in exchange for the end of Korean hostilities. It was greatly concerned that the conflict in Korea was weakening the West's position in Asia and, unless contained, could jeopardize its commercially vital colony of Hong Kong. It also feared the Korean War could conceivably lead to another world war involving the United States and the Soviet Union, much of which would be fought in Europe. Finally, London resented what it regarded as growing American intrusion into what it considered its own sphere of influence in Southeast Asia, and it was displeased by President Harry Truman's decision after hostilities broke out in Korea to extend the U.S. security blanket to protect Formosa against an invasion from the mainland. The following document makes clear the British government's concerns in August 1950 over American policy in Korea and, more generally, Washington's Asian policy. It also represents a succinct statement of Britain's own policy with respect to the region.

Document 12
CABINET REVIEW OF THE INTERNATIONAL SITUATION IN ASIA IN THE LIGHT OF THE KOREAN CONFLICT; "MEMORANDUM BY THE SECRETARY OF STATE FOR FOREIGN AFFAIRS," AUGUST 30, 1950

I am circulating separately for consideration by my colleagues memoranda on Korea and Formosa. In addition, I think it is necessary to review the whole position in Asia in the light of the Korean conflict, and to consider the policy of His Majesty's Government in relation to that part of the world. . . .

2. Since the end of the war, the policy of His Majesty's Government in South and South-East Asia has been to encourage the legitimate aspirations of the peoples of that area for independence. In accordance with this policy independence was given to India, Pakistan, Ceylon and Burma and with the exception of the last-named all these countries chose to remain in the Commonwealth. . . .

That the policy pursued by His Majesty's Government has been the right one there can be no doubt, and our support of nationalism in South and South-East Asia provides the best possible counter to communist subversion and penetration. The relations between the United Kingdom and the Commonwealth and foreign Governments of the area are cordial, and where matters of disagreement arise it can be said that it is possible to discuss these matters in an atmosphere conducive towards their settlement. There is a very strong fund of goodwill towards the United Kingdom in South and South-East Asia which should stand us in good stead.

The United Kingdom's position in the Far East was much weakened as a result of the war. The United States on the other hand, who played the principal part in the defeat of Japan, found themselves in the predominant position. The policy of his Majesty's Government in the Far East immediately after the war was to try to re-establish our commercial position in China and Japan and through the Far Eastern Commission to try to exercise such influence as was possible upon the post-surrender policies for Japan. In Korea the issue was almost entirely between the United States and the Soviet Union as occupying powers, and His Majesty's Government held what was little more than a watching brief.

This comparatively negative policy of the United Kingdom which was dictated by our post-war weakness and our many commitments elsewhere has meant that while on the one hand we were unable to exercise much influence upon the course of events, we were, on the other hand, less immediately involved in the debacle of China and Korea and are therefore to-day to some extent freer than the United States to determine our policy for the future in the Far East. . . .

The United States have tended since the war to regard South and South-East Asia as primarily a British interest . . . . Within the last year, however, the United States, largely owing to the Communist threat, have been disposed to take a closer interest in developments in South-East Asia to the extent of being prepared to give military and economic aid to certain countries within the scope of existing appropriations. It is hoped that they will eventually be prepared to take part in economic development in South and South-East Asia. In general the United States expect the United Kingdom to take the lead, and show a welcome disposition to consult His Majesty's Government before taking any kind of action. This is satisfactory and should be encouraged.

In the Far East, however, the United States have tended to be a law unto themselves since the end of the war, with results which have been far from happy. In Korea, up to the outbreak of the Korean conflict, United States policy had met with no great degree of success, and there is reason to believe that had South

Korea fallen a victim to the North by processes similar to those which over-
threw the existing Governments in Eastern Europe, the United States would
have accepted the fait acompli. In China, the late President Roosevelt's policy of cultivating the friendship of that country failed dismally for the reason
that American support was given to a regime which, through its failure to introduce promised reforms, eventually lost the confidence of the overwhelming majority of the Chinese people. . . . Thus it is true to say that the United
States lack all direction in their policy towards China. . . .

A similar lack of direction is apparent in United States policy towards Japan. Initially the disarmament and demilitarization of Japan was accom-
plished by General MacArthur with efficiency and despatch. But now, five
years after the end of the war with Japan, the United States appear to have no
clear idea as to the direction in which they are going. The Far Eastern Commission is virtually a dead letter, and consultation with other Powers is non-
existent, even though the United States are not entitled to settle the Japanese
problem by themselves. The dangers of such a situation need no emphasis.
Japan is a country of more than 80 million people which cannot be ignored in
the context of Asia. The treatment of Japan will determine whether in the future she is with us or against us. The lack of direction in United States policy
offers no guarantee that the treatment will be of the right kind, and clearly this
is a matter in which friendly Powers should be consulted and consulted soon.
Nor is there any need for the Korean conflict to preclude such consultation. . . .

The immediate reaction of Asian countries (excluding China) to the
North Korean aggression and to the United States intervention, which was
subsequently endorsed by the Security Council, was good as has been demonstrated by the measure of support given to the Security Council resolu-
tions. But second thoughts were induced not only by successive American
defeats in Korea but by the situation created by President Truman's declaration on Formosa. Nothing in United States' Far Eastern policy since the war
has inspired Asian countries with confidence, and the declaration on Formosa has caused both alarm and despondency because of the possibility
which it has created of a conflict between the United States and China, with
all the repercussions upon Asia which would be likely to follow. . . .

There is therefore a distinct possibility that, unless United States policy
towards China, Japan and Korea takes more account of Asian opinion and
Asian susceptibilities, we shall find that Asia is gradually alienated from the
West, which could only be of benefit to the Soviet Union. . . .

Unfortunately United States Far Eastern policy is bedevilled [*sic*] by internal politics. The bi-partisan foreign policy does not effectively extend to
the Far East. For some time past China has been the subject of increasingly

bitter controversy. The Korean conflict has given rise to accusations of unpreparedness and there has developed a tendency to search for scapegoats and to blame the Administrations for the failure of its Far Eastern policy, and to ignore the fact that it is precisely because the Far East has become a party political issue that the Administration's policy has been so negative. . . . The recent clash between President Truman and General MacArthur over the latter's statement on Formosa, which was published in spite of the President's veto, is likely to increase the party political tension. Added to all this is the fact that American public opinion is in a highly emotional state, which is attributable in part to the Korea situation itself and in part to the sense of frustration induced by the feeling that in fighting the North Koreans, Americans are not coming to grips with the real enemy. In such a state of mind the American public is likely to be irrational in its outlook, and unreasonable towards the United Kingdom where our policy diverges from that of the United States. . . .

The problem before us is to seek, at a time when the general atmosphere in the United States is least favourable for such a course, to persuade the United States Administration not to adopt policies in relation to the Far East which will fail to command general support amongst friendly nations and which will antagonise Asia. The immediate issues are those of Korea and Formosa and the question of Chinese representation in the United Nations. . . . [A]s regards Korea, it is essential to try to maintain intact the solidarity which has already been demonstrated by the 53 members of the United Nations Organisation. On China, including Formosa, the United States are likely to be more intractable, and it is on Chinese questions that the greatest difficulties are likely to be experienced in view of the atmosphere in the United States which I have just described. No effort is likely to succeed which, just before elections, has the result that the United States Administration appears to have given way to United Kingdom pressure. . . .

The position is by no means hopeless. For the first time since the war the United States Administration have shown a desire to consult with us on Far Eastern affairs and to give consideration to the views which we express, and they are also showing signs of appreciating the importance of Asian . . . opinion in dealing with these matters. . . .

Though the United States Administration . . . will not change its politics in response to purely British suggestion, it may be willing to modify those policies in response to a majority view in the United Nations Assembly, provided an agreed view emerges as a result of debate and consultations.

I have it in mind, therefore, after the discussions which are going on with the State Department, to try to get them to agree to consult with other Powers, in particular with Commonwealth countries, with France and possibly with some other European countries. If the support of these can be secured, the next step would be to try to get the broad agreement of other friendly members of the United Nations, and thus build up a common front against any manoeuvres of the Soviet Union whose main purpose will be to create a split.

The task will obviously be a difficult one, but it offers the best hope for reconciling United States and Asian opinion and of enabling the Commonwealth to keep in line with the United States. Only by pursuing this course can we hope to avoid open divergence with the United States on China and the related question of Formosa, and the unfortunate consequences which might ensure in the present highly-charged atmosphere in the United States.

I invite my colleagues to endorse the course of action which I propose.

E[rnest] B[evin]

Source: CAB 129/41, Public Records Office, London.

The military conflict in Korea took a major turn following the enormously successful amphibious operation at Inchon on September 15 and the simultaneous breakout of UN forces from the Pusan perimeter. With the North Korean forces retreating above the 38th parallel that divided North Korea from South Korea, the Truman administration was faced with the decision as to whether to have UN forces stop their advance at the 38th parallel, having achieved the military objective of containing communist expansion, or to seize the opportunity to roll back communism by driving North Korean forces all the way back to the Yalu River. In a document dated September 9, 1951, and known as NSC 81/1, the National Security Council had already strongly suggested that, should North Korean troops be forced to retreat from South Korea, UN forces should be allowed, subject to the response from Moscow and Beijing, to move north of the 38th parallel. Although Truman did not give his final approval for a crossing by MacArthur into North Korea until September 27, preliminary approval was given a day earlier in draft instructions transmitted from Secretary of Defense George Marshall to Secretary of State Dean Acheson and contained in the following "top secret" telegram from Acting Secretary of State U. Alexis Johnson to the United States Mission at the United Nations.

Document 13
THE ACTING SECRETARY OF STATE TO THE UNITED STATES MISSION AT THE UNITED NATIONS, SEPTEMBER 26, 1950

For [John] Allison from Johnson. Fol[lowing] is text of draft JCS directive to MacArthur which will be formally transmitted from Secy Defense to

Secy State this afternoon for approval and subsequent transmission to Pres for approval:

1. This directive, based on NSC 81/1, is furnished in order to provide amplifying instructions as to further military actions to be taken by you in Korea. These instructions, however, cannot be considered to be final since they may require modification in accordance with developments. In this connection, you will continue to make special efforts to determine whether there is a Chinese Communist threat to the attainment of your objective, which will be reported to the Joint Chiefs of Staff as a matter of urgency.

2. Your military objective is the destruction of the North Korean armed forces. In attaining this objective you are authorized to conduct military operations, including amphibious and airborne landings at ground operations north of the 38 parallel in Korea provided that at the time of such operation there has been no entry into North Korea by major Soviet or Chinese Communist forces, no announcement of intended entry, nor a threat to counter our operations militarily in North Korea. Under no circumstances, however, will your forces cross the Manchurian or USSR borders of Korea and, as a matter of policy, no non-Korean ground forces will be used in the northeast provinces bordering the Soviet Union or in the area along the Manchurian border. Furthermore, support of your operations north or south of the 38th parallel will not include air or naval action against USSR territory.

3. In the event of the open or covert employment of major Soviet units south of the 38th parallel, you will assume the defense, make no move to aggravate the situation and report to Washington. You should take the same action in the event your forces are operating north of the 38th parallel and major Soviet units are openly employed. You will not discontinue air and naval operations north of the 38th parallel merely because the presence of Soviet or Chinese Communist troops is detected in a target area but if the Soviet Union or the Chinese Communists should announce in advance their intention to reoccupy North Korea and give warning, either explicitly or implicitly, that their forces should not be attacked, you should refer the matter immediately to Washington.

4. In the event of the open or covert employment of major Chinese Communist units south of the 38th parallel, you should continue the action as long as action by your forces offers a reasonable chance of successful resistance.

5. In the event of an attempt to employ small Soviet or Chinese Communist units overtly south of the 38th parallel, you should continue the action.

6. You should immediately make an intensive effort, using all information media available to you, to turn the inevitable bitterness and resentment of the war-victimized Korean people away from the United Nations and to direct it

toward the Korean Communists, the Soviet Union, and depending on the role they play, the Chinese Communists.

7. On the principle that the treatment of POW's shall be directed toward their exploitation, training and use of psychological warfare purposes, you should set up on a pilot-plant scale interrogation, indoctrination and training centers for those POW's now in your hands in Korea.

8. When organized armed resistance by the North Korean forces has been brought substantially to an end, you should direct the Republic of Korea forces to take the lead in disarming remaining North Korean units and enforcing the terms of surrender. Guerrilla activities should be dealt with primarily by the forces of the Republic of Korea, with minimum participating by UN contingents.

9. Circumstances obtaining at the time will determine the character of and the necessity for occupation of North Korea. Your plans for such occupation will be forwarded for approval to the Joint Chiefs of Staff.

10. You will submit your plan for future operations north of the 38th parallel to the Joint Chiefs of Staff for approval.

11. The Joint Chiefs of Staff understand that instructions are now being formulated on the Governmental level regarding:

a. Armistice terms to be offered by you to the North Koreans in the event of sudden collapse of North Korean forces; and

b. Course of action to be followed and activities to be undertaken during the Post-hostilities period.["]

Source: Foreign Relations of the United States. Volume VII. *Korea* (Washington, DC: Government Printing Office, 1976): 781–82.

General Douglas MacArthur's outspoken views on the Far East and his egomaniacal personality continued to be a major problem for the Truman administration and for U.S. relations with its European allies, especially after the rapid advance of UN forces into North Korea following the Inchon invasion. At the same time, public adulation in the United States for the seemingly invincible general was never greater. Anxious in an election year to regain—or, at least, share in—the political spotlight that shone on MacArthur, concerned by an incident involving an air raid against a Soviet airfield sixty-two miles from Korea for which the United States later apologized, wanting to state personally to the general his administration's Asian policy, and never having met MacArthur, President Truman decided to make an 18,000 mile trip to Wake Island in the Far Pacific to confer with his commander. Although the meeting lasted only ninety-six minutes, it was important because it left the president persuaded by MacArthur that UN forces could continue their advance without fear of Soviet or Chinese military intervention, though the meeting did not wholly allay Truman's personal concerns about MacArthur's political judgment and respect for presidential authority.

Document 14
STATEMENT BY THE PRESIDENT ON HIS MEETING WITH GENERAL MacARTHUR AT WAKE ISLAND, OCTOBER 15, 1950

I have met with General of the Army Douglas MacArthur for the purpose of getting firsthand information and ideas from him. I do not wish to take him away from the scene of action in Korea any longer than necessary and, therefore, I came to meet him at Wake. Our conference has been highly satisfactory.

The very complete unanimity of view which prevailed enabled us to finish our discussions rapidly, in order to meet General MacArthur's desire to return at the earliest possible moments. It was apparent that the excellent condition coordination which has existed between Washington and the field, to which General MacArthur paid tribute, greatly facilitated the discussion.

After I had talked with General MacArthur privately, we met together with out advisors. These joint talks were then followed by technical consultations. . . .

Primarily we talked about the problems in Korea which are General MacArthur's most pressing responsibilities. I asked him for information on the military aspects. I got from him a clear picture of the heroism and high capacity of the United Nations forces under his command. We also discussed the steps necessary to bring peace and security to the area as rapidly as possible in accordance with the intent of the resolution of the United Nations General Assembly and in order to get our armed forces out of Korea as soon as their United Nations mission is completed.

We devoted a good deal of time to the major problem of peaceful reconstruction of Korea which the United Nations is facing and to the solution of which we intend to make the best contribution of which the United States is capable. This is a challenging task which must be done properly, if we are to achieve the peaceful goals for which the United Nations has been fighting. The success which has attended the combined military effort must be supplemented by both spiritual and material rehabilitation. It is essentially a task of helping the Koreans to do a better job which they can do for themselves better than anyone else can do it for them. The United Nations can, however, render essential help with supplies and technical advice as well as with the vital problem of rebuilding their educational system.

Meanwhile, I can say I was greatly impressed with what General MacArthur and Ambassador [John] Muccio told me about what has already been done and is now being done to bring order out of chaos and to restore to the Korean people the chance for a good life in peace. . . .

I asked General MacArthur also to explain at first hand his views on the future of Japan with which I was already generally familiar through his written reports. As already announced, we are moving forward with preliminary negotiations for a peace treaty to which Japan is entitled. General MacArthur and I look forward with confidence to a new Japan which will be both peaceful and prosperous.

I also asked General MacArthur to tell me his ideas on the ways in which the United States can most effectively promote its policies of assisting the United Nations to promote and maintain international peace and security throughout the Pacific area.

On all these matters, I have found our talks most helpful, and I am very glad to have had this chance to talk them over with one of America's great soldier-statesmen who is also now serving in the unique position of the first commander in chief of United Nations peace forces. We are fully aware of the dangers which lie ahead but we are confident that we can surmount these dangers with three assets which we have: first, unqualified devotion to peace; second, unity with our fellow peace-loving members of the United Nations; third, our determination and growing strength.

Source: The Military Situation in the Far East: Hearings before the Committee on Armed Services and the Committee on Foreign Relations, U.S. Senate, 82nd Congress, 1st Session (Washington, DC : Government Printing Office, 1951), 3553–58.

The entry of the Chinese communists into the Korean War in full force at the end of November 1950 changed the complexion of the war once more. As UN forces retreated again below the 38th parallel, prophets of gloom and doom could be heard in the United States. A climate of crisis and conspiracy developed throughout the country. Even the White House was shocked by the rapid retreat of UN forces as a result of the Chinese onslaught, especially as it came in the wake of forecasts by General Douglas MacArthur that the war would be over by Christmas. At a news conference on November 30, which was to have international repercussions, including an unplanned visit to the United States by British Prime Minister Clement Attlee to seek assurances that nuclear weapons would not be used in the conflict without London's sanction, President Truman refused to discount the possibility of using atomic weapons against the Chinese. But the European reaction to the president's remarks was so immediately negative that the

White House had to issue a statement the same day, qualifying what Truman had told the press just a few hours earlier.

The president also used his news conference to argue the need to expand and integrate Germany into NATO, to seek increased spending for the military, and to defend General Douglas MacArthur against his European critics. But it was his comments on the atomic bomb that made his meeting with the press so important.

Document 15
THE PRESIDENT'S NEWS CONFERENCE, NOVEMBER 30, 1950

THE PRESIDENT. Good Morning, everybody. Sit down.

I have got a statement I want to read to you. . . .

[Reading] Recent developments in Korea confront the world with a serious crisis. The Chinese Communist leaders have sent their troops from Manchuria to launch a strong and well-organized attack against the United Nations forces in North Korea. This has been done despite prolonged and earnest efforts to bring home to the Communist leaders of China the plain fact that neither the United Nations nor the United States has any aggressive intentions toward China. Because of the historic friendship between the people of the United States and China, it is particularly shocking to us to think that Chinese are being forced into battle against our troops in the United Nations command.

The Chinese attack was made in great force, and it still continues. It has resulted in the forced withdrawal of large parts of the United Nations command. The battlefield situation is uncertain at this time. We may suffer reverses as we have suffered them before. But the forces of the United Nations have no intention of abandoning their mission in Korea. . . .

If the United Nations yields to the forces of aggression, no nation will be safe or secure. If aggression is successful in Korea, we can expect it to spread throughout Asia and Europe to this hemisphere. We are fighting in Korea for our national security and survival.

We have committed ourselves to the cause of a just and peaceful world order through the United Nations. We stand by that commitment.

We shall meet the new situation in three ways.

We shall continue to work in the United Nations for concerted action to halt this aggression in Korea.

We shall intensify our efforts to help other free nations strengthen their defenses in order to meet the threat of aggression elsewhere.

We shall rapidly increase our own military strength.

In the United Nations, the first step is action by the Security Council to halt this aggression. And Ambassador Warren Austin is pressing for such action. We shall exert every effort to help bring the full influence of the United Nations to bear on the situation in Korea.

Some had hoped that the normal peaceful process of discussion and negotiation, which is provided through the United Nations, could be successfully entered into with the present Chinese Communist delegation at [the UN]. There is, however, no indication that the representatives of Communist China are willing to engage in this process. Instead of discussing the real issues, they have been making violent and wholly false statements of the type which have often been used by the Soviet representatives in an effort to prevent the Security Council from acting.

We hope that the Chinese people will not continue to be forced or deceived into serving the ends of Russian colonial policy in Asia.

I am certain that, if the Chinese people now under the control of the Communists were free to speak for themselves, they would denounce this aggression against the United Nations.

Because this new act of aggression in Korea is only a part of a worldwide pattern of danger to all the free nations of the world, it is more necessary than ever before us to increase at a very rapid rate the combined military strength of the free nations. It is more necessary than ever that integrated forces in Europe under a supreme commander be established at once.

With respect to our own defense, I shall submit a supplemental request for appropriations needed immediately to increase the size and effectiveness of our Armed Forces. The request will include a substantial amount for the Atomic Commission in addition to large amounts for the Army, the Navy, the Air Force. . . .

Q[uestion from the press]. Did you or the State Department raise the question of whether this offensive would affect the chances of a negotiated settlement with the Peiping [Beijing] government?

THE PRESIDENT. The whole matter was clearly discussed with General MacArthur every day.

Q. Mr. President, there has been some criticism of General MacArthur in the European Press—

THE PRESIDENT. Some in the American press, too, if I am not mistaken.

Q.—particularly in the British press—

THE PRESIDENT. They are always for a man when he is winning, but when he is in a little trouble, they all jump on him with what ought to be done, which they didn't tell him before. He has done a good job, and he is continuing to do a good job. . . .

Q. Mr. President, will the United Nations troops be allowed to bomb across the Manchurian border?

THE PRESIDENT. I can't answer that question this morning. . . .

Q. Mr. President, will attacks in Manchuria depend on action in the United Nations?

THE PRESIDENT. Yes, entirely.

Q. In other words, if the United Nations resolution should authorize General MacArthur to go further than he has, he will—

THE PRESIDENT. We will take whatever steps are necessary to meet the military situation, just as we always have.

Q. Will that include the atomic bomb?

THE PRESIDENT. That includes every weapon that we have.

Q. Mr. President, you said "every weapon that we have." Does that mean that there is active consideration of the use of the atomic bomb?

THE PRESIDENT. There has always been active consideration of its use. I don't want to see it used. It is a terrible weapon, and it should not be used on innocent men, women, and children, who have nothing whatever to do with this military aggression. That happens when it is used. . . .

Q. Mr. President, I wonder if we could retrace the reference to the atom bomb? Did we understand you clearly that the use of the atomic bomb is under active consideration?

THE PRESIDENT. Always has been. It is one of our weapons.

Q. Does that mean, Mr. President, use against military objectives, or civilian—

THE PRESIDENT. It's a matter that the military people will have to decide. I'm not a military authority that passes on those things.

Q. Mr. President, perhaps it would be better if we are allowed to quote your remarks on that directly?

THE PRESIDENT. I don't think—I don't think that is necessary.

Q. Mr. President, you said this depends on United Nations action. Does that mean that we wouldn't use the atomic bomb except on a United Nations authorization?

THE PRESIDENT. No, it doesn't mean that at all. The action against Communist China depends on the action of the United Nations. The military commander in the field will have charge of the use of the weapons, as he always has.

Later the same day the White House issued the following press release:

The President wants to make certain that there is no misinterpretation of his answers to questions at his press conference today about the use of the atom bomb. Naturally, there has been consideration of this subject since the outbreak of the hostilities in Korea, just as there is consideration of the use of all military weapons whenever our forces are in combat.

Consideration of the use of any weapon is always implicit in the very possession of that weapon.

However, it should be emphasized that, by law, only the President can authorize the use of the atom bomb, and no such authorization has been given. If and when such authorization should be given, the military commander in the field would have charge of the tactical delivery of the weapon.

In brief, the replies to the questions at today's press conference do not represent any change in this situation.

Source: Public Papers of the Presidents of the United States: Harry S Truman, 1950 (Washington, DC: Government Printing Office, 1965): 724–28.

Although President Truman had defended General MacArthur at his news conference of November 30 against his European critics, they remained concerned that the UN commander would try to expand the Korean conflict to include a land war against China. Truman himself grew increasingly annoyed with his insubordinate general, especially after MacArthur sabotaged a White House peace initiative in March 1951. The president came very close to firing the general. But what finally convinced Truman and the Joint Chiefs of Staff that MacArthur had to be relieved of all his commands was a letter MacArthur wrote to the Republican minority leader in the House of Representatives, Joseph W. Martin, on March 20, 1950. The short letter, which Martin read to the House, seemed to challenge not only the administration's conduct of the Korean Conflict but its entire Far Eastern policy. Furthermore, MacArthur wrote the letter despite a directive from the White House the previous December to coordinate with Washington all public statements concerning Korea. Although Truman defended his action with a succinct statement of the administration's objectives in Korea, his firing of MacArthur touched off one of the greatest political brouhahas in the nation's history and made an already unpopular president even more unpopular. MacArthur's eloquent farewell statement to a joint session of Congress on April 19, 1951, only added to the intense dislike for the president across the country. Following joint congressional hearings on MacArthur's firing, however, cooler heads prevailed, and even Republican leaders in Congress recognized that Truman had been right in firing MacArthur because he had challenged the president's constitutional authority as commander in chief. What follows are MacArthur's letter to Martin, Truman's defense of his Korean policy, and MacArthur's concluding remarks in his April 19 address to Congress, all reprinted as part of the hearings.

Document 16
GENERAL DOUGLAS MacARTHUR'S LETTER TO
HOUSE MINORITY LEADER JOSEPH W. MARTIN,
MARCH 20, 1951

Dear Congressman Martin: I am most grateful for your note of the 8th forwarding me a copy of your address of February 12. The latter I have read with much interest, and find that with the passage of years you have certainly lost none of your old-time punch.

My views and recommendations with respect to the situation created by Red China's entry into the war against us in Korea have been submitted to Washington in most complete detail. Generally these views are well known and clearly understood, as they follow the conventional pattern of meeting force with maximum counter-force as we have never failed to do in the past. Your view with respect to the utilization of the Chinese forces on Formosa is in conflict with neither logic nor this tradition.

It seems strangely difficult for some to realize that here in Asia is where the Communist conspirators have elected to make their play for global conquest, and that we have joined the issue thus raised on the battlefield; that here we fight Europe's wars with arms while the diplomats there still fight it with words; that if we lose the war to communism in Asia the fall of Europe is inevitable, win it and Europe most probably would avoid war and yet preserve freedom. As you pointed out, we must win. There is no substitute for victory.

Document 17
PRESIDENT HARRY TRUMAN'S SPEECH TO THE
NATION EXPLAINING HIS DECISION TO RELIEVE
MacARTHUR OF HIS COMMANDS, APRIL 11, 1951

We do not want to see the conflict in Korea extended. We are trying to prevent a world war—not to start one. The best way to do that is to make it plain that we and the other free countries will continue to resist the attack.

But you may ask why can't we take other steps to punish the aggressor? Why don't we bomb Manchuria and China itself? Why don't we assist Chinese Nationalist troops to land on the mainland of China?

If we were to do those things we would be running a very grave risk of starting a general war. If that were to happen, we would have brought about the exact situation we are trying to prevent.

If we were to do these things, we would become entangled in a vast conflict on the continent of Asia and our task would become immeasurably more difficult all over the world.

What would suit the ambitions of the Kremlin better than for our military forces to be committed to a full scale war with Red China?

It may well be that, in spite of our best efforts, the Communists may spread the war. But it would be wrong—tragically wrong—for us to take the initiative in extending the war.

The dangers are great. Make no mistake about it. Behind the North Koreans and Chinese Communists in the front lines stand additional millions of Chinese soldiers. And behind the Chinese stand the tanks, the planes, the submarines, the soldiers, and the scheming rulers of the Soviet Union.

Our aim is to avoid the spread of the conflict.

The course we have been following is the one best calculated to avoid an all-out war. It is the course consistent with our obligation to do all we can to maintain international peace and security. Our experience in Greece and Berlin shows that it is the most effective course of action we can follow.

First of all, it is clear that our efforts in Korea can blunt the will of the Chinese Communist to continue the struggle. The United Nations forces have put up a tremendous fight in Korea and have inflicted very heavy casualties on the enemy. Our forces are stronger now than they have been before. These are plain facts which may discourage the Chinese Communists from continuing their attack.

Second, the free world as a whole is growing in military strength every day. In the United States, in western Europe, and throughout the world, free men are alert to the Soviet threat and are building their defenses. This may discourage the Communist rulers from continuing the war in Korea—and from undertaking new acts of aggression elsewhere.

If the Communist authorities realize that they cannot defeat us in Korea, if they realize it would be foolhardy to widen the hostilities beyond Korea, then they may recognize the folly of continuing their aggression. A peaceful settlement may then be possible. The door is always open.

Then we may achieve a settlement in Korea which will not compromise the principles and purposes of the United Nations.

I have thought long and hard about this question of extending the war in Asia. I have discussed it many times with the ablest military advisers in the country. I believe with all my heart that the course we are following is the best course.

I believe that we must try to limit the war to Korea for these vital reasons: To make sure that the precious lives of our fighting men are not wasted, to see that the security of our country and the free world is not needlessly jeopardized and to prevent a third world war.

A number of events have made it evident that General MacArthur did not agree with that policy. I have, therefore, considered it essential to relieve General MacArthur so that there would be no doubt or confusion as to the real purpose and aim of our policy.

It was with the deepest personal regret that I found myself compelled to take this action. General MacArthur is one of our greatest military commanders. But the cause of world peace is more important than any individual.

The change in commands in the Far East means no change whatever in the policy of the United States. We will carry on the fight in Korea with vigor and determination in an effort to bring the war to a speedy and successful conclusion.

The new commander, Lieut. Gen. Matthew Ridgway has already demonstrated that he has the great qualities of leadership needed for this task.

We are ready, at any time, to negotiate for a restoration of peace in the area. But we will not engage in appeasement. We are only interested in real peace.

Real peace can be achieved through settlement based on the following factors:

One: The fighting most stop.

Two: Concrete steps must be taken to insure that the fighting will not break out again.

Three: There must be an end to the aggression.

A settlement founded upon these elements would open the way for the unification of Korea and the withdrawal of all foreign forces.

In the meantime, I want to be clear about our military objective. We are fighting to resist an outrageous aggression in Korea. We are trying to keep the Korean conflict from spreading to other areas. But at the same time we must conduct our military activities so as to insure the security of our forces. This is essential if they are to continue the fight until the enemy abandons its ruthless attempt to destroy the Republic of Korea.

That is our military objective—to repel attack and to restore peace.

In the hard fighting in Korea, we are proving that collective action among nations is not only a high principle but a workable means of resisting aggression. Defeat of aggression in Korea may be the turning point in the world's search for a practical way of achieving peace and security.

The struggle of the United Nations in Korea is a struggle for peace.

The free nations have united their strength in an effort to prevent a third world war.

That war can come if the Communist rulers want it to come. But this nation and its allies will not be responsible for its coming.

We do not want to widen the conflict. We will use every effort to prevent the disaster. And in so doing, we know we are following the great principles of peace, freedom, and justice.

Document 18
GENERAL DOUGLAS MACARTHUR'S SPEECH TO A JOINT SESSION OF CONGRESS: PERORATION, APRIL 19, 1951

Once war is forced upon us, there is no other alternative than to apply every available means to bring it to a swift end. War's very object is victory—not prolonged indecision. In war, indeed, there can be no substitute for victory.

There are some who for varying reasons would appease Red China. They are blind to history's clear lesson. For history teaches with unmistakable emphasis that appeasement but begets new and bloodier war. It points to no single instance where the end has justified the means—where appeasement has led to more than a sham peace. Like blackmail, it lays the basis for new and successively greater demands, until, as in blackmail, violence becomes the only other alternative. Why, my soldiers asked of me, surrender military advantages to an enemy in the field? I could not answer. Some may say to avoid spread of the conflict into an all-out-war with China; others, to avoid Soviet intervention. Neither explanation seems valid. For China is already engaging with the maximum power it can commit and the Soviets will not necessarily mesh its actions with our moves. Like a cobra, any new enemy will more likely strike whenever it feels that the relativity in military or other potential is in its favor on a world-wide basis.

The tragedy of Korea is further heightened by the fact that as military action is confined to its territorial limits, it condemns that nation, which is our purpose to save, to suffer the devastating impact of full naval and air bombardment, while the enemy's sanctuaries are fully protected from such attack and devastation. Of the nations of the world, Korea alone, up to now, is the sole one which has risked its all against communism. The magnificence of the courage and fortitude of the Korean people defies description. They have chosen to risk death rather than slavery. Their last words to me were "Don't scuttle the Pacific."

I have just left your fighting sons in Korea. They have met all tests there and I can report to you without reservation they are splendid in every way. It was my constant effort to preserve them and end this savage conflict honorably and with the least loss of time and a minimum sacrifice of life. Its growing bloodshed has caused me the deepest anguish and anxiety. Those gallant men will remain often in my thoughts and in my prayers always.

I am closing my 52 years of military service. When I joined the Army even before the turn of the century, it was the fulfillment of all my boyish hopes and dreams. The world has turned over many times since I took the oath on the plains at West Point, and the hopes and dreams have long since vanished. But I still remember the refrain of one of the most popular barracks ballads of that day which proclaimed most proudly that—

"Old soldiers never die; they just fade away." And like the old soldier of the ballad, I now close my military career and just fade away—an old soldier who tried to do his duty as God gave him the light to see that duty.

Good-by[e].

Source: The Military Situation in the Far East: Hearings before the Committee on Armed Services and the Committee on Foreign Relations, U.S. Senate, 82nd Congress, 1st Session (Washington, DC: Government Printing Office, 1951), 3543–44, 3550–58.

News of President Harry Truman's decision, in April 1951, to relieve MacArthur of all his commands was greeted with great enthusiasm by America's European allies. By the end of April, following the collapse of the Chinese Communists' most ambitious offensive since entering the war in November, the military conflict had also pretty much stabilized along a line approximating the 38th parallel. The Truman administration believed that the time was opportune to undertake another peace initiative, which eventually resulted in the opening of armistice negotiations in July. These developments were also welcome in Europe. But significant differences still existed between Washington and London over recognition of the Beijing government and the United States's continued support for the Chinese Nationalist government on Formosa. There were also disagreements over the conduct of the war, such as the air attack on August 25, 1951, by thirty-five B-29 bombers against the North Korean port city of Rashin only a few miles from the Soviet border. Nevertheless, the British were even willing to concede "hot pursuit" across the Manchurian border, provided that they were consulted before such attacks took place.

Document 19
CABINET DEFENCE COMMITTEE, *MILITARY ACTION IN KOREA IN THE EVENT OF A BREAKDOWN IN THE ARMISTICE TALKS,* REPORT BY THE CHIEFS OF STAFF, TOP SECRET, SEPTEMBER 7TH, 1951

We have considered the military action in Korea in the event of a breakdown in the armistice talks, and our report is at annex.

2. We would draw the attention of the Defence Committee to the point in paragraph 2 of this report that it may become necessary to consider "hot pursuit" by air across the Manchurian frontier, and that if this situation does arise we consider the agreement of participating Governments should first be sought.

Recommendation

3. We recommend that the Defence Committee take note of the point referred to in paragraph 2 above and the conclusions contained in paragraph 13 of the report at annex.

ANNEX
MILITARY ACTION IN KOREA IN THE EVENT
OF A BREAKDOWN IN THE ARMISTICE TALKS

2. The object of this paper is to examine what course of military action we consider should be pursued in Korea in the event of a breakdown in the present armistice talks. We have assumed that it would still be our intention to limit the war, and that it would not therefore be possible to resort to military action in Manchuria or elsewhere in China. The United Kingdom Government, however, have agreed in principle, subject to confirmation at the time, to the bombing of air bases in Manchuria if there are heavy air attacks from bases in China on U.S. Forces in Korea. The four older Commonwealth countries have agreed with this policy. The time may come when it may become necessary to consider hot pursuit by air across the frontier; if this situation does arise it will require the agreement of the participating Governments.

We examine this problem under two headings:-
a. The establishment of a naval blockade.
b. The future action in Korea. . . .

Conclusions

13. We conclude that:
a. A sea blockade is only likely to be effective as a long term measure, and would require the deployment of large UN naval and air forces. To be fully effective this blockade would need to include Russian ports, a step which could not be taken without incurring a very grave risk of global war. We therefore consider that the efforts and risks involved, even with a partial blockade, would considerably outweigh the value of the results likely to be achieved.

b. The UN forces would be quite inadequate to hold the Chinese frontier even if they were able to advance to it, particularly since, as we have assumed, it would still not be permissible to launch air attacks against Chinese territory.

c. The best course of action would be for the UN forces to base their defence on their present strong position in the Kansas line and inflict maximum casualties on the Chinese should they launch a new offensive. In the meantime the UN air offensive combined with active raiding operations and limited ground attacks should be intensified.

d. Should a Chinese offense collapse and the Chinese are thrown into disorder, General Ridgway should have discretion to undertake tactical advances as is thought militarily desirable to follow up the retreating Chinese. Should he wish to make a major advance such as to advance as far as the Northern waist this will require the approval of Governments.

Source: Foreign Office, Public Records Office, PREM 8/1405, London, England.

> The one issue that kept the negotiators at Panmunjom from reaching an agreement ending the Korean War for almost two years was the return of prisoners of war (POWs). This issue is discussed at length in Chapter 5. Suffice it to say here that even though the Geneva Convention of 1949 required the repatriation of all POWs, President Harry Truman refused to agree to their forced repatriation. Despite an opposing view even within his own administration that the United Nations Command (UNC) was required by international law to return all POWs even if their return was carried out against their will, Truman remained convinced that it would be morally wrong for the UNC to return to the communists POWs who feared for their lives if they were repatriated. For the Chinese and North Koreans, however, the issue was not so much a moral one as one of saving face since surveys of POWs held by the UNC indicated huge defections on the part of these prisoners if they were given the option of nonrepatriation. With some justification, communist leaders also believed that many of the POWs who chose nonrepatriation had been coerced into doing so by their captives and by Chinese Nationalist POWs, who had been impressed into the military following the victory of the communists in the Chinese Civil War and were later captured by UN forces. Complicating the POW issue even more was the fact that the North Koreans conscripted captured South Korean forces into their army, a practice to which the UNC objected as being contrary to the rules of war. The following statement on the exchange of POWs and civilians, delivered to the communist negotiators at Panmunjom on January 2, 1952, by Rear Admiral R. E. Libby, spells out clearly the differences between the two sides at the negotiations that would delay a trust in Korea for another eighteen months.

Document 20
PRISONER OF WAR PROBLEMS, JANUARY 2, 1952

Certain areas of agreement and certain differences of opinion have emerged from our exchange of views on the prisoners of war problem during the period it has been under discussion. Among them are these:

First, your side wants all the POWs to be released following the signing of the armistice. The UNC agrees that this should be done, under an equitable formula.

Second, your side has incorporated into your army many thousands of our soldiers who fell into your hands as POWs. From your standpoint, your action in this connection was in accordance with your traditional policy toward POWs. According to you, the POWs were "reeducated" and "released at the front." The fact that practically all of them later reappeared in your own army is explained away by the alleged fact that they exercised their own volition in joining it.

From our standpoint, the wholesale incorporation of POWs into your army is contrary to the rules of warfare and a violation of the rights of the men concerned, since there is reasonable doubt that the prisoners were free from duress in making this decision. The rules of warfare and the rights of the individual under those rules require that you refrain from using POWs in work connected with military operations and that you shelter the prisoners from the effects of military operations. Manifestly, these requirements are not met by the incorporating of POWs into your own military forces. It is the view of the UNC that all former soldiers of the Republic of Korea Army who were incorporated into your army through your mechanism of impressment should be returned to their status as POWs.

Moreover, since the outbreak of hostilities on 25 June 1950 your side has conscripted many civilian nationals of the ROK and accepted a certain number of deserters from the ROKA[rmy] into your army. Both of these practices are consistent with your doctrines of warfare. But both are inconsistent with ours. It is our view that deserters, just as involuntary captives, should be accorded a POW status. . . .

Third, your side takes the position that all POWs should be returned to the side with which they were identified when they were captured. The UNC, on the other hand[,] takes the view that all bona-fide residents of the ROK as of 25 June 1950 are nationals of that state. From that fact they derive certain rights and have certain responsibilities which are not set aside by the accident of war. Consequently, the disposition of persons of this category who have been taken into custody by the UNC while fighting against the ROK is a matter for our side alone to determine. It is of no concern whatever to your side.

Fourth, the tides of warfare in Korea have displaced many civilians of both sides from their homes. Sometimes this resulted from accident, sometimes from military necessity. Whatever the cause, many former residents of the Democratic People's Republic of Korea are now in the territory under the control of the ROK and vice versa. Your side has alluded frequently during these discussions to the conditions under which these refugees are living. You have expressed the thought that these displaced civilians should be permitted to return to their homes as soon as the armistice is signed. The UNC, too, sees no reason why displaced civilians should not be permitted, if they so desire, to return to their former homes under the armistice agreement. Moreover, it considers that failure on the part of the armistice delegations to insert a permissive provision in the Armistice Agreement would be to disregard the needs of these people unnecessarily.

In determining its opinion on the question of release and exchange of POWs the UNC has accorded recognition to the viewpoints of both sides as set forth above and has developed a proposal which in large measure reconciles them. Our proposal provides for the release of all POWs. In this respect it is consistent with the principle advocated by your side. With respect to repatriation, the UNC proposal differs from yours in that it expressly provides that all repatriation will be voluntary.

To accomplish this, the UNC proposal embodies the principle, advanced and advocated by your side, that a soldier from one side who becomes a POW of the other side can, upon his "release," exercise his individual option as to whether he will return to his own side or join the other side. However, the application of this principle of freedom of choice as regards repatriation is extended, under the UNC proposal, to include all personnel who are, or should be[,] eligible for repatriation under concepts held by either side. The proposal extends to the right of individual self-determination to former ROKA soldiers who came under your control and who are now in your army. It extends to the residents of the ROK who were inducted into the Korean People's Army following the outbreak of war. It extends it to nations of the ROK who fought on your side but who are now in our hands as interned civilians or as POWs. Finally, it extends it to displaced civilians on both sides. Specifically, the principle is applied to the following groups:

A. Approximately 16,000 nationals of the ROK who were identified with the KPA [Korean People's Army] and the Chinese People's Volunteers and whom the UNC now holds as POWs.

B. Approximately 38,000 nationals of the ROK who were incorrectly classified initially as POWs and who have since been reclassified as interned persons.

C. All former ROKA soldiers who came into the custody of the KPA and CPV and who were subsequently incorporated into the KPA.

D. All bona-fide residents of the ROK who were inducted into the KPA subsequent to 25 June 1950.

E. Approximately 11,000 soldiers of the UN and of the ROKA who are now held as POWs by the UNC.

F. Approximately 116,000 soldiers of the KPA and CPV who are now held as POWs by the UNC.

G. Foreign civilians interned by either side.

H. All civilians who, on 25 June 1950, were bona-fide residents of the territory under control of one side and who are, at the same time of the signing of the armistice, within the territory under control of the other side.

The principle of individual self-determination is a valid principle only if adequate machinery is provided to insure that the decision of the individual is made freely and without duress. Neither side would be satisfied that persons were accorded an opportunity to express their desires on repatriation freely and without duress if the interviewing process was conducted by or under the unilateral aegis of one of the respective belligerents. Thus, there is a requirement under the UNC proposal for an impartial neutral organ to conduct and supervise the interview in which the individual expresses his choice as regards repatriation.

The fact that both sides have, to a degree, accepted the services of the International Committee of the Red Cross suggests that this agency, which is ideally suited and fully qualified, perform this function. Therefore, the UNC proposal provides that the ICRC be requested to supervise the exercise of the right of individual determination as relates to both POWs and displaced civilians. To afford additional assurances to both sides, the proposal provides that, in the case of POWs, the individual expression of choice of repatriation will be made at the exchange point or points. There the process will be under the close scrutiny of representatives of both belligerents.

In order that neither side will gain a military advantage through the exchange of POWs under the Armistice Agreement, the UNC proposal contains a parole feature. Under this provision, POWs repatriated by one side after all POWs held by the other side have been exchanged will be required to give their parole not to bear arms against the captor in the future. The delivery of the POW is subject to acceptance of this agreement by the military authorities of the side to whom the POW is delivered.

The UNC proposal is as follows:

1. POWs who elect repatriation shall be exchanged on a one-for-one basis until one side has exchanged all such POWs held by it.

2. The side which thereafter holds POWs shall repatriate all those POWs who elect to be repatriated in a one-for-one exchange for foreign civilians interned by the other side, and for civilians and other persons of the one side who are at the time of the signing of the armistice in the territory under control of

the other side, and who elect to be repatriated. POWs thus exchanged shall be paroled to the opposing force, such parole to carry with it the condition that the individual shall not again bear arms against the side releasing him.

3. All POWs not electing repatriation shall be released from POW status and shall be paroled, such parole to carry with it the condition that the individual will not again bear arms in the Korean conflict.

4. All remaining civilians of either side who are, at the time of the signing of the armistice, in territory under control of the other side, shall be repatriated if they so elect.

5. In order to insure that the choice regarding repatriation is made without duress, delegates of the ICRC shall be permitted to interview all POWs at the point of exchange, and all civilians of either side who are at the time of the signing of the armistice in territory under the control of the other side.

6. For the purposes of paragraphs 2, 4 and 5, civilians and other persons of either side are defined as those who on 25 June 1950 were bona-fide residents of either ROK or the DPRK.

In summary, the UNC proposal provides for the release of all POWs, including soldiers of the other side who may have been incorporated into the army of the detaining power. Thus, it is consistent with the first principle advanced by your side that all POWs be released. As regards repatriation, it permits freedom of choice on the part of the individual, thus insuring that there will be no forced repatriation against the will of an individual. It provides repatriation not only for POWs alone but for those other victims of war, the displaced civilians. All those who desire it are permitted to return to their former homes. Finally, the proposal provides for a supervisory organ to interview the persons involved to insure that, whatever their choice, such choices will be made freely and without duress.

Source: Department of State, *Bulletin* 26 (January 7, 1952), 105–6, 111.

Dwight D. Eisenhower's election as president in 1952 greatly concerned Washington's European allies because they feared that the right-wing of the Republican party, which sought an expansion of the Korean conflict, including the unleashing of Chiang Kai-shek's Nationalist forces on Formosa to attack the Chinese mainland, would now have easier access to the White House. Sometimes strident remarks by the new secretary of state, John Foster Dulles, and indeed, by President Eisenhower himself who had made clear during the campaign his determination to end the Korean conflict one way or the other, only deepened their concern. The new administration's decision, soon after taking office, to withdraw the Seventh Fleet from the Formosa Straits seemed to confirm their worst fears, notwithstanding the fact that London had been informed of the decision before it was carried out. In effect, Eisenhower appeared to be unleashing the Chinese Nationalists to invade the mainland. British Foreign Secretary Anthony Eden lodged an official protest with the Department of State. Whether or not this was mainly "for the record" as an official at the British embassy believed, there is little question that London was greatly concerned about a possible escalation of the war in Korea under the new Republican administration.

Document 21
SECRET SECURITY INFORMATION MEMORANDUM FOR THE PRESIDENT

February 2, 1953

The following message from Mr. Eden, with respect to the decision to change the orders of the 7th Fleet, was delivered to me last night by an officer of the British Embassy. After informing Acting Secretary of State [H. Freeman] Matthews the text was cabled to Mr. Dulles in Paris. The message follows:

"Her Majesty's Government regret this decision which they consider will have unfortunate political repercussions particularly in the United Nations. They do not think that it will carry with it compensating military advantages or will help in any way towards a solution of the Korean conflict.

"I expect to be questioned in the House of Commons on the attitude of Her Majesty's Government. I shall have to make it clear that we were informed in advance of the United States's decision and immediately took steps to make known to the United States Government our serious misgivings. We had indeed only a week or two before drawn their attention to apparent infringements of President Truman's 1952 declaration and had expressed the hope that the doctrine of neutralization of Formosa would be maintained without modification."

In forwarding the above message to Secretary Dulles I pointed out that the British Embassy officer who delivered it had expressed the personal view that the message was mainly "for the record." The officer also agreed that the last sentence in the message is misleading as the British have not in fact officially expressed to us the hope that the neutralization policy would be maintained. Mr Dulles was told that the British Embassy was cabling the fact to London.

In forwarding the above for your information, Mr. Matthews wishes to have it made clear that the Department of State is not in any manner suggesting there should be any change in the decision to modify the orders of the 7th Fleet.

John Allison

Source: Records of the Department of State, Division of Far Eastern Affairs, 1953. Record Group 59. "Miscellaneous Subject Files for the Year, 1953," Box 2, File "Formosa Book—Korea Cease-Fire Negotiations." National Archives, Washington, DC.

In May 1953, the communist negotiators at Panmunjom offered a new proposal for resolving the repatriation issue that represented an important breakthrough in the negotiations, although it was not realized at the time. Five weeks of delicate negotiations followed, but by the beginning of July, the negotiators were near a final agreement ending the Korean conflict. The greatest obstacle to peace now was South Korean President Syngman Rhee who did not want any peace short of the reunification of Korea under his government. On June 18, he tried to sabotage a peace agreement by unilaterally freeing 25,000 North Korean POWs from four prison camps guarded by South Koreans. In response, the Chinese launched a massive assault that bloodied South Korea's ill-prepared Fifth and Eighth Divisions. At the same time, the United States followed a carrot-and-stick policy toward the Seoul government, warning that South Korea would have to fight alone if it continued to undermine the chances for peace but offering a mutual security pact and substantial economic and military assistance if it agreed to abide by an armistice agreement. Although Rhee refused to be signatory to such a pact, he did promise to abide by its terms. On that basis, the United Nations Command was able to sign an agreement with the Chinese and North Koreans on July 27, 1953, ending the three-year-old conflict. The following letter from Secretary of State John Foster Dulles to Rhee indicates some of the difficulties the United States continued to have with the South Korean president up to the eve of the armistice. It also makes clear the concessions Rhee was able to get from the United States in return for his pledge not to be obstructive.

Document 22
THE SECRETARY OF STATE TO THE PRESIDENT OF THE REPUBLIC OF KOREA (RHEE), JULY 24, 1953

CONFIDENTIAL

My dear President Rhee: I have your message of July 24. I have read it to President Eisenhower. We are both surprised at your statement that "before deciding on the position of my government it is of utmost importance to have your answers to two vital questions which at present remain in an uncertain status." Our surprise is two-fold. We thought you have decided and we thought you had the answers.

First, in your letters of July 11, 1953, to President Eisenhower and to me, you gave explicit assurances with reference to the position of your Government. Thus, in your letter to President Eisenhower you said "as you know, I have decided not to obstruct in any manner the implementation of the terms in deference to your request." In your letter to me, you said with reference to the truce "I have granted almost every request that has been made upon me. My only qualification is that if the means which you have chosen do not prove to be successful, we must be allowed the final right to do what we can do to retrieve our nation from the situation that will exist when the Communists refuse to grant in peace what the allies have refrained from accomplishing in war. The truce will now be signed. We shall abide by our agreement to give the United Nations yet another chance to try out in our nation its prescribed method of political negotiation."

The "only qualification" to which you referred is recognized. Thus, we believed, and were surely entitled to believe, that the attitude of your government toward a truce was already decided.

Second, the position of our Government on your questions was set forth in Assistant Secretary [Walter] Robertson's *aide-memoire* of July 2, 1953. Upon his return to Washington, he discussed both questions with President Eisenhower, myself and Congressional Committees, and you were advised under date of July 21, when I communicated with you through our Embassy and when Mr. Robertson through the same channels wrote you personally.

If in violation of the armistice the Republic of Korea is subjected to unprovoked attack you may of course count upon our immediate and automatic military reaction. Such an attack would not only be an attack upon the Republic of Korea but an attack upon the United Nations Command and U.S. forces within that Command.

So far as concerns a military security pact, as Mr. Robertson explained to you at Seoul and as was confirmed in the two July 21 communications above referred to, the pact in order to secure ratification would in our opinion have to adhere rather closely to the draft which was submitted to you on July 4 and which as you were then advised had been discussed with Congressional leaders. This provides that our action must be in accordance with our constitutional processes. Of course, the President would within his executive powers act instantly to aid a friendly nation with whom we had a security pact which was the victim of unprovoked aggression. But under our Constitution only Congress can declare war. We believe that your country can feel confident that the treaty we propose will deter aggression.

With reference to your inquiry regarding moral and material support of your possible military effort which might follow a collapse of the political conference, this is not a matter where the President can give any blanket commitment in advance. As pointed out in Mr. Robertson's letter of July 21 the President does not wish to curtail the liberty of action to take whatever steps may be indicated by the conditions then existing. But as Mr. Robertson also said in his letter to you the U.S. commitment to withdraw from the political conference under the circumstances set forth in Mr. Robertson's *aide-memoire* of July 2 still stands.

I promised you that, upon the signing of the armistice I would promptly come and talk with you to settle a common policy in relation to the political conference. I eagerly look forward to seeing you again and I have every confidence that we shall be able to arrive at an agreed program which will embody every honorable means of accomplishing the unification of your country.

I believe that the many assurances of cooperation which have been given you and which go to the limit of our governmental power should be a complete demonstration of the sincerity of our purpose and the strength of our determination. Never in all its history has the U.S. offered to any other country as much as is offered to you.

During recent days many people and many countries have been slandering you and alleging that such promises as you have given the President and me could not be depended upon. We have indignantly rejected these insinuations and have insisted that we had complete confidence that you would adhere to the position which you communicated to us. As I said in a public statement day before yesterday these are times when we must have confidence in our friends and when our friends can have confidence in us. My final plea is that you should share this sentiment. You did not find us lacking in the past and you can I believe trust us for the future.

From your good friend

Foster Dulles

Source: Papers Relating to the Foreign Relations of the United States: 1952–1954 XV (Washington, DC: Government Printing Office, 1984): 1430–32.

Glossary of Selected Terms

AMG (American Military Government): Military government established by the United States after World War II for its zone of occupation in Korea. Headed by General John Hodge, the AMG worked closely with anticommunist forces in South Korea and helped train South Korean military forces (the ROK Army).

Big Switch: Code name given to the exchange of prisoners of war (POWs) by both sides at the end of the Korean conflict.

Brinkmanship: Also known as "massive retaliation" was a foreign policy of the Eisenhower administration predicated on the threat of nuclear retaliation (going to the brink of a nuclear war) at a place of the United States's own choosing against communist aggression. The assumption behind brinkmanship was that communist aggression would be deterred by the potential consequences of such action.

China Lobby: Politicians and others who believed that the United States had allowed China to "fall" to the Communists in 1949 and who lobbied for increased military and economic support for the Nationalist government of Chiang Kai-shek on Formosa. Closely tied to the right wing of the Republican party, they were generally critical of the Truman administration for making Europe rather than Asia the primary focus of its foreign policy.

Cinunc: An acronym for Commander in Chief, United Nations Command.

Containment: This was the strategy the United States followed during most of the Cold War period. The person most closely associated with the containment doctrine, George Kennan, intended that the United States contain communist expansion by rebuilding western Europe after World War II. But containment soon took on a more military and global posture and was the basis for American intervention into Korea in 1950.

DPA (Defense Production Act): This piece of legislation, which was approved by Congress in September 1950, gave the president sweeping powers to mobilize the economy for wartime purposes.

DPR (Democratic People's Republic of Korea): Established in September 1948 in the area of the Korean peninsula above the 38th parallel and more commonly known as North Korea.

EDC (European Defense Community): Part of an effort to rearm Germany and to integrate its military forces into a European defense force. A European Defense Community Treaty was signed in May 1952, and the United States strongly supported the establishment of an EDC during the Korean War. But the end of the Korean War and the defeat of the French, who remained strongly opposed to the rearming of Germany, rejected the treaty. Instead, Germany was rearmed within the structure of NATO.

Greater Sanction Policy: A secret understanding between the United States and Britain during the Korean War that if a truce was reached ending the war, China would be warned that a major violation of the agreement would result in renewed hostilities, which would not be limited to the Korean peninsula. Following the signing of the armistice agreement in July 1953, the sixteen nations with armed forces in Korea signed the "greater sanction" statement but it was not made public until August because of growing allied opposition to the policy.

Iron Triangle: A heavily defended area in Korea encompassed by a triangle with Pyonggang (not to be confused with the North Korean capital city of Pyongyang) at the northern angle, Chorwon at the left angle, and Kumhwa at the right angle. Much of the military fighting in Korea after the failure of the communist offensive in April 1951 took place within the Iron Triangle.

Kaesong: Initial site of armistice negotiations beginning in July 1951. Following a series of incidents by both sides in the talks, the negotiations were moved in October to Panmunjon, a village about five miles to the east.

Little Switch: Code name given to the exchange of sick and wounded POWs begun on April 20 and completed on May 3, 1953. The successful carrying out of Little Switch persuaded the Eisenhower administration that the communists were sincere in their effort to resolve the eighteen-month POW question and reach an armistice agreement.

Massive Retaliation: *See* **Brinkmanship**.

Munich Syndrome: In late September 1938, British Prime Minister Neville Chamberlain and French Premier Edouard Deladier concluded an agreement with Germany's leader Adolf Hitler, which dismembered Czechoslovakia by ceding large parts of the country with German populations to Germany. The agreement, which was an effort to preserve peace by trying to "appease" Hitler, gave the term "appeasement" an ugly connotation. The lesson of Munich seemed to be that appeasement only encourages aggression, and this conclusion (the Munich Syndrome) deeply affected the U.S. reaction to the North Korean invasion of South Korea in 1950.

NATO (North Atlantic Treaty Organization): Approved by Congress in 1949, NATO was the first military alliance signed by the United States since the American Revolution. It provided for a unified command structure and military force for the defense of western Europe. The Korean conflict made the development of a militarily strong NATO an even higher priority than it had already been.

Panmunjom: A village near the 38th parallel where armistice negotiations were conducted after they were moved in October 1951 from Kaesong about five miles to the west.

POWs (Prisoners of War): The issue of the status of the POWs after the Korean War ended was the most contentious issue of the negotiations to end the conflict. The communist negotiators insisted on the repatriation of all POWs as required by the Geneva Convention of 1949, but the UNC opposed forced repatriation. The issue probably delayed an armistice agreement by eighteen months.

PRC (People's Republic of China): After the communists won the civil war in China in 1949, they declared communist China the People's Republic of China.

Red Scare: Name given to the widespread fear in the United States in the 1940s and early 1950s of an internal communist conspiracy against the United States. The successful testing of an atomic bomb by the Soviet Union in September 1949 and the final victory of the communists in the Chinese Civil War a month later seemed to many Americans to confirm the existence of such a conspiracy. But the person most closely associated with the "red scare" was Senator Joseph McCarthy of Wisconsin who claimed to have a list of communists working for the State Department. The Korean War, especially after the Chinese entered the war and drove UN forces behind the 38th parallel, fueled the already flaming fears of a communist conspiracy to take over the world.

UNC (United Nations Command): The name of the command under which the United States and its allies fought the Korean War. It reflected the fact that, technically, the war was waged as a United Nations action against communist aggression even though all major military (and political) decisions were made by the United States and the Command was always under American control.

UNTCOK (United Nations Temporary Commission on Korea): Established in October 1947 by the United Nations in order to carry out legislative elections as the first step toward bringing about the unification of Korea. But the Soviet Union, which occupied the area of Korea above the 38th parallel, claimed that UNTCOK was dominated by the United States and its allies. They were also aware that two-thirds of the elected delegates to the National Assembly would be from South Korea because the new legislature would be based on proportional representation. Accordingly, Moscow denied UNTCOK permission to hold elections in the communist-controlled part of Korea. Over the objection of even some of America's own allies, including Australia and Canada, the Commission held elections in South Korea in 1948 which led to the appointment of Syngman Rhee as the first president of South Korea.

Annotated Bibliography

BIBLIOGRAPHIES AND HISTORIOGRAPHIES

Cumings, Bruce. "Korean-American Relations: A Century of Conflict." In *New Frontiers in American-East Asian Relations: Essays Presented to Dorothy Borg*, ed. Warren Cohen, 237–82. New York: Columbia University Press, 1983. Strong on foreign sources.

Foot, Rosemary. "Making Known the Unknown War: Policy Analysis of the Korean Conflict in the Last Decade." *Diplomatic History* 15 (Summer 1991): 411–31. Stresses the many facets of the Korean War hitherto unknown such as civil nature of the war and role of the Soviet Union and People's Republic of China in the events leading to the North Korean invasion of South Korea.

Hajoon, Kim. "Trends in Korean War Studies: A Review of the Literature." In *Korea and the Cold War: Division, Destruction, and Disarmament*, ed. Kim Chull Baum and James A. Matray, 106–15. Claremont, CA: Regina Books, 1993. Especially good on the new literature on Soviet and Chinese policy with respect to the war.

McFarland, Keith D. *The Korean War: An Annotated Bibliography*. New York: Garland Press, 1986. A comprehensive bibliography of the literature on the Korean War through the early 1980s.

McMahon, Robert J. "The Cold War in Asia: Toward a New Synthesis?" *Diplomatic History* 12 (Summer 1988): 307–27. Delineates between radical and liberal interpretations of United States policy in the Far East and suggests development of a synthesis.

Warner, Geoffrey. "The Korean War" *International Affairs* 56 (January 1980): 98–107. Reviews fifteen books examining the question of who started the

Korean War and why the Chinese communists later intervened in the conflict. Also uses primary sources.

West, Philip. "Interpreting the Korean War." *American Historical Review* 94 (February 1987): 80–96. A balanced review essay of six books on the Korean War. Emphasizes historians' need to know more about the Chinese side of the war.

GENERAL HISTORIES

Alexander, Bevin. *Korea: The First War We Lost*. New York: Hippocrene, 1986. Highly critical of the United States. Argues that Washington should have read better Beijing's warnings that it intended to enter the war if UN forces did not stop their advance toward the Yalu River.

Berger, Carl. *The Korean Knot: A Military-Political History*. Philadelphia: University of Pennsylvania Press, 1964. Short account of the war with emphasis on political aspects.

Blair, Clay. *The Forgotten War: America in Korea, 1950–1953*. New York: Times Books, 1987. A popular account of the war.

Fehrenbach, T. R. *This Kind of War: A Study in Unpreparedness*. New York: MacMillan, 1963. Maintains that the United States was not prepared militarily or even psychologically for fighting a limited war in Korea.

Foot, Rosemary. *The Wrong War: American Policy and the Dimensions of the Korean Conflict, 1950–1953*. Ithaca, NY: Cornell University Press, 1985. Emphasizes the influence that America's allies, particularly Britain, had in restraining the United States from expanding the war.

———. *A Substitute for Victory: The Politics of Peacemaking at the Korean Armistice Talks*. Ithaca, NY: Cornell University Press, 1990. An account of the two years of negotiations leading to the armistice agreement of 1953. Emphasizes concessions made by the communists in the talks.

Goulden, Joseph C. *Korea: The Untold Story of the Korean War*. New York: McGraw Hill, 1982. The first book to use newly opened diplomatic records and records of the Joint Chiefs of Staff at the National Archives. But the book's treatment of the war is weak after 1951.

Hastings, Max. *The Korean War*. New York: Simon and Schuster, 1987. A concise, well-written account of the Korean War, especially excellent on the military history of the war.

Henderson, Gregory. *Korea: The Politics of the Vortex*. Cambridge, MA: Harvard University Press, 1968. History of Korea from the Yi dynasty to the mid-1960s with special emphasis on the post–World War II period. Stresses the homogeneity and centralization of Korean society. Critical of U.S. policy toward Korea.

James, D. Clayton. *Refighting the Last War: Command and Crisis in Korea, 1950–1953*. New York: The Free Press, 1993. The theme of the book is evident from its title.

Kaufman, Burton I. *The Korean War: Challenges in Crisis, Credibility and Command*, 2nd edition. New York: McGraw Hill, 1997. A general account of the Korean conflict stressing the three themes indicated in its title.

Kim, Joungwon A. *Divided Korea: The Politics of Development, 1945–1972*. Cambridge, MA: Harvard University Press, 1975. Good account of the political development of North and South Korea with particular emphasis on the political leaders in both countries.

Lowe, Peter. *The Origins of the Korean War*. London: Longmann, 1986. Strong on the geopolitical context of the war.

MacDonald, Callum. *Korea: The War before Vietnam*. London: Macmillan, 1986. Readable and balanced account of the war.

Nam, Koon Woo. *The North Korean Communist Leadership, 1945–1965: A Study of Factionalism and Political Consolidation*. University, AL: University of Alabama Press, 1974. Trace's Kim Il Sung's consolidation of power over two decades. Interesting because of the emphasis it places on factional nature of North Korean society in the years immediately following World War II.

O'Ballance, Edgar. *Korea: 1950–1953*. London: Faber, 1969. Still useful military history of the war by a prominent military historian who has written on other wars as well.

Oh, John Kie-Chiang. *Korea: Democracy on Trial*. Ithaca, NY: Cornell University Press, 1968. Discusses establishment of Republic of Korea. Highly critical of Syngman Rhee because of his repressive government in the 1940s.

Rees, David. *Korea: The Limited War*. New York: Hamish Hamilton, 1964. The first comprehensive account of the Korean War. Argues that the North Korean invasion of South Korea was simply a brazen attack inspired by Moscow. Remained standard interpretation for twenty years.

Rose, Lisle A. *Roots of Tragedy: The United States and the Struggle for Asia, 1945–1953*. Westport, CT: Greenwood Press, 1976. Shows the United States's reluctant but growing ties to the Syngman Rhee government by 1948.

Scalapino, Robert A., and Chong-Sik Lee. *Communism in Korea*. 2 Volumes. Berkeley, CA: University of California Press, 1972. Examines development of communism both from a historical as well as an economic, social, and cultural perspective. Strong on the communist movement under Kim Il Sung.

Stueck, William, Jr. *The Korean War: An International History*. Princeton, NJ: Princeton University Press, 1997. A comprehensive account of the war that places it in an international perspective. Based heavily on archival research in the United States, Great Britain, and Australia.

Suh, Dae-Sook. *The Korean Communist Movement, 1918–1948*. Princeton, NJ: Princeton University Press, 1967. Stresses the two conflicting societies that had developed in Korea by 1948.

Whelan, Richard. *Drawing the Line: The Korean War, 1950–1953*. Boston: Little, Brown and Co., 1990. An interesting and informative history of the war, which argues that the conflict was a world war in miniature.

OFFICIAL MILITARY HISTORIES

Appleman, Roy. *South to the Naktong, North to the Yalu*. Washington, DC: Government Printing Office, 1961. Deals with diplomatic as well as military operations in Korea during the first six months of the war. Makes extensive use of oral interviews as well as archival materials.

Condit, Doris. *The Test of War*. Washington, DC: Government Printing Office, 1984. A thoroughly documented history of the Office of Secretary of Defense through the Korean War. Condit makes it clear that the role of the Joint Chiefs of Staff vis-à-vis Secretary of Defense George Marshall remained unclear throughout the Korean War.

Field, James A., Jr. *History of United States Naval Operations: Korea*. Washington, DC: Naval History Division, 1962. Comprehensive account of naval operations during the Korean War based on U.S. naval records. Excellent on decision-making process during the war.

Hermes, Walter G. *Truce Tent and Fighting Front*. Washington, DC: Government Printing Office, 1961. Official Army account of the armistice negotiations at Kaesong and Panmunjom.

Montrose, Lynn, Nicholas A. Canonza et al. *U.S. Marine Operations in Korea*. 5 Volumes. Washington, DC: Historical Branch, U.S. Marine Corps, 1954–1972. Thoroughly documented official account of U.S. Marine operations during the Korean War.

Schnabel, James F. *Policy and Direction: The First Year*. Washington, DC: Government Printing Office, 1972. Focuses on period through June 1951. Based primarily on U.S. Army records.

OTHER MILITARY HISTORIES

Appleman, Roy E. *Disaster in Korea: The Chinese Confront MacArthur*. College Station, TX: Texas A&M University Press, 1989. The first of three volumes that together provide the definitive military account of the Korean War during the critical period November 1950 to April 1951. Covers period through December 1950. Challenges conventional view that the Chinese took advantage of the gap between the Eighth Army and X Corps. Highly critical of Lt. General Walton H. Walker.

———. *Escaping the Trap: The U.S. Army X Corps in Northeast Korea, 1950*. College Station, TX: Texas A&M University Press, 1990. Brilliant account of the X Corps escape from their trap at Chosin Reservoir in Northeast Korea.

———. *Ridgway Duels for Korea*. College Station, TX: Texas A&M University Press, 1990. Covering the period January–April 1951, Appleman attributes much of the turnaround in the war to the gallant leadership of Matthew Ridgway.

Futrell, Robert Frank. *The United States Air Force in Korea, 1950–1953*. New York: Office of Air Force History, 1961. Well-documented and comprehensive account of Air Force operations during the war. Makes use of oral interviews. Extensive bibliography.

Gugeler, Russell A., ed. *Combat Actions in Korea*. Washington, DC: Office of the Army Chief of Military History, 1954. Detailed illustrative accounts of small unit operations during the war.

Hoyt, Edwin P. *On to the Yalu*. New York: Stein and Day, 1984. A popular account based on published source of the advance of UN forces toward the Yalu River following the successful amphibious operation at Inchon. Stresses how MacArthur threw caution to the wind as he set off in pursuit of the retreating North Koreans.

Marshall, S.L.A. *The River and the Gauntlet: The Defeat of the Eighth Army by Communist Forces*. New York: Morrow, 1968. Excellent account by a leading military authority on the Korean War of the Eighth Army's retreat toward the 38th parallel following the Chinese invasion of Korea at the end of 1950.

Stewart, James T., ed. *Air Power: The Decisive Force in Korea*. Princeton, NJ: Princeton University Press, 1957. Collection of essays drawn from *Air University Quarterly Review*. Covers such varied matters as role of photo reconnaissance, airfield construction, and air rescue operations.

ORIGINS OF THE WAR

Baum, Kim Chull, "U.S. Policy on the Eve of the Korean War: Abandonment of Safeguard." In *Korea and the Cold War: Division, Destruction, and Disarmament*, ed. Kim Chull Baum and James A. Matray. Claremont, CA: Regina Press, 1993. Emphasizes bureaucratic conflict between the Department of State and the Pentagon over the withdrawal of U.S. forces from Korea in 1949.

Cho, Soo-Sung. *Korea in World Politics, 1940–1950*. Berkeley, CA: University of California Press, 1967. Argues that although American intentions toward Korea after World War II were good, its policies were harmful and made the Korean War almost inevitable.

Cumings, Bruce. "American Policy and Korean Liberation." In *Without Parallel: The American-Korean Relationship since 1945*, ed. Frank Baldwin, 39–108. New York: Pantheon, 1973. Sees root causes of the Korean War in the civil and revolutionary struggle in Korea after World War II.

———. *The Origins of the Korean War, I: Liberation of the Emergence of Separate Regimes*. Princeton, NJ: Princeton University Press, 1981. Cumings makes extensive use of Korean-language materials to stress the civil nature of the Korean War.

————. *The Origins of the Korean War, II: The Roaring of the Catarac, 1947–1950*. Princeton, NJ: Princeton University Press, 1981. A continuation of Volume I through the North Korean invasion of 1950. Doubts even that the Soviet Union played much of a role in Kim Il Sung's decision to attack South Korea. Cumings's two volumes on the origins of the Korean War are not without controversy, but they are generally recognized as two of the most important works on the Korean War in the last twenty years.

————. "Introduction: The Course of Korean-American Relations, 1943–1953." In *Child of Conflict: The Korean-American Relationship, 1943–1953*, ed. Bruce Cummings, 3–55. Seattle: University of Washington Press, 1983. A concise statement of his thesis on the civil nature of the Korean conflict.

Dobbs, Charles M. *The Unwanted Symbol: American Foreign Policy, the Cold War, and Korea, 1945–1950*. Kent, OH: Kent State University Press, 1981. Argues that Korea came to symbolize for the United States its determination to defend the free world against communist aggression, especially after the communist victory in China in 1949.

Gaddis, John L. "Korea in American Politics, Strategy and Diplomacy, 1945–1950." In *The Origins of the Cold War in Asia*, ed. Yonosuke Nagai and Akira Iriye, 277–98. New York: Columbia University Press, 1977. Emphasizes errors of policy toward Korea by the big powers after World War II.

————. "The Strategic Perspective: the Rise and Fall of the 'Defensive Perimeter,' 1947–1951." In *Uncertain Years: Chinese-American Relations, 1947–1950*, ed. Dorothy Borg and Waldo Heinrichs, 61–118. New York: Columbia University Press, 1980. Traces shift after World War II of the U.S. strategic perimeter. Notes fragility of the consensus on the defensive perimeter strategy.

Kim, Joungwon, A. *A Divided Korea: The Politics of Development, 1945–1972*. Cambridge, MA: Harvard University Press, 1975. A history of the development of North and South Korea. Strong on political leaders in both countries.

Kolko, Joyce, and Gabriel Kolko. *The Limits of Power: The World and United States Foreign Policy, 1945–1954*. New York: Harper and Row, 1972. Attributes North Korean invasion of South Korea in June 1950 to the military imbalance in favor of South Korea.

Masao, Okonogi. "The Domestic Roots of the Korean War." In *The Origins of the Cold War in Asia*, ed. Yonosuke Nagai and Akira Iriye, 299–320. New York: Columbia University Press, 1977. Maintains that domestic differences in Korea after World War II were internationalized as a result of the Cold War and were at the root of the Korean War.

Matray, James A. "An End to Indifference: America's Korean Policy during World War II." *Diplomatic History* 2 (Spring 1978): 181–96. As title in-

dicates, Matray shows how World War II marked an end to American indifference toward Korea. Discusses President Franklin Roosevelt's
decision to establish a trusteeship for Korea.

———. "Captive of the Cold War: The Decision to Divide Korea at the 38th Parallel." *Pacific Historical Review* 50 (May 1981): 145–68. Attributes the
decision to divide Korea at the 38th parallel largely to the deterioration of
U.S.-Soviet relations and President Truman's unwillingness to allow the
Soviet Union to occupy the entire Korean Peninsula.

———. "Korea: Test Case of Containment in Asia." In *Child of Conflict*, ed.
Bruce Cumings, 169–93. Seattle: University of Washington Press, 1983.
Rejects notion that President Truman's interest in the reconstruction of
Europe after World War II diverted his interests away from Asia, includ-
ing Korea.

———. "Cold War of a Sort: The International Origins of the Korea War." In *Korea and the Cold War: Division, Destruction, Disarmament*, ed. Kim
Chull Baum and James I. Matray, 35–62. Claremont, CA: Regina, 1993.
As in his other writings, Matray places decisions made about Korea by
the United States and Soviet Union after World War II in the context of
their Cold War struggle.

McClothen, Ronald. "Acheson, Economics, and the American Commitment in
Korea, 1947–1949." *Pacific Historical Review* 58 (February 1989):
21–53. Argues the importance that Secretary of State Dean Acheson attached to Korea as a source of rice and a market for Japan.

Meade, Edward Grant. *American Military Government in Korea*. New York: Columbia University Press, 1951. Discusses American occupation of South
Korea after World War II.

Merrill, John. "Internal Warfare in Korea, 1948–1950: The Local Setting of the
Korean War." In *Child of Conflict: The Korean-American Relationship,
1943–1953*, ed. Bruce Cumings, 133–62. Seattle: University of Washington Press, 1983. Examines guerrilla warfare in South Korea prior to 1950.
Notes lack of Korean support for Rhee government.

Paul, Mark. "Diplomacy Delayed: The Atomic Bomb and the Division of Korea,
1945." In *Child of Conflict: The Korean-American Relationship,
1943–1953*, ed. Bruce Cumings, 67–91. Seattle: University of Washington Press, 1983. Maintains that at the Potsdam Conference Truman delayed discussion of Asian issues, including the future status of Korea,
until he knew the status of the atomic bomb. As a result, when World War
II ended, hasty decisions were made regarding Korea that contributed to
the coming of the Korean War.

Simmons, Robert R. "The Korean Civil War." In *Without Parallel: The
American-Korean Relationship since 1945*, ed. Frank Baldwin, 143–78.
New York: Pantheon, 1974. Makes the point that the North Korean inva-
sion of South Korea was part of an ongoing civil war in Korea.

Stone, I. F. *The Hidden History of the Korean War*. New York: Monthly Review Press, 1952. Early revisionist account of the outbreak of the Korean conflict, which holds South Korea responsible for starting the war.

Stueck, William Whitney, Jr. "Cold War Revisionism and the Origins of the Korean War: The Kolko Thesis." *Pacific Historical Review* 42 (November 1973): 537–75. Rejects argument of Joyce and Gabriel Kolko that South Korea and the United States were responsible for the Korean War.

———. *The Road to Confrontation: American Policy toward China and Korea, 1947–1950*. Chapel Hill, NC: University of North Carolina Press, 1981. Maintains that although Korea did not have much military importance for the United States, it did become increasingly important in terms of maintaining American credibility as a world leader.

U.S. RESPONSE TO OUTBREAK OF HOSTILITIES

Bernstein, Barton J. "The Week We Went to War: American Intervention in the Korean Civil War." *Foreign Service Journal* 54 (January 1977): 6–9 and (February 1977): 8–11. Two-part article, the first of which focuses on White House concerns about Soviet intentions in Korea and the second on the events leading to the U.S. decision to commit American ground forces to Korea.

George, Alexander L. "American Policy-Making and the North Korean Aggression." *World Politics* 7 (January 1955): 208–32. States that Truman intervened in Korea because he feared that inaction might lead to further Soviet aggression elsewhere.

Halperin, Morton H. "The Limiting Process in the Korean War." *Political Science Review* 78 (March 1963): 13–39. Remarks that Truman was concerned about negative impact of inaction in Korea on western Europe.

Matray, James I. "America's Reluctant Crusade: Truman's Commitment of Combat Troops in the Korean War." *Historian* 42 (Fall 1980): 437–55. Argues that Truman's decision to intervene in Korea flowed naturally from his concern about Soviet expansion.

May, Ernest. *Lessons of the Past: The Use and Misuse of History in American Foreign Policy*. New York: Oxford University Press, 1973. Argues that President Truman's determination to avoid the mistakes of the past, particularly by not repeating the failed policy of appeasement, influenced his decision to go to war.

Paige, Glenn D. *The Korean Decision*. New York: Free Press, 1968. An almost hourly account of the U.S. reaction to news that South Korea had been invaded.

Pelz, Stephen. "U.S. Decisions on Korean Policy, 1943–1950: Some Hypotheses." In *Child of Conflict: The Korean-American Relationship, 1943–1953*, ed. Bruce Cumings. Seattle: University of Washington Press, 1983. Suggests that besides considerations growing out of the Cold War, Truman intervened in Korea because of domestic political consequences if he did nothing.

Yonosuke. "The Korean War: An Interpretative Essay." *The Japanese Journal of American Studies* 1 (1981): 151–74. Maintains that the Korean War gave the United States an opportunity to end ambiguity about its policy with respect to the Far East.

THE PEOPLE'S REPUBLIC OF CHINA, THE SOVIET UNION, AND THE WAR

Cohen, Warren. "Research Note: Conversations with Chinese Friends: Zhou En-lai's Associates Reflect on Chinese-American Relations in the 1940s and the Korean War." *Diplomatic History* 11 (Summer 1987): 283–89. Emphasizes dominance of Mao Zedong's power at the time of the Korean War and the lack of Chinese intelligence about U.S. policy toward Asia.

Farrar-Hockley, Anthony. "The China Factor in the Korean War." In *The Korean War in History*, ed. James Cotton and Ian Neary, 4–10. Atlantic Highlands, NJ: Humanities Press, 1989. Describes Mao Zedong's concerns about a North Korean attack on South Korea.

Goncharov, Sergei N., John Lewis, and Xue Litai. *Uncertain Partners: Stalin, Mao, and the Korean War*. Stanford, CA: Stanford University Press, 1993. Emphasizes differences between Moscow, Beijing, and Pyongyang prior to the North Korean invasion. One of a number of recent works that point out the reluctance of Stalin to allow North Korea to invade South Korea.

Hunt, Michael. "Beijing and the Korean Crisis, June 1950–June 1951." *Political Science Quarterly* 107 (Fall 1992): 453–78. Notes indecision and uncertainty in Beijing about policy to pursue with respect to the Korean War. Challenges rational actor theory of crisis management.

Jian, Chen. *China's Road to the Korean War: The Making of the Sino-American Confrontation* New York: Columbia University Press, 1994. Important reinterpretation of reasons behind China's decision to intervene in the Korean War. Stresses revolutionary nationalism of Mao Zedong. Argues that the decision to intervene was made in August 1950, even before the Inchon invasion and the movement of UN forces across the 38th parallel.

Kim, Hak Jonn. "China's Non-Involvement in the Origins of the Korean War: A Reassessment of the Traditionalist and Revisionist Literature." In *The Korean War in History*, ed. James Cotton and Ian Neary, 11–19. Atlantic Highlands, NJ: Humanities Press, 1989. A balanced treatment of the conflicting literature on Beijing's support for a North Korean invasion of South Korea.

Merrill, John. "The Origins of the Korean War: Unanswered Questions." In *Korea and the Cold War: Division, Destruction, and Disarmament*, ed. Kim Chull Baum and James I. Matay, 95–108. Claremont, CA: Regina Press,

1993. Argues that North Korea's invasion of South Korea was a rational response on its part to a growing military and political imbalance on the Korean peninsula in favor of South Korea.

Nakajima, Mineo. "The Sino-Soviet Confrontation: Its Roots in the International Background of the Korean War." *Australian Journal of Chinese Affairs* I (January 1979): 19–47. Argues that Chinese subordination to Stalinist policy with respect to the Korean War contributed to their growing confrontation after the war.

Pollack, Jonathan D. "The Korean War in Sino-American Relations." *Sino-American Relations, 1945–1955: A Joint Reassessment of a Critical Decade*, ed. Harry Harding and Yuan Ming, 213–37. Wilmington, DE: Scholarly Resources, Inc., 1989. Maintains that China had little choice other than to enter the Korean War, albeit reluctantly, after the U.S. decision to cross the 38th parallel. Notes also the effect of the war on Sino-Soviet relations.

Qingzhao, Hua. *From Yalta to Panmunjom: Truman's Diplomacy and the Four Powers, 1945–1953*. Ithaca, NY: Cornell University Press, 1993. Points to security concerns as the reason China intervened in the Korean War.

Sheng, Michael M. "Beijing's Decision to Enter the Korean War." *Korea and World Affairs* 19 (Summer 1995): 294–313. Argues against thesis that security reasons motivated China into intervening in the Korean War.

Simmons, Robert R. *The Strained Alliance: Peking, Pyongyang, Moscow, and the Politics of the Korean War*. New York: Free Press, 1975. One of the first accounts to analyze the Korean War from the vantage point of the communist side. Argues that, contrary to public opinion, North Korea acted on its own and without the approval of the Soviet Union in invading South Korea.

Spurr, Russell. *Enter the Dragon: China's Undeclared War against the U.S. in Korea, 1950–51*. New York: Newmarket Press, 1988. Account by a former correspondent in Beijing of the Chinese intervention in Korea through December 1950. Includes discussion of China's motivation for entering the war.

Stueck, William, Jr. "The Soviet Union and the Origins of the Korean War." In *Korea and the Cold War: Division, Destruction, and Disarmament*, ed. Kim Chull Baum and James A. Matray, 111–24. Claremont, CA: Regina Press, 1993. Makes point that Stalin agreed to North Korea's invasion of South Korea in part because he did not think that the United States would intervene in the conflict.

Whiting, Allen S. *China Crosses the Yalu: The Decision to Enter the Korean War*. Stanford, CA: Stanford University Press, 1968. Argues that Beijing played no role in North Korea's invasion of South Korea. China's decision to enter the war came only after UN forces crossed the 38th parallel.

Yufan Hao, and Zhai Zhihai. "China's Decision to Enter the Korean War: History Revisited." *China Quarterly* 121 (March 1990): 94–115. Argues that

China entered the war primarily for security reasons. Criticizes both Mao Zedong and Truman for not reading the signals from the other side.

Zhang, Shu Guang. *Deterrence and Strategic Culture: Chinese-American Confrontations, 1949–1958*. Ithaca, NY: Cornell University Press, 1993. Emphasizes strategic and cultural differences between China and the United States that increased the chances of conflict between them in places like Korea. Makes use of Chinese Communist Party records.

DECISION TO CROSS THE 38TH PARALLEL

Bernstein, Barton J. "The Policy of Risk: Crossing the 38th Parallel and Marching to the Yalu." *Foreign Service Journal* 54 (Fall 1981): 16–22, 29. Regards decision to cross into North Korea as fundamentally a political one by the White House.

LaFeber, Walter. "Crossing the 38th: The Cold War in Microcosm." In *Reflections on the Cold War*, Lynn H. Miller and Ronald W. Pruessen, 71–90. Philadelphia: Lippincott, 1974. Points out that the decision to cross the 38th parallel marked an important shift in the Cold War policy of containment.

———. "American Policy-Makers, Public Opinion, and the Outbreak of the Cold War, 1945–1950." In *The Origins of the Cold War in Asia*, ed. Yonosuke Nagai and Akira Iriye. New York: Columbia University Press, 1977. Argues that Truman made decision to cross 38th parallel as early as July 1950.

Matray, James L. "Truman's Plan for Victory: National Self-Determination and the Thirty-Eighth Parallel Decision in Korea." *Journal of American History* 66 (September 1979): 314–33. States that President Truman's decision to cross the 38th parallel grew out of his concern that the Korean conflict was part of a worldwide Soviet-American confrontation, and was also motivated by an idealistic concern for Korean self-determination.

McClellan, David S. "Dean Acheson and the Korean War." *Political Science Quarterly* 83 (Spring 1968): 16–39. Critical of Acheson for misreading Chinese intentions in supporting the decision to cross the 38th parallel.

THE NUCLEAR ISSUE

Anders, Roger M. "The Atomic Bomb and the Korean War: Gordon Dean and the Issue of Civilian Control." *Military Affairs* 52 (January 1988): 1–6. Discusses struggle of the chairman of the Atomic Energy Commission, Gordon Dean, to preserve civilian control over the U.S. nuclear arsenal.

Bernstein, Barton J. "Truman's Second Thoughts on Ending the Korean War." *Foreign Service Journal* 57 (November 1980): 31–32. An almost humorous account of Truman's private rumination of dropping atom bombs on major Soviet and Chinese cities.

———. "New Light on the Korean War." *International History Review* 3 (April 1981): 256–77. Argues that the United States gave serious thought to using the atomic bomb in Manchuria following the Chinese invasion of Korea.

Calingaert, Daniel. "Nuclear Weapons and the Korean War." *Journal of Strategic Studies* 11 (June 1988): 177–202. Points out limitations on using nuclear weapons during the Korean conflict.

Dingman, Roger. "Atomic Diplomacy During the Korean War." *International Security* 13 (Winter 1988–89): 50–91. Important article that challenges conventional views about the importance Eisenhower attached to the possible use of atomic weapons to end the war but also makes clear that Truman gave more thought to their use than generally acknowledged.

Ryan, Mark A. *Chinese Attitudes toward Nuclear Weapons: China and the United States during the Korean War.* New York: M. E. Sharpe, 1989. Maintains that China had a realistic understanding of the limitations of nuclear weapons during the Korean War and that the nuclear weapons threat was not a factor in its decision to end the conflict.

ALLIES, THE UN, OTHER COUNTRIES, AND THE KOREAN WAR

Belmonte, Laura. "Anglo-American Relations and the Dismissal of MacArthur." *Diplomatic History* 19 (Fall 1995): 641–67. Although conceding that Truman fired MacArthur for internal strategic and political reasons, notes Britain's indirect influence on the president's decision that MacArthur had to go.

Dockrill, M. L. "The Foreign Office, Anglo-American Relations and the Korean Truce Negotiations July 1951–July 1953." In *The Korean War in History*, ed. James Cotton and Ian Neary, 100–19. Atlantic Highlands, NJ: Humanities Press, 1989. Points out that although London generally went along with U.S. decision-making in the Korean War, it did not always do so happily. Moreover there was significant divergence in the views of the two allies on the basic question of future Chinese-Western relations.

Farrar, Peter N. "A Pause for Peace Negotiations: The British Buffer Zone Plan of November 1950." In *The Korean War in History*, ed. James Cotton and Ian Neary, 66–72. Atlantic Highlands, NJ: Humanities Press, 1989. Discusses British proposal for, and American rejection of, a buffer zone between China and Korea following China's invasion of Korea in November 1950.

Foot, Rosemary. "Anglo-American Relations in the Korean Crisis: The British Effort to Avert an Expanded War, December 1950–January 1951." *Diplomatic History* 10 (Winter 1986): 43–57. As in several of her other articles and books, Foot stresses the restraining influence London exerted on U.S. policy with respect to the Korean War.

Goodrich, Leland M. *Korea: A Study of U.S. Policy in the United Nations.* New York: Council on Foreign relations, 1956. Critical of the United States for not following a forceful enough policy with respect to South Korea politically and diplomatically.

Kaplan, Lawrence S. *The United States and NATO: The Formative Years*. Lexington, KY: University of Kentucky Press, 1984. Argues that the Korean War was a turning point in the formation of NATO.

LaFeber, Walter. "NATO and the Korean War: A Context." *Diplomatic History* 13 (Fall 1989): 461–77. Disagrees somewhat with Kaplan by arguing that the transformation of NATO and the military buildup in Europe began ten months earlier.

Lowe, Peter. "The Frustrations of Alliance: Britain, the United States and the Korean War." In *The Korean War in History*, ed. James Cotton and Ian Neary, 93–96. Atlantic Highlands, NJ: Humanities Press, 1989. Points out divisive impact of Korean war on Anglo-American relations.

MacDonald, Callum. *Britain and the Korean War*. London: Macmillan, 1990. States that Britain's involvement in the Korean War was a result of both the Cold War and the special relationship it had with the United States. Like Washington, London viewed the North Korean attack on South Korea as a Soviet initiative that demanded a response to prevent further Soviet aggression.

Melady, John. *Korea: Canada's Forgotten War*. Toronto: Macmillan of Canada, 1983. Good military analysis of Canada's contribution to the fighting in Korea.

Millar, Thomas B. "Australia and the American Alliance." *Pacific Affairs* 37 (1964): 148–60. Discusses how the Korean War strengthened ties between the United States and Australia.

O'Neill, Robert. *Australia and the Korean War, 1950–1953*. Canberra: Australian Government, 1981. Discusses Australia's military commitment to the conflict.

Soward, F. H. "The Korean Crisis and the Commonwealth." *Pacific Affairs* 24 (1951): 115–30. Although generally supportive of U.S. policy with respect to the Korean War, the Commonwealth countries sometimes disagreed with that policy.

Stairs, Denis. *The Diplomacy of Constraint: Canada, the Korean War and the United States*. Toronto: University of Toronto Press, 1974. A first-rate analysis of Canada's diplomatic role in the Korean War.

Steinberg, Blema S. "The Korean War: A Case Study in Indian Neutralism." *Orbis* 8 (Winter 1965): 937–54. Good summary of India's diplomacy at UN to end the war.

Wood, Herbert Fairlie. *Strange Battleground: The Operations in Korea and Their Effects on the Defense Policy of Canada*. Ottawa: Queen's Printer, 1966. Official account of the Canadian Army during the Korean War.

DOMESTIC SIDE OF WAR

Caridi, Ronald J. *The Korean War and American Politics: The Republican Party as a Case Study*. Philadelphia: University of Pennsylvania Press, 1968. Highly critical of Republican Party's partisanship during the war.

Detzer, David. *Thunder of the Captains: The Short Summer of 1950*. New York: Crowell, 1970. A narrative on American society in the two weeks following the outbreak of the war.

Kepley, David R. *The Collapse of the Middle Way: Senate Republicans and the Bipartisan Foreign Policy, 1948–1953*. Westport, CT: Greenwood Press, 1988. Argues that the Korean War contributed to the breakdown of congressional bipartisanship on foreign policy.

Schlesinger, Arthur M., Jr. *The Imperial Presidency*. Boston: Houghton Mifflin, 1973. Discusses the constitutional issues raised by the war.

Wiltz, John Edward. "The Korean War and American Society." In *The Korean War: A 25-Year Perspective*, ed. Francis H. Heller, 112–58. Lawrence, KS: University Press of Kansas, 1977. Notes that although the war was a frustrating experience for Americans, positive developments resulted from the war, such as the confirmation of civilian control over the military and the stimulation of the economy.

TRUMAN-MacARTHUR CONTROVERSY

Higgins, Trumbull. *Korea and the Fall of MacArthur: A Precis in Limited War*. New York: Oxford University Press, 1960. Attributes MacArthur's dismissal to a fundamental disagreement between the general and President Truman on military strategy for Korea based on their differences on the military objectives of the war.

Rovere, Richard H., and Arthur M. Schlesinger, Jr. *The MacArthur Controversy and American Foreign Policy*. New York: Farrar, 1965. A strong defense of Truman's decision to fire MacArthur in April 1951.

Ryan, Halford R. "Harry S Truman: A Misdirected Defense for MacArthur's Dismissal." *Presidential Studies Quarterly* 11 (December 1981): 576–82. Argues that it would have been better for Truman in explaining his reasons for firing MacArthur to spend less time defending his own policy with respect to Korea and more in defending his decision to fire MacArthur.

Spanier, John W. *The Truman-MacArthur Controversy and the Korean War*. Cambridge, MA: Harvard University Press, 1959. Another strong defense of the president's decision to fire MacArthur. Also argues for the need of the United States to abandon its concept of military victory.

Wiltz, John E. "The MacArthur Hearings of 1951: The Secret Testimony." *Military Affairs* 39 (December 1975): 167–73. A synopsis of the joint Senate hearings on MacArthur's dismissal, which were not declassified and published until 1973.

———. "Truman and MacArthur: The Wake Island Meetings." *Military Affairs* 42 (December 1978): 168–75. Notes that Truman went to Wake Island primarily for domestic political benefits.

END OF THE WAR

Bacchus, Wilfrid A. "The Relationship between Combat and Peace Negotiations: Fighting While Talking in Korea." *Orbis* 17 (Summer 1973): 547–74. Notes how difficult it is to obtain an armistice in a limited war. Emphasizes need to threaten forceful military action if peace negotiations lead nowhere.

Bernstein, Barton J. "The Origins of America's Commitment in Korea." *Foreign Service Journal* 55 (March 1978): 10–13, 34. Describes America's dealings with Syngman Rhee, including plans for his overthrow, in an effort to win South Korea's acceptance of an armistice agreement, in return for which the United States agreed to a defense pact with Rhee.

———. "Syngman Rhee: The Pawn as Rook: The Struggle to End the Korean War." *Bulletin of Concerned Asian Scholars* 10 (January–March 1978): 38–47. Examines the negotiations to end the war. Points to the difficulties that both Presidents Truman and Eisenhower had in dealing with President Syngman Rhee.

———. "The Struggle over the Korean War Armistice: Prisoners or Repatriation." In *Child of Conflict: The Korean-American Relationship, 1943–1953*, ed. Bruce Cumings, 261–307. Seattle: University of Washington Press, 1983. Discussion of the major disputes during the two years of armistice negotiations that finally ended the war. Excellent summary.

Blechman, Barry M., and Robert Powell. "What in the Name of God is Strategic Superiority?" *Political Science Quarterly* 97 (Winter 1982–83): 589–602. Argues that Chinese fear of an escalated war rather than a nuclear threat led to the end of the war.

Brands, Henry W. "The Dwight D. Eisenhower Administration and the 'Other' Geneva Conference of 1954." *Pacific Historical Review* 61 (February 1987): 78–99. The other conference to which Brands refers is the post-armistice conference dealing with Korea.

Friedman, Edward. "Nuclear Blackmail and the End of the Korean War." *Modern China* 1 (January 1975): 75–91. Rejects Secretary of State John Foster Dulles's claim that the threat to use nuclear weapons against China led to the armistice agreement.

Gittings, John. "Talks, Bombs, and Germs: Another Look at the Korean War." *Journal of Contemporary Asia* 5 (Spring 1975): 205–17. Rejects Communist claims with respect to the UN's alleged use of bacteriological and chemical warfare and its lack of good faith in the armistice negotiations.

Keefer, Edward C. "President Dwight D. Eisenhower and the End of the Korean War." *Diplomatic History* 10 (Summer 1986): 267–89. Points out Eisenhower's lack of a plan to end the war when he assumed office and his willingness to use nuclear weapons against China if Beijing would not agree to an acceptable armistice.

———. "The Truman Administration and the South Korean Political Crisis of 1952: Democracy's Failure." *Pacific Historical Review* 60 (May 1991):

145–68. Critical of Truman's failure to support a planned coup against Rhee.

Vatcher, William H., Jr. *Panmunjom: The Story of the Korean Military Armistice Negotiations*. New York: Praeger, 1958. A UN advisor to the negotiations at Panmunjom, Vatcher maintains that UN negotiators were hamstrung by their lack of authority and by the limits placed on battlefield operations.

BIOGRAPHIES

Ambrose, Stephen E. *Eisenhower: The President*. New York: Simon and Schuster, 1984. The second of a two-volume biography of Eisenhower by his leading biographer. Argues that Eisenhower did not need to threaten the Chinese directly with the use of nuclear weapons against them because they already knew that was an option he was considering.

Donovan, Robert J. *Tumultuous Years: The Presidency of Harry S Truman*. New York: Norton, 1982. The second of a two-volume biography of Truman. Donovan provides a good overview of Truman's response to the North Korean invasion of South Korea and his conduct of the war. Donovan was a White House correspondent during the Truman and Eisenhower administrations.

Hamby, Alonzo L. *Man of the People: A Life of Harry S Truman*. New York: Oxford University Press, 1995. The latest and best biography of Truman. Hamby regards Truman as a great, but often flawed, president whose good instincts usually prevailed.

James, D. Clayton. *Triumph and Disaster, 1945–1964*. Boston: Houghton Mifflin, 1985. The third of James's three-volume definitive biography of Douglas MacArthur. Thorough coverage of MacArthur's stormy relations with Truman, his firing and recall, and the political brouhaha that it caused.

Manchester, William. *American Caesar: Douglas MacArthur, 1880–1964*. Boston: Little, Brown and Co., 1978. A generally favorable biography of the general that is particularly good at capturing some of the complexity and contradictions in his personality. Very readable.

McCullough, David. *Truman*. New York: Simon and Schuster, 1992. A sympathetic and well-written biography by one of the nation's most highly read and respected popular historians.

Schaller, Michael. *Douglas MacArthur: The Far Eastern General*. New York: Oxford University Press, 1989. Documents the reluctance of the Joint Chiefs of Staff to challenge MacArthur on Korea.

MEMOIRS

Acheson, Dean. *Present at the Creation: My Years in the State Department*. New York: Norton 1969. An extensive account and spirited defense by Acheson of his stewardship as secretary of state. Makes clear the interrelationship between U.S. European policy and developments in Korea.

Allison, John M. *Ambassador from the Prairie or Allison in Wonderland.* Boston: Houghton Mifflin, 1973. Memoirs by the Assistant Secretary of State for Far Eastern Affairs during the Korean War. Good character studies of Acheson and MacArthur.

Attlee, Clement R. *As It Happened.* New York: Viking Press, 1954. In these memoirs, the former British prime minister discusses his concern in 1950 and 1951 that the Far Eastern war be confined to Korea.

Bohlen, Charles E. *Witness to History, 1929–1969.* New York: Norton, 1973. A career diplomat, Bohlen criticizes the United States for overextending its commitments in Europe.

Bradley, Omar N., and Clay Blair. *A General's Life.* New York: Simon and Schuster, 1983. A highly useful account of major foreign policy decisions involving the military. Highly critical of General MacArthur.

Clark, Mark W. *From the Danube to the Yalu.* New York: Harper, 1954. Critical of U.S. military policy in Korea. Believes the war could have been won militarily if Washington had had the determination to do so.

Collins, Joseph Lawton. *War in Peacetime: The History and Lessons of Korea.* Boston: Houghton Mifflin, 1969. A view of the Korean War from inside the Pentagon.

Eden, Anthony. *Full Circle: The Memoirs of Anthony Eden.* Boston: Houghton Mifflin, 1960. Good discussion by Britain's foreign secretary under Winston Churchill of Britain's position with regard to the "greater sanction" statement.

Eisenhower, Dwight D. *Mandate for Change, 1953–1956.* Garden City, NY: Doubleday, 1963. Makes clear Eisenhower's determination to end war when he took office, including using nuclear weapons if necessary.

Goodman, Allen E., ed. *Negotiating While Fighting: The Diary of Admiral C. Turner Joy at the Korean Armistice Conference.* Stanford, CA: Hoover Institute Press, 1978. A companion to the admiral's memoirs listed next.

Joy, C. Turner. *How Communists Negotiate* New York: Macmillan, 1955. The chief UN negotiator at Kaesong and Panmunjom until May 22, 1952, Joy details his frustrations in negotiating with his communist counterparts.

MacArthur, Douglas. *Reminiscences.* New York: McGraw, 1964. Disappointing. Relies mainly on MacArthur's own speeches. But clearly establishes the general's own vanity.

Panikkar, K. M. *In Two Chinas.* London: Allen, 1959. Discusses activities of India's ambassador to China to negotiate an end to the Korean War.

Ridgway, Matthew B. *The Korean War.* Garden City, NY: Doubleday, 1967. Balanced. Argues that because all future wars will be limited ones. The United States must learn how to fight a limited war.

Talbott, Strobe, ed. *Khrushchev Remembers.* Boston: Little, Brown, 1970. In these recollections, the former Soviet premier comments on Moscow's reluctant approval of Kim Il Sung's plans to invade South Korea.

Taylor, Maxwell D. *Swords and Plowshares*. New York: Norton, 1972. Explains why atom bombs were not used in Korea.

Truman, Harry S. *Memoirs: Years of Trial and Hope*. Garden City, NY: Signet, 1956. Extensive coverage of the Korean War from the perspective of the Oval Office.

FILMS ON THE KOREAN WAR

Back at the Front. Starring Tom Ewell and Harvey Lemback. Directed by George Sherman. Universal Studios. 1952. A light-hearted comedy about the adventures of G.I.s Willie and Joe in Korea. What makes this film of passing interest is that it continues the exploits of two of the most popular cartoon figures of World War II, Willie and Joe, and reflects some of the anger of World War II veterans at being recalled to service during the Korean War. In this film, Willie and Joe do everything possible to avoid going to Korea.

The Bamboo Prison. Starring Robert Francis and Dianne Foster. Directed by Lewis Seiler. Plot revolves around premise that some American POWs during the Korean War, who supposedly became enemy collaborators, were actually American intelligence agents.

MacArthur: The Rebel General. Starring Gregory Peck. Directed by Joseph Sargent. Universal Studios. 1977. A generally favorable biography of MacArthur, which accurately portrays the general's clash with President Truman during the Korean War.

The Manchurian Candidate. Starring Frank Sinatra. Directed by John Frankenheimer. United Artists. 1962. This film captures the concern many Americans felt after the Korean War about the ability of their communist captors to "brainwash" UN POWs and the Cold War obsession with communist plots to overthrow the government.

MASH. Starring Donald Sutherland and Elliott Gould. Directed by Ingo Preminger and Leon Ericson. TCF/Aspen. 1970. A film of black humor that emphasizes the idiocy of war by describing the antics of a group of dedicated doctors and nurses trying to stay sane as they deal daily with the human gore of war.

Pork Chop Hill. Starring Gregory Peck. Directed by Lewis Milestone. United Artists. 1959. A film based on one of the most famous battles of the Korean War. In the film, UN forces take Pork Chop Hill but then find it difficult to hold onto it.

Prisoner of War. Starring Ronald Reagan and Steve Forrest. Directed by Andrew Morton. MGM Studios. 1954. In this film, Reagan portrays an American officer who parachutes into North Korea and purposely allows himself to be captured in order to investigate allegedly brutal communist treatment of American POWs. Based on actual interviews with former prisoners.

Tokyo File. Starring Florence Marly and Robert Peyton. Directed by Dorrell McGowan and Steve McGowan. RKO Studios. 1951. In this film, an

American agent tries to uncover a communist spy ring in Japan during the Korean War.

VIDEO ON THE KOREAN WAR

Korea, the Forgotten War. Hosted by Robert Stack. Directed by Don Horan. Low Reda Production. 1987. A 92-minute documentary that covers the major military and political events of the Korean conflict. Based on rare archival footage.

WEB SITES

Asian Studies. WWW. Virtual Library. Australian National University:
http://coombs.anu.edu.au/WWWVL-AsianStudies.html

The Harvard-Yenching Library:
http://www.fas.harvard.edu/~della/hylhome.html

The Korea Institute. Harvard University:
http://www.fas.harvard.edu/~korea/index_home.html

Korea National Library:
http://203.237.248,5/index,html

Korean Studies. Bibliographic Data Base Project:
http://www.fas.harvard.edu/~korbib/

The Korean War Project:
http://www.onramp.net/~hbarker

North Korea Page. University of Oregon:
http://darkwing.uoregon.edu/~felsing/kstuff/nkshelf.html

Online Catalog of Korean Books at the University of California Berkeley:
http://www.lib.berkeley.edu/EAL/ealk2.html

Register of Leading Asian and Pacific Studies E-Journals:
http://coombs.anu.edu.au/WWWVLPages/AsianPages/Asian
E-Journals.html

Index

About the Author

BURTON I. KAUFMAN is Dean of the School for Interdisciplinary Studies at Miami University in Oxford, Ohio. He is author of two previous Greenwood Press books, *Efficiency and Expansion* (1974) and *Oil Cartel Case* (1978).